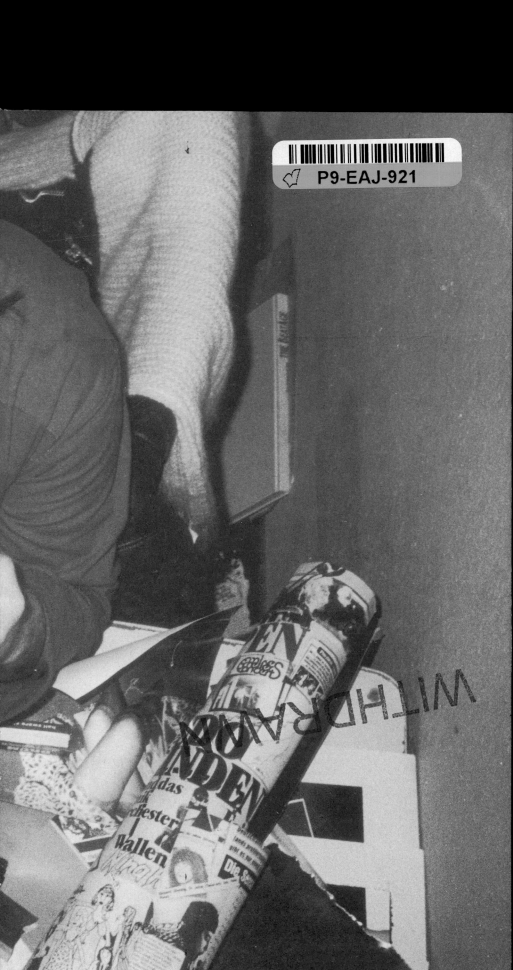

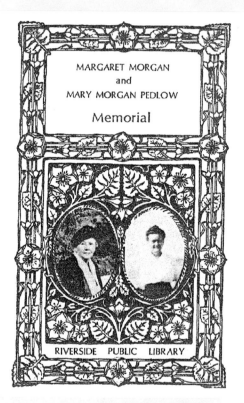

MARGARET MORGAN
and
MARY MORGAN PEDLOW

Memorial

RIVERSIDE   PUBLIC   LIBRARY

don't let me be misunderstood

Eric Burdon
with J. Marshall Craig

Thunder's Mouth Press
New York

Published by
Thunder's Mouth Press
An Imprint of Avalon Publishing Group Incorporated
161 William St., 16th floor
New York, NY 10038

Book design: Sue Canavan

frontispiece photo: Barry Jenkins and I take in the wonders of Central Park. Photo by Linda McCartney.

Library of Congress Cataloging-in-Publication Data
Burdon, Eric, 1941-
    Don't let me be misunderstood: a memoir/by Eric Burdon with Jeff Craig.
    p. cm.
    ISBN 1-56025-330-4 (cloth)
    1. Burdon, Eric, 1941- 2. Rock musicians–England–Biography. I. Craig, Jeff. II. Title.

ML420.B883 A3 2001
782.42166'092–dc21
[B]
                                                                2001048043

Printed in the United States of America
Distributed by Publishers Group West

In memory of my grandmother, Clara Taylor, who had the first singing voice that inspired me, and is in no small way responsible for the great road I chose.

introduction

"There is a house in New Orleans, they call the Rising Sun
It's been the ruin of many a poor boy, and God I know I'm one."

It turns out the most famous line I've ever sung is true. There *is* a House of the Rising Sun. From the morning the Animals recorded the song that knocked the ruling Beatles down the pop chart a notch to the night I finally walked through its door was a journey of thirty years.

This book is about that journey, and more. It's about the life I've led since 1962, much of it on the road. It's been a life filled with such extraordinary memories that sometimes, looking back, I wonder if it all really happened. I didn't keep a diary, and I didn't take notes. But then I'll be at a show somewhere, or at a party, and someone from my deep past will suddenly appear and say, "Hey, do you remember that time when. . . ." and recount the wildest tale. Just like I'd remembered it. And like I've written it here.

There's been triumph, some glory and fame and achievement—and also times of true misery. But I'm not seeking sympathy. And I'm certainly not here to apologize. It's been a hell of a ride and continues to be.

don't let me be misunderstood

A few years ago I found out that my gold records, which I'd assumed were destroyed along with my photographs, scrapbooks and recordings in a house fire, had in fact been recovered. That someone was trying to sell them added insult to injury. But thanks to the efforts of some fans they were returned to me in the fall of 1999. Looking at them brought a world of memories flooding back. Like when Graham Bond passed me my first marijuana joint. It was, no kidding, the night I learned that "House of the Rising Sun" had gone to No. 1. I'd smoked hash before that, but real grass was a rarity in England in those days.

"Son," he told me, "you're gonna be famous, the whole world's gonna know your name, but if you take up the blues, you'll never have any money."

He was right.

I lost all the money. Millions. But I have been blessed to have good friends. I wish I could have had both, but between the two, let me tell you, friends are more valuable.

Despite mountains of grief and regrets, I must extend my thanks to the original Animals: Alan Price, Hilton Valentine, John Steel, and the late Chas Chandler. My thanks to the second generation New Animals: John Weider, Danny McCulloch, Barry Jenkins, Dave Briggs, Andy Summers, Zoot Money (and not forgetting his wife Ronni); my late first wife, Angela King; Danny and Pat, my friends from Africa; Pete Townshend; the late Brian Jones, who was years ahead of his time (and the rest of the Stones); the Beatles, especially the enormously missed John; Keith Altham; Georgie Fame; the Geordie Boys; Mark Knopfler and the former members of Dire Straits; Sting; Brian Johnson; George "Sunblessed" Pearson; the lads in the Squatters.

In the U.S., there's been Neil Young; John Trudell; Floyd "Red Crow" Westerman; the late Bill Graham; Mike Egan; Dr. Martin Jack Rosenblum; Brummbaer and Robin; the boys in my band: Dean Restum, Martin Gerschwitz, Aynsley Dunbar, Dave Meros and his wife, Rose, and, of course, the late, great guitarist Larry Wilkins; Snuffy Walden, Tony Braunagle and the other dozen or so talents I've had the pleasure of working with in America over the years; The Bear, Blind Owl, and all the boys in Canned Heat, especially Fito de la Parra; David Marks; the good cops I've known; Chuck "Grand Master" Farley; Frank Norbert Gerlich, and the Three Musketeers; Ken and Kathy Kroesch; in New Orleans: Jan Densmore, Keith and the Brit boys, Annie Davis, the mighty Neville brothers, Snooks Eaglin, and Darlene Jacobs. The late, great Jimmy Witherspoon; Taj Mahal; the missed Frank Zappa; Karen Monster; Chesley Millikin; the late, great Rolling Thunder; Brian Auger and his family; Sean Riley; Sonny Ridley and his wife Fuji; Jean Moreau; Arthur Berggren; Philip Payne; Chet Helms; Chocolate George; Oliver Reed.

In Germany, there's been the Gyory family, Christian Granderath, Thorston Schmidt, Rhaman Nadjasi. All the guys in the Linberg Panik Orchestra; the staff of my German agency; Thelma Houston, Ada Montano, Robert Gordon; Connie Kolle; Barbara Rudnick; Julie Carmen; Stephie Stephan; Frank Oswald; Orlando; Heide the cook.

In Spain, Carlos Carreras Moise and his family; Amando the Fisherman; Marcelo Nova and family in Brazil.

There have been les girls—Anna-Lena Karlsson; Judit Andras; Yvonne Gyory; Kathy Andrews; Anna-Bella Karube; Judy Wong; Alvenia Bridges; Ming Lowe. I love you all.

My special inspirations: Jimi Hendrix, Rahsaan Roland Kirk, Dana Fox, Linda McCartney, my mother and my father, my Aunt Nora, my Aunt May and Uncle Alf.

I must offer special thanks here to my secretary Jeri Vogelsang and her partner Les Starks, who have been great in keeping my marriage to the road as trouble-free as can be expected.

Journalist and screenwriter J. Marshall Craig took years of memories, yards of tape and boxes of writing and helped conjure their essence into this book. He was inspiring and tireless, and we killed off many bottles of wine together in the process—but even he couldn't convince me to repeat my New York mob story. There are some tales you just don't tell!

A special thanks to the children of the future: my daughter, Alexandria; granddaughters, Keaira, Justice, and my grandson, the little Eric. My thanks and love also to my sister Irene. We were never close but in recent years, after many visits together in California, we've finally developed a deep bond; she's even found the courage to join me onstage on several occasions.

Finally, to my fans all over the world: Without you I'd be lost, especially Marianna Proestou in Athens. You're the reason I'm still here. Simple. In a world that grows ever colder, where personal freedoms are fading even in America, I have the luxury of being able to go to work, where I gaze out into the sea of faces before me, and, with the help of my band, touch them in some way with music, to make a difference—if only for a couple of hours. It's therapy for me, too. Rock music can be the fountain of youth. . . if it doesn't kill you first!

Like just about every performer, I got screwed by the businessmen. But it's only money. There's always more of that out there on the road. At least I'm alive to write about it—and alive to sing about it. As I've said before: I'm just a soul whose intentions are good. Please don't let me be misunderstood.

Eric Burdon
St. Gregory's Day, 2000
White Water, California

acknowledgments

My thanks, first of all, to Eric for having the courage to turn me loose with the amazing amount of material he'd prepared over the years. It's not like I was there to witness his incredible life . . . he was playing a London club with the original Animals the night I was born . . . a continent away. Through it all he's become a true friend. Chesley Millikin needs a nod here, too, for bringing Eric and me together. Editor David Stanford deserves the thanks that all behind-the-scenes people deserve yet few receive. I knew we were in good hands when our publishers brought in a cat who'd edited Jack Kerouac, someone whose work Eric and I both admire greatly. Finally, I must thank my wife, Christine, who does the impossible every day . . . lives with a writer.

—J. Marshall Craig

chapter 1

unethical treatment of animals

F ucked from the get-go.

Not a terribly graceful way to begin my tale, but it's true. The Animals never had a chance when it came to protecting ourselves from the vampires in the music business.

There were stupid contracts and bad decisions, but I'll tell you how bad it was even at the peak of our early success and fame. Following our third appearance on "The Ed Sullivan Show," Alan Price, John Steel, Hilton Valentine, Chas Chandler, and I slipped out of the CBS studios, protected from the screaming fans by a flank of NYPD uniforms and private security. We jumped into the deep leather of our limo's seats, heavy TV makeup still caked on our faces, feeling very much like showbiz veterans.

Our East Coast promo guy, Frank Mancini, was already in the car, tucked away in a shadowy corner behind dark sunglasses, munching on salted peanuts.

As we pulled away from the curb, a young white kid ran toward us, our new album in one hand and a big black marker in the other. He was looking at the limo instead of where he was going, and ran smack into a light pole, and fell onto the sidewalk. Frank yelled at the driver to stop, and he rolled down his window. The kid sat up, blood trickling down his forehead.

"You all right, son?" Frank hollered.

"Yeah, I think so," the kid said.

"Good, good," Frank called out. "Remember, kid, buy the records. Buy the records!"

He rolled up the window and told the driver to move on.

The band chuckled for a moment, then Frank said, "You guys feel like your shit is gold. . . top of the world, eh? Well, just remember that we put you there."

"What do you mean?" I asked.

"The record company bought enough copies of "House of the Rising Sun" to make it go No. 1. We put you on top, and we can tear you down just as fast."

Talk about a bubble bursting. I know now that this has gone on for years—record companies routinely buy up their own product to make it chart higher. But it was a hell of a bringdown for us. After all, we'd just made the second triumphant landing of the so-called British Invasion bands, preceded by the Beatles, and to be followed by the Stones.

By now it's all painfully clear to me: The nightmare part of the rock 'n' roll dream is the business—the money. The Beatles got ripped-off, even the savvy Mick Jagger and the Stones got screwed out of royalties in the early 1970s. The rock 'n' roll highway is dotted with little white crosses marking the casualties, some literal, many more financial.

The great American blues band Canned Heat, in fact, *didn't* get ripped-off only once in its career. That was when, for a brief time, they hired a member of the Hell's Angels to manage them. Their gigs were always great, they always got paid what they'd been promised, when they'd been promised it—and nobody fucked with them.

What does that tell you? To survive in the music business, you can trust the mob and outlaw bikers, but put yourself in the hands of lawyers, accountants, and executives and you're a goner. But what are you gonna do? Applause junkies need a constant fix. Once you taste the stage it's pretty hard to give up. Once you have felt the power of music, and seen first hand that you are capable of touching the hearts and souls of people all over the world, the magic is something you can never forget.

Then there's fame and how it affects people. I learned about that even back in Newcastle, when I was singing with local bands prior to the formation of the Animals.

One of my first experiences was a girl with dark, flashing eyes who made sure we connected one night at Newcastle's Downbeat club. She lived on the coast and the last train from Newcastle was at 1 A.M. I walked her to the train and was shocked when, as casually as saying good night, she devoured me in a cold, windy corner of the sparsely populated station.

The following week, I was sitting in with Mighty Joe Young's jazz band at the Rex Hotel on Whitley Bay. Friday nights down there in the summer, people went wild and the crowd would spill out onto the sea front.

A note was passed to me onstage while the saxman played his sleaziest solo of the night. She waited there for her latest target. . . her newfound secret lover. . . the singer in the band—me!

Leaving the heat of the ballroom and its mirrored walls for the chill of the North Sea breeze, I found my willing fan—and her jilted lover, who begged me to leave her alone.

I took the last train from the coast and jumped off at Newcastle Central, then walked to the Downbeat through the West End in the drizzling rain, the hood from my duffel coat over my head. I was as happy as a lark. I was who I was supposed to be, a poverty-stricken art student. Not a care in the world, a spotty-faced teenage animal living on fish and chips and Newcastle Brown Ale. What a life.

Back at the Downbeat the minions hired to run the joint had just about finished cleaning out from the first set. That's when the all-nighter would begin. I couldn't afford the entrance fee so I explained to one of the bouncers that I had to go upstairs to retrieve some equipment that was left there from the previous set. Once inside I hid underneath the stage and waited in silence until the place filled up with older people who'd come to listen to jazz, drink their whisky, and catch up on the latest gossip.

I crouched there in the darkness watching people coming and going. Ronnie Scott's drummer, Phil Seaman, set up his kit onstage right there in front of me. He was a legendary percussionist and junkie, staggering around assembling his kit. But even with an arm full of smack, he was probably Britain's finest jazz drummer. And soon Ronnie Scott himself strolled onto the stage, cigarette dangling from the corner of his mouth and tenor sax hanging around his neck.

"Test, one, two, one, two, test," he said into the massive silver microphone. People took their seats, and there was a buzz as the jazzmen got ready to play. Ronnie made an announcement, introduced the band, and told the same joke he told every night. People laughed as they always did. The band began, marking my opportunity to emerge from beneath the stage. I casually brushed myself down, stepped out into the light and walked across the stage, bowing toward Ronnie and the band. No one in the audience seemed surprised or even cared. I took the first empty seat, sat down, relaxed, and soaked up everything the jazzmen from London had to offer.

It was on such a night in the Downbeat, three stories up underneath the shadow of the high-level bridge, that my mates and I first talked about putting our own band together. We'd fallen in with a local gang of wild guys called the Squatters who drank hard, played hard, and were among the first to embrace American music. We were like a motorcycle gang. . . without the motorcycles.

We were regulars at the Downbeat on weekends, and we began looking for other players outside of our college. Our first group was a jazz outfit called the Pagan Jazzmen. It didn't last long as we were soon

Chas Chandler and I tear it up on the original Animals'
first American tour.

5

taken over by R&B—and we dropped the "Jazzmen" portion of the band's name and became the "Pagans."

Less than a year later, the magical combination of the Animals fell into place.

One key find for the band was Chas Chandler. Chas, the oldest member of the group, had played bass and sung backup with an outfit called the Contours. When we met he certainly seemed an unusual bloke. He didn't go out to the music clubs much, preferring workin' man's clubs, playing darts, staining his custom Burton's suits with tobacco smoke. Always in a sharp necktie and spit-polished shoes, Chas was a big guy, standing head and shoulders above us all. He'd worked in a machine shop and had made a great copy of a Fender guitar, which impressed us all. He was clever, and among the things I picked up from him was the lifelong habit of never being without a book.

There was one bad moment between us—one that Chas never forgot. One night after a gig in the Midlands, we were all climbing aboard the old army ambulance we used in those days as band transport. Everyone was there except Chas. We'd heard the news that we were about to depart for London and possibly fame and fortune.

A discussion ensued, sparked by the other band members, about Chas's inability to play like other bass players we'd seen, such as Jack Bruce.

Of course, we didn't realize at the time that Chas's approach of underplaying was key to the original Animals' sound. But with Chas's real and strong ability to function as a manager, why, we thought, don't we make him full-time manager and get another player to step in on bass?

Everyone agreed. But who was to tell him? Without really thinking, I, as the band's lead singer, volunteered.

When Chas got in the van, I told him. The others went white. "We didn't mean it," Alan said. "It was only an idea."

Thanks a fuckin' lot, guys. I felt like a real bastard when I saw tears in the big guy's eyes. From then on I was known as the guy who'd wanted to ax Chas. And I was seen as the shit-stirring, irresponsible maniac.

Despite this sore spot between us, Chas and I certainly had our share of fun. One night when the Animals were playing Barcelona, Chas and I went out carousing after the show and picked up two beautiful Filipino sisters who were on a Catholic tour of Europe. We invited them back to our hotel for drinks. As we went up to our room, the hotel clerk called in the law. I guess the girls looked a little too young, besides which, it was against Spanish law then for an unmarried couple to share a room. By the time the cops arrived the booze was flowing, and the sisters had shed most of their clothing. Nothing quite like a Catholic girl away from home. When they banged on the door, big Chas flew into action, first throwing the girls' clothes on top of a huge bureau near a window. Then, as I slid open the massive drawers, he lifted each of the petite creatures up and gently slipped them inside, putting his finger to his pursed lips.

Chas and me on stage at the Joseph Stalin Hall of Culture in Warsaw . . . the first Western rockers to play there.

Mick Jagger, one of many girlfriends, and me on the town in Manhattan in 1965.
© michael ochs archives.com

"Shhhh."

The cops weren't regular—they were the Guarde Seville—and they came barging in, their massive, bayonetted .303 rifles nearly scratching the plaster off the ceiling as they looked around, perplexed, unable to figure out what had happened to the girls. There were four vodkas and orange juice in the room, a detail that didn't escape their notice.

"Señors," I explained, "We are alcoholics. . . and the service in this stinking hotel is so *slow*!"

Still, they looked under the beds and in the bathroom before leaving.

Early in our careers, the Animals were appearing on the British television show "Ready, Steady, Go!" along with the Rolling Stones, and the two bands shared a dressing room. There was a line down the middle of the room dividing us. The place was piled high with clothing, open cases, shoes, boots, underwear, and shirts. Chas and I sparked a joint and huddled in a corner near an air vent. We had the sound on the TV monitor turned down so we could hear anyone coming. It was nice and quiet waiting for the moment we had to hit the stage and perform live on television for the whole nation.

Silly from the weed, Chas wandered over to Mick Jagger's open case, on top of which was a new Pentax camera Mick had bought in New York. He handed it to me, and I pulled the lens cap off as Chas pulled his prick out of his pants. I snapped a glorious wide-angle shot, advanced the film and put the camera back in its place among Mick's white shirts and dandelion-stripped pants.

A few days later we got an irate phone call from the Stones' office. Seems Mick's girlfriend, Chrissy Shrimpton, had taken the film around to the chemists to have it developed. Mick knew who'd over-exposed himself because Chas's big turquoise ring was in the shot!

Drummer John Steel and I hit it off from the moment we met in class at the Newcastle Art College. He was a wealth of information about jazz, while I turned him onto the blues, and we shared a love for radical movies. He was always smartly dressed, clean and crisp. He had a dry sense of humor, laughing at even the most trying of situations, and was always the one able to think and talk his way through problems. He was probably the most house-trained of the Animals. We spent a lot of time together. One day, we were hanging out on the Left Bank in Paris during the summer break from college when we caught sight of Chet Baker standing in a doorway, jonesing while waiting for his connection. There were so many artists on the run in the city, and we got to know the locals well, watching Memphis Slim tickle the keyboards in the Trois Mallet, crowding around jukeboxes in cafes listening to Ray Charles, Elmore James, Bobby Blue Bland, James Brown, Etta James, and Charles Brown. John and I told them that we'd be back to storm the city with our own blues band and sell out the great Olympia Theater— and that our records would be on those jukeboxes.

It wasn't too long before the dream came true. But John didn't stay an Animal for more than the first few years. In the spring of 1966, he

met the rest of us in a pub—all band business was conducted in pubs—
and said he was leaving the Animals because he was getting married.
While we were all shocked and disappointed, there wasn't one of us
who didn't understand: John and his gal, Ann, were, and are, such a
perfect couple. We knew then it was a sure thing and that their marriage would last, and it has.

My biggest love-hate relationship was always with keyboardist Alan
Price. As it turned out, we were in competition with each other from the
moment we met.

In the wild northwest end of Newcastle, not far from the college, was
an old '50s dance place called the Majestic Ballroom, which featured a
terrific, large, tobacco-stained sign that read "No Jivin'." It was a great
place to hang, as pretty local office girls liked to congregate there for
lunch. Besides, there was always a chance the DJ would play some real
American rock 'n' roll, which in 1962 was something we could normally
only hear on jukeboxes down at the coast.

So after a pint and a ploughman's lunch, we'd head over to the ballroom and its wooden floor, coffee bar, and spinning spotlights.

In the showband was a trombone player named Ronnie who told me
that there was a talent competition and suggested that I should enter.
Just for laughs, I thought I'd do it. Hell, there could be a few quid and
maybe a gig out of it. So one rainy afternoon I asked for application
forms and stuffed them in my coat.

Come competition night, I showed up at the ballroom—and was
stunned. I'd never been there in the evening and it was hopping. I
handed in my application and met with the band leader, his hair slicked
back and as shiny as his stage clothes.

He asked if I had sheet music. No. What key I was going to sing in?
"The best one you got," I answered.

Then, thankfully, the horn player Ronnie came up and settled things, telling the band leader that he'd jammed with me on "Going to Chicago" and "Roll 'Em Pete."

I went back to the bar for a bottle of Brown ale, amazed at the lurid makeup of the overdressed local girls.

While I was checking them out, I saw a list of the other competitors. One name stood out, and I caught a glimpse of him at the bar. His name was Alan Price. I'd seen him before at the Methodist Church Hall, doing Larry Williams's "She Said Yeah!" with a group fronted by Thomas Hedly. He was fucking good. And on this night, he was planning to do his rendition of Jerry Lee Lewis's "Whole Lotta Shakin'." I kind of knew then that I was sunk. This guy sang *and* played piano. I figured I didn't stand a chance just singing with a big band, especially with such a straight crowd.

I got another Brown ale and waited, letting my eyes settle on all those bra straps and seamed nylons. Then the band leader announced the competition.

I knew before either of us went on who was going to take the show.

At the side of the stage, Alan came up and said hello. He told me that he'd been playing with Hedly's group, but that he was playing guitar, not piano, which he would have preferred.

"Well," I told him, "We're thinking about putting a real R&B band together. You can play piano with us anytime."

When the band leader announced Alan's name he climbed onstage, headed right for the big black Steinway, and the 88s began to roll. Microphone stand between his legs, hair flopped over his forehead, Alan got into it, speeding up at the end and throwing off the big-band drummer, just like Jerry Lee.

When he walked off, Alan seemed surprised at the enthusiasm of the applause, but this was a basically straight crowd seeing and hearing live rock and roll for the first time!

At least he warmed them up, I thought as I was called next.

The band kicked it off—all I had to do was fall right in. Through sheer fear and adrenaline, I imagined I was alone, just singing in front of the world's largest record player, and closed my eyes.

"Well, you're so beautiful
but you gotta die some day.
Yeah, you're so beautiful,
you gotta die some day.
All I want is a little lovin'
before you pass away."

There was a flurry of horn solos. The band was on fire. And so was I, which prompted them to keep going. I spat out some improvised lines to fit the riffs. We rocked until sweat and natural timing brought us to an incredible climax.

The audience went fucking nuts. I couldn't believe it myself.

It surprised me even more when I walked off with the first prize that I thought Alan had already earned. I'd won. Very soon we'd be on the same team: the Animals. But the competition never really ended.

Alan was not a native son, which means he was from the twin city of Sunderland. This meant Alan supported the Sunderland football club instead of Newcastle's United. And he drank Sunderland's Double Maxim beer rather than the famous Newcastle Brown. As petty as this sounds, in terms of the Newcastle of my youth, this was quite a distinction. Despite this, however, we needed Alan and knew that he'd fit in. We'd wanted to put together an R&B band Newcastle could call its own.

I was filled with enthusiasm as I'd been down to London where I met Alexis Korner at the club where he played out in the Thames Valley. His band of pioneering players included guys like Ginger Baker and Jack

Bruce, Cyril Davies on electric harp, and Dick Hexal Smith on saxophone. Within the hungry and appreciative crowd I'd seen Brian Jones, Mick Jagger, and Keith Richards. R&B was what was happening and we figured if we got a band together ourselves, we could play all the local clubs, most of which were owned and run by one guy, Mike Jeffery.

While we looked for the rest of the players we needed, I was happy going to art school and jamming around the clubs wherever I could with whomever I could. I sang with rock bands and folk bands, at jazz clubs and dance halls. It was a crash course on how to sing with any band, any style of popular music.

We'd heard of a guy down at the coast who played rock guitar. He had his own amplifier and he also had an echo unit, which was like a secret weapon back then. He had the unlikely name of Hilton Valentine. Hilton was perhaps the trippiest member of the Animals, though he was certainly not without a temper. One time, annoyed at constant knocks on the dressing room door, he fired a pistol off—narrowly missing the manager of the venue and getting us banned for life at every theater in the company's chain.

There were a few weird things I could never figure out about Hilton. At one point, in the early days, he'd had glasses made out of car reflector lenses. They were a deep red, so deep that he couldn't really see where he was going most of the time, a condition made all the worse by the fact that for a period of about six or eight months Hilton was continually tripping on LSD. What a trip he must have had, wandering around half blind, the distorted lights coming through those lenses.

He then joined the Beatles in all that Maharishi Yogi crap and went on to develop a curious phobia about never changing the strings on his guitar—if one broke, it was replaced; otherwise, they didn't get touched.

But we'd come up with the magic combination: me, Chas, Hilton, John, and Alan. We knew we had a shot at making it. Another local,

The original Animals in our very first publicity photo after landing our first record deal. © michael ochs archives.com

Hank D. Marvin, had become the first Geordie to make it big in the music business, playing guitar for Cliff Richard.

Since Presley had been drafted into the army, there was at the time a serious Elvis gap in England, and Cliff Richard came along and filled it. America's black music had become the new secret underground teen language. It seemed to us the best of American culture, and though Americans seemed determined to ignore or discard it, we were happy to pick it up, dust if off, shine it, and give it a new twist.

We had also embraced Beat writers and poets. I avidly read people like Jack Kerouac, Lawrence Ferlinghetti, William Burroughs, anything I could get my hands on. The wonderful thing was to find that there was a connection between these writers, these books, and this music.

Our first London gigs were at the Scene Club, which was tucked away in a back alley. The Animals played there during the club's transitional period from jazz to rock. It was hip, frequented by U.S. servicemen and much of the black London crowd. This mix, usually involving a girl, led to vicious fights, which added to the excitement. The dance floor was tiny, and would hold only about 100 people, while the stage was barely large enough for the band and me. Part of the problem was that there was a white piano hogging the stage. It was old, beat up, and never tuned—no one ever played the thing. It was a cumbersome relic from the days when the club had been a jazz lounge.

One raucous night, I was having trouble finding room on the stage and, fueled by speed and alcohol, I decided to take things into my own hands. Or feet, as it were.

While the band rocked, I climbed up on top of the piano in my thick-soled cowboy boots and just started stomping. The crowd went wild as my feet went through the piano, which crashed to the stage floor. The audience grabbed for bits of it, completing the demolition.

The club's house band at the time was called the High Numbers, which soon changed its name to the Who. Pete Townshend was probably in the crowd that night, and I've always believed that the crowd's reaction to my piano stomp gave him the idea to start the instrument-smashing gimmick the Who became famous for.

One of our great early experiences was going out on the road with Gene Vincent. Well, it was mostly great. Gene will always be one of my heroes but, man, was he a handful. I always liked to joke that he was exactly the kind of guy the American Bureau of Alcohol, Tobacco, and Firearms was created for: He smelled of all three all of the time. The dirtiest of the white boys. Sure, Elvis could move his hips and lips— Gene quivered. Always leather-clad and greasy, Gene and his band had once been thrown out of the Reprise studios by Frank Sinatra himself because of the way they looked.

Seeing Gene on the big screen in *The Girl Can't Help It* was one thing, but to see him live with the English backup band Sounds Incorporated was quite another. He had a permanent limp, and wore leather gloves on stage.

The first time I saw Gene in person, the show was great—he and Eddie Cochrane cooked. But on the road some days after they'd played the Newcastle Empire, somewhere near York, they crashed their car. Eddie died and Gene limped away. Undaunted, Gene stormed the country in the weeks that followed, playing live gigs and appearing on television. He was the leader of the pack for awhile.

Peter Grant, the first Animals road manager—and later the brains and brawn behind Led Zeppelin's success—loved to talk about his time on the road with Gene on an Italian tour featuring Brenda Lee and Sounds Incorporated.

One night, outside of Milan, a bad promoter was giving Grant some trouble over the fee. Grant, however, had to leave his meeting with the guy because a fight had broken out on the tour bus. Gene's wife, Margie, had him by the hair and was banging his head against the windows. Grant boarded the bus and screamed at them to stop, but the tables turned as Gene grabbed Margie's hair and started slamming her head against the windows. Grant yelled at the drummer, the biggest boy in the bunch, to separate the two and sit on Gene until he could get back with the band's money.

The drummer complied a little too enthusiastically, seriously injuring Gene's good leg in the process.

Since there was only one more night of the tour, it was decided not to entrust Gene to some Italian country doctor, but to wait until they could get him back to London. So Gene got Demerol, Wild Turkey, and heroin to ease the pain of his swelling leg.

The opening act on the final night was Nero and the Gladiators. They were playing a real Roman amphitheater, complete with a moat on the inside, and Nero decided to enter with a bang. He rented a flatbed wagon and some horses and staged a grand entrance, with the band on the wagon. A drum solo announcing their entrance. He wanted to steal the show from Gene Vincent.

Only he'd assumed the horses would enjoy a rock 'n' roll drum solo going on behind them. When it began, they bolted. The wagon careened into the stadium, and the band and its equipment were unceremoniously dumped into the moat.

Backstage, Gene's ever-swelling leg had his leather pants straining at the seams, and Grant bumped him up with speed and another round of pain killers. The band kicked off with "Race with the Devil." But Gene was so out of it he couldn't stand steady and promptly slid to the floor. Grant and a roadie got some rope and tied the rocker to his mike stand. Four or five numbers later it was all over and the next day Gene was back in London getting the medical treatment he needed.

Gene toured endlessly—often not even knowing where he was. Peter loved to tell the story of Gene's heading homeward from a long tour and scheduling to make a connecting flight in Seattle on his way to Los Angeles. Tired, stoned, and confused, Gene mistakenly got off the plane in Seattle, climbed into a cab, and ended up in a huge punchup with his driver when he accused him of taking the wrong route to his house. Home, of course, was actually nine hundred miles south, in the San Fernando Valley outside of L.A.

It was in 1963 that the Animals really struck gold. Our growing reputation as a rhythm and blues band landed us the great opportunity to play with Sonny Boy Williamson on a New Year's show that became a classic recording, *The Animals With Sonny Boy Williamson*. It's probably our best live recording—although somehow we've never received a dime in royalties from it. This was the first of many times the Animals would get fucked out of our money.

Still, playing with Sonny Boy was the first of many honors. What a character. He once bolted from a gig he was playing when he saw sheriff's deputies coming through the door to bust him for draft evasion. Sonny Boy went through a window behind the stage and hightailed it home by cab—a ride that cost him more than $500!

He was also one suspicious cat. He always cooked his own meals. Even at fancy dinner parties like those hosted by Giorgio Gomelski and his wife—both gourmet cooks—Sonny Boy would, as politely as possible, go off into a corner with a little cookstove he had and boil up a pot of pig's feet. He was so paranoid that he'd be poisoned, like Robert Johnson, that he never ate a meal he didn't prepare himself.

The Animals' next big break was appearing with Jerry Lee Lewis, Little Richard and Gene Vincent in a big concert that was shown on TV as *Whole Lotta Shakin'*.

I always found you had to be careful approaching Gene when he was locked up in his dressing room. If yours was an unwelcome face you could be the subject of verbal abuse—or suddenly have a gun pointed at you. Onstage, Gene always seemed to have that thousand-yard stare. . . he'd look over his shoulder back to the band with a look that could kill.

Eventually, his handlers would rouse his wife to come and calm the beast. Between her temper and his, sometimes things just got worse.

When we toured with Gene, his paranoia was at an all-time high. Not a good thing for a gun-crazy man. The promoters thought that if Margie was on the road with him, he'd be a little easier to handle. Problem was that as soon as she arrived, Gene became convinced that everyone wanted to fuck her. Whenever he couldn't find her, he'd go on the prowl trying to catch her in the sack with someone. He never did, of course—it was all in his head.

One night we were staying at one of those old airless, Victorian railway hotels. (I don't remember whether it was Manchester or Birmingham.) I'd left my door open to allow some fresh air into the room. Suddenly, the door swung open and two men crept toward me in the dark. I just lay silent under a bundle of blankets as they looked around the room and poked at the lumps in the bed.

"I know she's in here somewhere, the bitch!"

It was Gene, with the hotel's concierge, looking for Margie.

don't let me be misunderstood

The biggest score for the early Animals was when Peter Grant, at that time working out of one of the top talent agencies, called us in Newcastle with the news that we'd been chosen for Chuck Berry's U.K. tour, which featured Jerry Lee Lewis and others. Every band in Britain had been hoping for that tour—the Yardbirds, the Stones. But the Animals scored.

What an experience it was, traveling from town to town on a little English bus with Chuck Berry and Jerry Lee Lewis; it was a four-wheeled microcosm of America's biggest social problems. There was the crazed Jerry Lee Lewis and the temperamental Chuck Berry, trustful of no one, just trying to survive the mad little world and hoard every penny he could. The two of them were at each other's throats constantly.

Those early tour buses were hardly a model of luxury. The seats were stiff and uncomfortable and didn't recline. There was just one sleeper seat on the whole bus, at the back. Peter Grant, who came on the road as the tour manager, tried to maintain the peace between Jerry Lee and Chuck.

"OK," Peter would say. "Jerry Lee, you had the sleeper last night and Chuck's gonna have it tonight. Besides, Chuck's song just went up in the charts so he outranks you."

Jerry Lee would have none of this and would start cursing and swearing. His roadie would pull his Colt .45 out of his shoulder holster and start waving it around. Chuck would come on the bus carrying his guitar, a rag tied around his head and the collar of his raincoat pulled up, and would make an attempt to walk by Jerry Lee without incident, but Jerry Lee would always snear under his breath something like "Yeah, get to the back of the bus, nigger, where you belong."

Then it would be mayhem—fists flying, everyone of us getting into the melee, heads bouncing off the bus windows. It was wild.

We couldn't wait for the excitement of America.

19

As we started the tour, the Animals discussed our performance strategy. We wanted to make the most of the opportunity, using the exposure of the tour to our best advantage. At the time our very first single, "Baby Let Me Take You Home," had hit No. 15 on the British charts. We knew that every band onstage would be trying its hardest to make an impression as aggressive rock players. But we realized it was hopeless to try and out-rock Chuck Berry and decided we'd make a more lasting impression if we finished our set with something slow and melodic. We'd been working on an arrangement of "House of the Rising Sun" and decided that this tour was the place to debut it. It was a smash. The audiences went wild.

We recorded it not long after. The day we went into the studio began at King's Cross Railway Station, 9:45 one Saturday morning. The overnight train from Manchester pulled into the massive Victorian palace of King's Cross. We stumbled with our luggage onto the platform—the five members of the Animals and our trusty roadie, Tappy R. Wright. As we walked toward the train's rear luggage compartment, Hilton saw a massive rubber-wheeled cart with a handle just right for off-loading our gear.

A rail employee came lurching out of the shadows. "Here, you can't use that," he said. "That's British Railways property. It can't leave the station, and it can't be used by people who are not employed by British Rail. It's more than me job's worth."

"It's more than me job's worth," we all repeated in unison, laughing at the uniformed intruder.

Chas pulled a five-pound note out of his trouser pocket and leaned forward, crumpling the note into the poor bugger's hand, sending him on his way. We began loading our equipment onto the handcart.

So it was that we six Geordies made our way through the morning streets of London's empty business district. It was like a scene from a sci-fi movie—desolate, just six guys, pushing our worldly goods and our wildest dreams on a British Railways handcart toward a future we were unable to imagine.

The recording studio was located in a basement on the edge of the financial district. Waiting downstairs in the cool gloom was our producer, Mickie Most, and a recording engineer, Dave, who'd never recorded anything electronic in his life. Until that morning, he had dealt only with classical music.

Baby-faced Mickie hailed from South Africa. His background was in performance, but he'd decided he would be better off doing something else, like turning raw talent into gold. While Mickie certainly had an ear for picking hit songs, I never thought he truly deserved the reputation he had as a producer. In fact, there was one occasion that has always stuck out in my mind as proof that he really didn't know what he was doing. We'd recorded some song—I don't remember which—and Mickie came over the intercom from the engineering room to say that the take was perfect, except for the guitar solo, so we'd have to do it again. Chas pointed out that with the four-track recorder we could just punch it in.

"You can?" said Mickie, surprised.

We were all so young at learning this new craft that the so-called megaproducer didn't even know about over-dubbing.

Naturally, we didn't make it any easier for Mickie. England was in the throes of a social revolution and suddenly it was fashionable to be northern and working class. For readers who didn't grow up in England in the 1950s and 1960s, there was a clear social distinction between coming from the north or being a native Londoner—and anyone from the north was truly looked down upon. The Animals were the rawest thing that Mickie had ever had on his hands, and he soon learned that one did not control the Animals: One guided us, made suggestions, but our basic makeup was to be out of control.

One of our biggest disagreements was, in fact, over "House of the Rising Sun." Mickie didn't want us to record it and even Jeffery, our manager, said it was a waste of effort and money. But the reception the song received on that Chuck Berry tour convinced the band to do it—although we certainly had no idea the track would go to No. 1 all around the world, would cause electronic feedback to seep into the fingertips of young Bob Dylan and spark him into going where he needed to go: electric. There was a tale that Dylan and Joan Baez were driving across America in a fishtail convertible Cadillac, and somewhere in Kansas they heard the Animals on the radio. Bob yelled to Joan to stop the car. He got out and banged on the front fender, "Electric!" he yelled, "Electric!"

Seemed like one of those funny old rock 'n' roll stories. John Steel recalls meeting Dylan, at his manager Al Grossman's apartment in New York, and Dylan told him that it was true: our recording of "House of the Rising Sun" is where he got the idea to go electric.

The song has its roots in a seventeenth-century British folk melody, but became what it is today after circulating among Southern American musicians. It was first recorded, in fact, by black bluesman Texas Alexander in 1928. Roy Acuff, Woody Guthrie, Big Bill Broonzy, Josh White, Dylan, and others recorded it before the Animals' version, in which I changed the lyrics to make it the story of a "poor boy" rather than a "poor girl," as it was originally written.

Yeah, this was the song that launched I don't know how many guitar players and planted the seed of countless babies in the back seats of Chevys. This is the song that has taken me down many a back alley, led me to women's prisons, shark fighters' conventions, dope dealers, radio stations, breakfasts with naked ladies, Mafia kingpins, be-ins, love-ins and a life on the road, of motels and hotels, a Spanish villa, and even an Israeli Army sleeping bag.

I remember the recording session well: Alan Price cranked up the Vox Continental, giving it that Jimmy Smith edge. Chas leaned over toward John's drum kit. Hilton had on his peaked cap, a style he'd copped from Donovan. He hit the opening notes, those magical notes.

don't let me be misunderstood

In the separation booth I squeezed the cans onto my head and held them tight with both hands. I saw Hilton's face, which always lights up when he plays the intro. Mickie gave us the signal. Needles began to bounce. David, the virgin rock 'n' roll engineer, put his glasses on, and we got down to business. A spark hit the room, was caught on the magnetic tape, and the magic began, all reflected through half-empty bottles of Newcastle Brown Ale.

We went halfway through the song so the engineer could adjust all the levels, the tape rolled, and then we played it through once. That was it. "House of the Rising Sun" took us 10 minutes and cost us less than four pounds to record—about 10 bucks, I guess. It sold millions.

During the rush to press the single and print up the labels, one of the most pivotal, disastrous moments of my life occurred. Jeffery came to the band and explained we had a problem. "House of the Rising Sun" was a traditional song that we as a group had arranged, but there wasn't enough room on a 45 label to print all of our names. Jeffery said we were to elect one name and put it on, just for the label, and that the legalities and sharing would all be worked out later. Jeffery suggested Alan Price's name and, insanely, we agreed. With the stroke of a pen, the rest of the Animals were screwed. Ripped off from the get-go—from inside. We should have known better than to trust Alan, who had once worked as a tax collector.

I think that's another reason John Steel left the band when he did. He recognized that we were all in for a fucking when the first check from "House of the Rising Sun" came in and Alan got every penny.

In all honesty, we probably would have signed anything to get onto the charts. In just two weeks, we had a No. 1 hit around the world. Soon, we were on a jet to New York.

The instant we were on U.S. soil, we found ourselves in a carnival of madness. We were hustled through customs and taken through a side exit because the fans out front had become so unruly that the security guards and cops were losing control. They didn't want another Beatles-like reception—but we did! Instead of putting us in limos, the record company arranged for each band member to be driven to the hotel in a new Mustang convertible, complete with a gorgeous model dressed up as a cuddly little animal in fishnet stockings and leopard-skin tails.

Ah, America! Step out into the light!

At our first press conference, the record company had arranged for a line of screaming teenage girls to come up to our table and get autographs. One girl came up, leaned over the table and told me, "Here, sign these," lifting her sweater to reveal two beautiful breasts. Before I could write my room number on her flawless skin, however, security spirited her away.

Our agency had booked us into the Paramount Theater in Times Square, which was about to be closed. We would be a part of its grand farewell, a long series of shows spread over a couple of weeks. The bill was filled with an incredible array of talent, but it was a bit disconcerting

The first Animals press conference and autograph session in America. © michael ochs archives.com

to find out that our "House of the Rising Sun" success meant we were headlining over. . . Chuck Berry! Other artists "supporting" us were Dionne Warwick, Dee Dee Sharp, the Dixie Cups, and Little Richard.

Richard was in a royal state of outrage, I remember. He was quite rightly insulted that he had a measly twenty minutes to play before the Animals took the stage. If he went over his time limit and caused the show to run late, warned stage manager Bob Levine, the theater would be fined $10,000 by the city. At the time, city ordinances dictated show curfews, but Richard didn't give a shit.

Every night during the run, he'd come offstage dripping in sweat, and get in the elevator that transported acts from the stage level up to the dressing rooms. One night, I was riding up with Richard, having watched from the wings while he performed.

"Great show, man," I told him as one of his entourage, a young, skinny black kid, fanned him with a big towel, trying to cool him down.

There was a big cop on security duty in one corner of the elevator, and he just stood there smoking a cigarette. Just before the elevator doors closed, Levine stepped through, yelling.

Richard had gone ten minutes over time. Levine warned him that he was taking time away from the Animals, and that if he did it again he'd be fired.

Richard exploded and he flew into a rage. With his high-pitched voice, he sounded like an old woman going berserk. He told Levine to go fuck himself and lunged at him, the young black kid trying to hold him back. Then the cop, who didn't move a muscle, spoke up and calmly told Richard he'd put a .38 between his eyes if he didn't shut up. Richard chilled. And, as I recall, he didn't break his twenty-minute time limit for the remainder of the Paramount run. And the young black kid? I'd meet up with him a few years later and we'd become best friends. His name was Jimi Hendrix.

The weeks at the theater were a great buildup for our rendezvous

Ed Sullivan gets playful after our third appearance on his show, the first with Dave Rowberry on keyboards, following the departure of Alan Price. © michael ochs archives.com

with history—following in the Beatles' footsteps, we were to appear on "The Ed Sullivan Show."

The screaming girls camped outside our hotel were always on the verge of being out of control, and we couldn't even risk showing ourselves. We found out how dangerous this could be when John Steel lifted his hotel room window and looked down at the fans massed on the street many stories below. As soon as the crowd saw him, it erupted, and there was a screech of brakes as a car narrowly missed hitting a girl who had run into the street screaming about having seen one of the Animals. Later, one girl had a finger chopped off in a door of the Sullivan theater as overzealous security guards slammed it shut.

There were three days of rehearsals before we appeared on "Ed Sullivan." For us Brits, the host was a truly American enigma. Ed was at the center of the burgeoning television monster and controlled the airwaves of American culture. Bands lucky enough to headline his shows had the whole of America for an audience.

Despite having so much power, he was very anti-showbiz. He didn't look or talk showbiz. Hell, somebody who looked and talked like Ed Sullivan probably couldn't get on television these days even if he were willing to pay for it! Richard Nixon always made me think of him: an old man with uplifted shoulders, a long, shallow jaw, dark eyes and gangly arms that would flap around like a traffic cop's. We soon found it was best to keep out of his way.

After rehearsals went well we thought everything was going to be fine. But on show night Sullivan screwed up and introduced us from stage left instead of stage right, so we all stumbled down from the wrong direction, looking like complete assholes. On the second of our six appearances, we wanted to go on and sing a new song we had written, called "I'm Crying." We figured that we didn't need more exposure for "House of the Rising Sun," but that's all Ed wanted. He told us to shut up—we would play "House" or not appear at all.

We agreed. Later, Ed came back in a better mood and gave us a second spot on the show so we could do our new song. But when we performed it, some fucker in the audience jumped up and started yelling anti-Vietnam, anti-Lyndon Johnson rants before being carted off by security.

Jamming at the Cafe Au Go Go with guitarist Danny Kalb of the Blues Project.
Photo by Linda McCartney.

don't let me be misunderstood

Immediately after, we were informed by the network censor that our segment would be cut because the network would never allow the anti-war protest to reach the public. That wasn't the worst thing that happened, either. That particular show also featured the Supremes, and at one point Ed had the beautiful singers in tears. I passed their dressing room and saw him screaming at all three of them, telling them that they'd never appear on his show again. I don't know what they'd done to offend him, but whatever it was it couldn't have warranted his boorish behavior.

I ended the night by taking the Supremes' Mary Wilson out to a club—the most pleasant experience I had during our time with Ed Sullivan. Of course, singing "House of the Rising Sun" in front of millions on the stage where Elvis had his hips censored was a thrill—and no doubt contributed to the song's popularity and success on the charts. I've been a rock 'n' roller for thirty-five years, spent a lifetime onstage and danced, lived with, and loved the bitch called fame. And it was that one song that fired me up, that opened the doors to my wildest dreams and lured me into the land of the blues.

I had more than a dozen other hit songs in the years that followed, but "House of the Rising Sun" burned its mark into my soul and changed my life forever.

CHAPTER 2

the fella in the dark glasses

Even in Newcastle's sunless, cold winter, he wore them. You couldn't miss him. "Hey, who's the fella with the dark glasses?"

"Oh, you mean M.J. He's the manager of the Downbeat, man."

As things turned out, M.J.—Mike Jeffery—was as much a creator of my early success as he was a personal demolition man.

I first met him shortly after I graduated from art school. I passed my final exams with honors, as much to my surprise as my family's. The first job I was offered was from the Pilkerton Glassworks ceramics company. Not terribly appealing. I was much more thrilled to hear that there was a club owner in Newcastle's west end who was opening a new place and looking for a designer.

I found the building and, stepping over construction materials, looked for the owner. Not much older than the rest of us, he was wearing a smart business suit, white shirt and tie, and prescription sunglasses. We hit it off, and it became my job to turn a Victorian barn into Ground Zero for the city's youth: the Club A Go Go.

For nearly two years, I was in the joint just about every day. Over morning cups of tea and cigarettes, Jeffery spun wonderful stories; he was filled with mystery and intrigue, and I was all ears. Nobody ever did learn much about his early background. He'd served in Egypt with the British Army and was the most worldly man we knew, filling our heads with tales of the mystic Middle East. He told of making fortunes from the sale of army newspapers, which he and his cohorts stole and resold to Arab merchants.

I'd wondered why he was in Newcastle, but I realized he enjoyed being the big fish in our small pond. And it was pretty cool to hang at the big fish's side. He had a lot of coin, and a lot went into the club. It was exciting for me to be able to bring in some of my art school chums to help out. Jeffery understood the need for entertainment: It was as if Vegas had come to Newcastle.

It was surprising that Jeffery managed to bring gambling into Newcastle at a time when gambling was frowned upon all over the British Isles. In those days there were only one or two gaming houses in the country.

But times were changing quickly due to the influence of New York mobsters. Their lifestyle was so appealing to the English criminal minds that the gang life soon crossed the Atlantic, and well-dressed, brutal thugs like the famous Kray twins started popping up.

Jeffery learned that a little intimidation could go a long way. His own mob sprang up around him like morning mushrooms—and was just as toxic. His main enforcer was The Turk, a nasty bastard whose tools of choice were an ax and two highly trained German shepherds.

Even my old man warned me about him. There had been a fire in Jeffery's other club, the Club Marimba. When I heard about the fire I took a city bus over to see what it was all about. I could see M.J. standing in the shadows dressed in his pajamas, bathrobe, and leather house slippers, his dark glasses on the bridge of his nose.

An electrical short was blamed for the fire, but it was my own father who'd done the wiring work, and he declared it arson.

"The man's crooked, I'm telling you," my father said. "It wasn't my electrical cables that were at fault. I jointed them meself. My work is good. It was a setup job, believe me. And if you're going to get involved with this bloke, you're asking for trouble."

Why did the Animals fall under the spell of this guy? He was the most worldly, intriguing, and powerful man we knew. He spoke several languages, had a naturally dark complexion that always made him attractive to women, while his weak eyes and corresponding dark glasses made him mysterious. Like most people with felonious intent, he was charming, attractive, and sometimes a riot to be around.

During the heights of the Animals' success, we spent quite a bit of time in Spain together. Once, I had my '64 Corvette and he had a Shelby Cobra flown in from America, and we decided to race, twenty-four hours straight, back to Newcastle. It was a blur of screeching tires and angry cops. He beat me to the coast, where I just missed the last ferry of the day. Thankfully, however, one of the locals told me about an air ferry that took off from an airfield about twenty miles away. My Corvette and I caught the flight—and beat Jeffery to Newcastle by hours!

The New Animals in one of our many performances at the Beat Club in Germany.

don't let me be misunderstood

We thought of him as our Brian Epstein, and, in a way, he was. He got us out of Newcastle and down to London. We didn't notice his flaws until our first trip to America. Bad enough that he hired a prancing choreographer to teach us how to move onstage—but it was appalling that he insisted we clean up and don shiny suits like the Beatles. The kids would have loved us more as what we were—rough scruffs from Newcastle. With the success of the Beatles, it suddenly became chic to be working-class. I could have died when he roped us into a fucking chewing gum commercial.

Jeffery's actions may have been objectionable, but the man himself never was. He had an alluring personality. Early on, I remember sitting in the back seat of his Humber Hawk as he drove me across town to see a doctor that he'd recommended. I was suffering my first encounter with a sexually transmitted disease. As he drove, Jeffery looked at me in the mirror and laughed about not wanting to catch "it." He was wickedly funny. Just turned nineteen, young and impressionable, I thought I was going to die. I'd heard stories at school about the Iron Umbrella, a nifty little medical instrument which was inserted into a stricken penis in severe cases of the clap. Once inside, it opened up like an umbrella and somehow cleaned out the patient, who was then put on a lengthy course of antibiotics. And if you had one taste of alcohol, the story went, you had to start all over again. I was terrified and M.J. enjoyed playing with my head.

The Newcastle music scene was wonderful. Almost every night of the week at some club or pub there was music going on, from folk to jazz. Life was pretty simple back then. With some spare change in my pocket, I'd jump on a westbound bus, read the evening *Chronicle* to find out where the action was, and head for the chosen gig of the night. Live jazz music: There's nothing like it. Plus it attracted the best girls. At a pub called the Corner House, I'd often see Mighty Joe Young's Jazzmen. Halfway through the night I'd get to feeling so good I'd slide up next to

Eric Burdon

the musicians on stage and tug on the trombone player's jacket. "Hey Ronnie, can I sings a blues tune?" Before they could question my boldness, I'd yell in their ears, "Just a few lines of 'Beale Street Blues.' I know the 'St. Louis Blues,' too. How about 'See See Rider'?"

"Yeah, let the kid do a song," people in the audience would murmur.

"Okay, wait around."

As soon as I saw an opening, I was in, onstage, out there, doing it.

Jeffery began promoting dances for the Newcastle University and soon ended up ruling the city's live music scene. His university dances got to be so successful that he abandoned studying sociology and political science to become a full-time promoter.

Soon after opening his first club, the Downbeat, Jeffery had a run-in with two gangsters who came from London looking for new turf. I was in the Downbeat the day the Kray twins themselves appeared at the entrance to the upstairs dance room. About seven of Jeffery's heavies faced the two men in leather coats. Someone had called the law and it wasn't long before we heard the arriving police cars and the doors bursting open three floors below, I heard a metallic object skip across the dance floor. A small black pistol had been tossed by one of Jeffery's guys, and it slid under a seat on the far side of the room. Just then the doors opened and in came an inspector, with a sergeant and two other policemen behind him. They had passed the departing terrible twins on the stairs but chose not to mess with them.

"What's going on here?"

"Oh, nothing, officer," said Jeffery, pulling his black prescription lenses over the bridge of his nose. "Nothing at all. No problem. Just talking a little business."

And business was good. With the success of the Downbeat, he scraped enough money together to open a coffee shop called the Marimba, which was the club my father did the electrical work in.

After Jeffery had it torched and blamed bad wiring, he took the generous insurance settlement to pay for the completion of the Club A Go Go, just as I designed it. Second only to the Cavern in Liverpool, it became the home of northern music.

The Stones, John Lee Hooker, Sonny Boy Williamson, Graham Bond and Cyril Davies all came through Newcastle and played at the Club A Go Go. Often, we'd get the gig as the backing band.

The Animals played all of Jeffery's joints, and we'd begged him to manage our careers. He wasn't interested, despite the crowd reaction to us and the fact that we'd already recorded our first EP with local studio owner Phil Woods. Then, Graham Bond came to town and met us and played with us. When he returned to London, he told Yardbirds manager Giorgio Gomelski about the band. As soon as Jeffery learned that we had become popular enough for a London executive to be interested, he took notice and suddenly got territorial. He signed us immediately. Mickie Most was brought in as record producer, and Harold Davidson became our new agent. We were transported lock, stock, and barrel to London.

The group was housed in an apartment in Fulham, and Jeffery moved into his own place in the West End. From that point on, we were hardly seen in our hometown, and Mike was not seen at all. He was off making bad deals for the Animals. But we were too hot—for that short time—to be affected by any deals, good or bad.

I probably first heard the term "creative accounting" from the lips of Jeffery. He was always around, waiting in the background, hovering. He was the guy who set up the accounts and the tax shelter in the Bahamas, the most outstandingly bad of the bad deals.

Well, the Beatles had done it, so why not us? "Soon, you'll be touring the U.S.A.," said Jeffery, "and you don't want to pay American and U.K. taxes. But you'd better be quick, this deal has to be done overnight." So we signed on the dotted line. Millions of the Animals' money would disappear there, a huge sum in 1966.

We were sent out on the road to tour, tour, tour, and the money flowed in—into the Bermuda Triangle, that is. When I complained that MGM, our record company, was also a movie company and that we should be landing some movie gigs, Mike secured us a part in the goofy *Beach Party A Go Go.* Yes, I'm embarrassed—as you'll understand if you've seen it.

Jeffery's biggest coup came after I broke up the original Animals in 1966, and Chas decided to go into the production side of the business. In the fall of that year, he met Keith Richards's girlfriend, Linda Keith, in New York. Linda, in turn, introduced Chas to a twenty-three-year-old Jimi Hendrix at the Cafe Wha? in New York's Greenwich Village. Jimi was then in a band called Jimmy James and the Blue Flames. Chas was captivated and offered to take Hendrix to England to put together a new

Chas Chandler gives advice to his new rising star, Jimi Hendrix.

band. It was a masterstroke, as history confirms. I'd actually met Jimi some time earlier, back when he was playing with Little Richard—who treated him like a slave, but nevertheless had a huge influence on him. Jimi quickly outgrew Little Richard and everyone else. And on September 24, 1966, Chas, Jimi, and my former roadie Terry McVay boarded a plane for London and, as it turned out, a magical, tragic destiny.

Chas quickly hired English drummer Mitch Mitchell. Noel Redding had auditioned for my new band, but I'd passed on him. Jimi saw his potential and grabbed him immediately. With Chas at the helm, the Jimi Hendrix Experience was born. *Are You Experienced?* and *Axis: Bold As Love* followed in the next twelve months.

Because we'd lost all of our Animals money, Chas was hard-pressed to launch Hendrix properly. He'd hocked one of his own guitars for startup-cash, but to get the backing he needed he was willing to deal with the devil once more: Mike Jeffery. The deal was that Chas and Jeffery shared twenty-five percent of Jimi's earnings.

Chas asserted his primary influence in the studio, while Jeffery quickly became the man behind the scenes.

First of all, they set up a tour with Jimi opening for the Monkees. They knew how insane the pairing was, but counted on its attracting press attention. Then Chas concocted a bizarre story that the Daughters of the American Revolution were shocked and enraged by Jimi Hendrix, the wild, sex-addicted guitar player whom the British press began calling—disgracefully and in the most insultingly racist terms—the "Wildman of Borneo." Can you imagine? This shit happened within the last thirty years. We haven't come that far, have we?

Jeffery claimed to have once worked for British Army Intelligence. Whenever he was in New York he'd buy the latest gadgets and bugging devices and transmitters and the like.

The Animals went to Spain to do shows in support of the clubs Jeffery had been opening (with, as it turned out, our money). After we arrived, I ran into Jeffery on the beach, and he told me that he'd show me how to scuba dive at dawn the next morning.

"Oh, by the way," he said, "don't be surprised in the morning if you see a line of big ships out there. You see those lights?" He pointed toward distant twinklings on the horizon. "Well, the Americans came in. That's the Seventh Fleet out there, son. When the sun comes up, you'll see them in all their glory."

"What are they doing here?" I asked.

"You haven't heard about the atomic bombs?"

A week or so before, an American B-52 bomber carrying four nukes collided with its KC-135 jet tanker while refueling off the coast. Eight of the eleven crew members were killed as the tanker's forty thousand gallons of jet fuel ignited. Two of the nukes ruptured, scattering radioactive crap all over the local fields. A third landed intact near the village while the fourth was lost off the coast. The Yanks were out in full force to recover it, Jeffery said.

They'd so upset the locals with the radioactive contamination that Jeffery was raising the stakes, getting a perverse thrill out of inflaming the tensions.

Early the next morning I made my way down to the beach, where people were already gathering to bask in the beautiful weather. It wasn't long before I saw Jeffery emerge from the ocean, wetsuit on, flippers in his hand and tanks on his back.

"I've been up since six," he said as he approached. "The water's nice and clear."

As he had predicted, the huge American battle group was clearly visible, glowing in the light of the morning sun. When we got to his beach towel, he told me he had something to show me, and picked up a black box from among his belongings.

"What's that?" I asked.

"Just another of my little gadgets."

He crouched down, the box in his hands, and I saw there were connecting wires running toward a small battery. "Right," he said, looking out at the ships and the swimmers in the ocean. "I just have to wait for the right moment."

"Right moment for what?" I asked.

"I'll have to fill you in. You see those markers?"

He handed me a pair of binoculars. "Look. There's a net there under the water that divides the swimming area from the boating area. I dove out there this morning. Wait. . . the time's right." He turned the handle on the box and a series of explosions roared up from the water, sending smoke and spray showering all over the beach.

People ran in panic as Jeffery quickly gathered his little black box and scuba gear. He could barely contain himself from laughing as we scurried up the beach. As we got to the bar, people were speculating wildly. Had the Americans shelled the shoreline? Had the nuke in the ocean gone off? Everyone was clearing out, leaving the beach, furious at the American navy offshore. Jeffery was thrilled. He'd once told me that his specialty with the army had been in "creating civil unrest." His pyrotechnic display on the beach led to a huge riot, and ultimately the Americans were banned from Spanish ports for years. From then on I believed what Jeffery told me about his past.

Which doesn't mean I agreed with everything he did. For instance, the time he had Jimi Hendrix kidnapped in Upstate New York, just so he could make himself look good by liberating him. Jeffery paid one set of hoods to kidnap Jimi just so his own muscle could sweep in and save the day.

Jimi himself recalled the incident this way: "Before I realised what had happened I found myself forcibly abducted by four men. I was blindfolded and gagged and shoved rudely into the back of a car. I couldn't understand what the fuck was going on as I lay there sweating with someone's knee in my back. I was taken to some deserted building and made to believe that they really intended to hurt me. They never did tell me why they abducted me. The whole thing seemed very mysterious because after awhile I realized that if they really had intended to hurt me they would have already done it by this time. And the whole thing seemed even more mysterious when I was rescued by three men supposedly sent by the management. They really effected a story-book rescue."

Jimi was a quiet, soft-spoken guy who hated confrontation. He knew Jeffery was bad news but despite my years of warnings, it wasn't until the final months of his life he told me that he was finally going to fire Jeffery. He had hopes of bringing Chas, who had by then quit Jimi's management, back into the fold.

After Jimi's death, Jeffery tried to refute claims that he had an uncommon hold on Hendrix, telling *Rolling Stone* magazine "If he wanted to split, he would have split. As far as being artistically frustrated, Jimi had an incredible genius about him, and the common thing with most artists of that calibre is that they are constantly artistically frustrated."

Yeah, right. I was told that Jeffery ended up with a set of Jimi's tapes that no one else knew about and started going around to record companies pretending they were by some undiscovered genius. He claimed he'd found Jimi's successor but needed serious cash to develop this mystery talent.

The last time he left New York he was carrying a briefcase filled with the tapes—and several million dollars in cash.

After Jimi's death, producer Alan Douglas claimed there was a suite of music called *Black Gold* that was missing. It was, he claimed, an autobiographical, multi-song fantasy piece Jimi had been working on. Jimi intended it to accompany an animated feature about a black rock star—himself—on the road. Douglas described it as the best thing Hendrix ever wrote, forty minutes of fresh, new material that clearly demonstrated the direction Jimi was headed in.

According to Jimi's estate, there is a demo of a song called "Black Gold," but nothing more. Mitch Mitchell, on the other hand, has said that when Jimi died, there were at least six cassettes of material that Jimi was working on, and that a suite of songs, called *Black Gold,* was among them.

I never heard any of the music, but I remember Jimi telling me about his idea for *Black Gold.* He talked excitedly about the cartoon character he'd envisioned for it. So I know he did at least some work on the suite before he died. Who knows if that was the music Jeffery exploited to raise all that money in New York before his final flight to Europe. After stopping in Spain he was killed in a mid-air collision. Chas called me with the news, and I almost laughed at the irony. Jeffery always had a deep fear of flying and would do the most bizarrely compulsive things, which he superstitiously believed would prevent him from dying in a plane crash. He'd routinely change his itinerary at the last moment and fly strange routes. To get to England from Los Angeles, he'd go through Chicago, Paris, Bonn, Barcelona, and, finally, London. I always suspected it was actually a ruse to give him the opportunity to stop in Zürich and hide some of our cash in his private accounts.

As for his death, I'm not sure I ever fully believed it. I suspect Jeffery was on the ground in Spain and decided there was no way he was getting on that plane. At the time of the crash, there was a civil air traffic controller's strike in France, and the military had taken over. I believe he gave in to his gut feelings of fear and at the last moment decided not to board the aircraft, as he'd done dozens and dozens of other times at the last minute.

The plane, an Iberia DC-9, was over French/Spanish airspace when the lack of controllers resulted in it slamming into a Spantax Coronado. The Coronado limped back to an airfield, but the DC-9 spun out of control, killing all sixty-one passengers and seven crew listed on the manifest.

Jeffery realized that he was, technically, on the plane and its casualty list. He was a free man with a briefcase full of money. Yes, it may be my hard-won paranoia, but I think he's probably on a beach somewhere right now sipping a fruit drink and gently tanning the face of anonymity bought from some plastic surgeon. Maybe he's even reading this book and having the mother of all laughs; if so, I hope you choke on a mango, fucker.

"Eric, it's all in your head," they say. Maybe, but Jeffery was exactly the kind of person who could pull off a scam like that.

And what successful rock 'n' roll manager or agent isn't? You have to be a certain type of person to do it. Not necessarily evil or corrupt, but you have to have a certain. . . well, ruthlessness about you.

And I'll give you ruthless: Peter Grant, the one-time Animals road manager who went on to huge success with Led Zeppelin, told me a great story when we were traveling together on a long flight to New York from London. Before joining the Animals, he'd been working in Harold Davidson's booking office in London, when Little Richard hit

the top of the charts and embarked on his first English tour. It was a wild success, but Richard felt ripped off and vowed never to play England again. When it appeared that a follow-up release of Richard's was also going to hit the Top 10, Davidson's office begged him to return to England. Richard refused, fearing he'd get screwed again.

He only agreed, Grant said, after they offered to bring him and his band to England in style—aboard the QE2—to make up for the problems on the previous tour.

Two weeks later, Richard and his band showed up at Pier 29 in New York's harbor and boarded the world's most luxurious ocean liner. The chief purser met them at the top of the gangway, passenger list in hand, and welcomed them on board. He then told them their first show of the evening began at 8:30 in the main ballroom. Davidson had booked them to play twice nightly to pay for their passage!

Grant howled at the story. A giant of a man, he'd been a wrestler in England before getting into show business, and his legendary fierceness was there from the beginning. One night in London I was late. . . I'd bought a sportscar so I could drive myself to the Animals' gigs alone. When I walked into the dressing room, the other Animals just gave me an icy stare, but Grant exploded.

"Where the fuck d'ya think you've been?" he hollered.

"Er, been driving to the gig, ain't I?"

"Well, you're late!"

"So, I'm late. I drove here as fast as I could."

"Well, you fucking leave earlier the next time, you cunt!"

He picked me up and threw me about 10 feet into a wall. I slid to the floor. I was never late again.

Peter Grant and Mike Jeffery—two fierce and ruthless men who had a huge impact on my early career.

The one music legend—I wouldn't call him fierce or ruthless, but his reputation certainly preceded him—that I never did work with was Phil Spector. We came close, however. In the early 1970s in Los Angeles, I got a call that he wanted to meet with me at his Sunset Strip offices.

I walked in from the harsh late-afternoon sun, and was escorted by two huge men whose white dress shirts were framed by shoulder-holstered automatic handguns. They took me into Spector's dark second-floor office, where the producer, wearing dark glasses and a black cap, was sitting in a huge velvet chair. The heavy drapes behind were drawn, allowing only a crack of light through, which silhouetted Spector at his desk. It was lighting by Francis Ford Coppola! As he began talking, I interrupted him and asked if the armed guards were really necessary. He dismissed them.

Then he told me that there were three singers in the world he wanted to work with: John Lennon, Bob Dylan, and me. Was I interested?

Well, sure, I thought—Spector was a god among producers. Then I heard the deal: He was to get fifty percent of all revenues and would maintain ownership of the master tapes. I thanked him for the offer and said I'd consider it and get back to him. With that, the short, intense meeting was over and I was back out on L.A.'s sunny streets, hardly believing what had just happened.

In the end, I declined the offer. It wasn't the right time for me. I was scared to get into bed with any new producer or manager, and the cut he wanted seemed excessive.

I don't know if Spector ever approached Dylan or not. I've never asked him. Lennon, of course, found himself in a world of confusion after he and Spector recorded what would eventually be released as the *Rock and Roll* album. They battled it out in court and Lennon eventually had to cough up nearly $100,000 to Spector before the album could be released.

I don't assume I would have ended up in the same boat. A union with Spector may have yielded spectacular results that would have benefited us both. I have always wondered what my voice would have sounded like up against his famous "wall of sound."

I figured I'd never see him again—he's reclusive in the extreme. But just before New Year's Eve 2000, I was playing a gig with Nancy Sinatra at the Whisky in Hollywood, and who was in the crowd, surrounded as always by an entourage, but Spector.

He got word to me that he wanted to meet after the show. Backstage, when he appeared in his ever-present dark glasses, he was his usual self: soft-spoken, friendly, and enormously generous with his praise.

One of the most talented enigmas in rock history.

CHAPTER 3

animal planet

There's really no gentle or polite way to ask if you've had your dick dipped in plaster. By this, of course, I refer to the countless times people have asked me whether I was captured in full-mast perpetuity by the legendary Cynthia Plaster Caster, who managed to immortalize the members of many, including that of Jimi Hendrix.

"Well, they tried," I always joke. "Didn't have enough plaster."

The truth is that the day Cynthia set her sights on the Animals, the conditions were less than favorable. We were aboard an old twin-engine Martin. The plane spewed black fumes and sparks from one engine cowling as if the carb mix were wrong. And the pilot was perpetually running on vodka and tanked himself up before each flight with pure oxygen.

On this particular day, Hilton was at the front of the plane tearing down a brick of Columbian weed. Behind him was Barry Jenkins, the drummer who joined the band after John left for a sane, domestic life.

On the plane with us were Herman's Hermits and Peter Grant, all playing poker among the stash of amps and equipment, which was sliding around and shifting the balance of the plane through all the turbulence.

Cynthia was aboard with her kit of plaster, vaseline, and goodies to make our best friends immortal. She was accompanied by a girlfriend assistant with a mouth bathed in bright red lipstick. She looked like she could swallow the Chicago Cubs infield.

Alas, for posterity this was far too turbulent and frightening, not exactly the ideal environment for maintaining, shall we say, full attention. What's more, Cynthia hadn't used enough vaseline on me and the hardening plaster began yanking out my pubic hair. Hardly the conditions that would encourage one to maintain the sort of hard-on you'd like to have represent you on the shelf for years to come.

So that encounter was a bust. We ran into Cynthia again, soon after, backstage somewhere in the Northeast, but didn't have enough time before our performance to immortalize our johnsons.

"We'll see you in L.A.," Cynthia said.

I was on the road a lot in those days, but I maintained a flat in Dalmeny Court in London's West End, a stone's throw away from the Royal Palace. I was right above the Indica Gallery, Ham Yard, St. James. This was Yoko Ono's place of business, into which strolled one day the ever-inquisitive John Lennon. He came looking for something to hang on his wall and left in love for the rest of his life.

My place was a five-minute walk from Piccadilly, the very heart of the busiest section of London. I had an Italian restaurant downstairs fix me breakfast. I had my black Corvette parked in an underground garage one block away. I always seemed to be on the run, at high speed, on my way to TV, radio, and magazine interviews. The Animals were hot stuff. I was a bad boy, we were all bad boys, and the musical press followed our antics weekly. Life was fun, one big fucking joke.

I recall staggering out of the Scotch of St. James one night with two beautiful black girls, one on each arm, tripping toward my Corvette. On the street we passed Sean Connery, in his Savile Row-tailored suit. He looked at me sideways and said, "Fuck me, I'm in the wrong business."

Before the Beatles stopped performing in 1966, John Lennon and I often hung out together at the Scotch, exchanging tales from our most recent tours. He was always keen to hear updates, sniffing, "You guys seem to have more fun." The Beatles didn't have the freedom the Animals did. They were always surrounded by security and followed by nearly as many reporters as fans.

I always liked John. He was a sweet guy and actually quite shy in private; he used the sarcastic facade to protect himself in public.

This was a great time for us all—exciting and new. As John himself told *Rolling Stone* magazine in one interview, "This was the best period . . . We created something. . . . We didn't know what we were doing, but we were all talking, blabbing over coffee, like they must have done in Paris, talking about paintings. Me, Burdon, and Brian Jones would be up night and day talking about music, playing records, and blabbing and arguing, and getting drunk."

I miss those days. I miss John. I always liked the boys in the Beatles, but I have to say that it was John I could relate to the most. One of my fondest memories of him was at a party we'd crashed in London. The hosts were an Anglo-German couple with a young son. John kept his rapt attention all evening—by speaking to him in German. Of course, Lennon had a streak of the bad boy in him. One night in the Scotch of St. James, Princess Margaret was dancing, and John slid up behind her and whispered something outrageous in her ear. He was in hysterics about it, but wouldn't tell me what he'd said. The next day, the owner of the Scotch got a stern warning from the Palace that if he couldn't control his patrons, the authorities might investigate further and shut the place down.

We had some great times together, something John gave a nod to in his song "I Am The Walrus." It may be one of my more dubious distinctions, but I was the Egg Man, or, as some pals called me, "Eggs." The nickname stuck after a wild experience I'd had at the time with a Jamaican girlfriend named Sylvia. I was up early one morning cooking breakfast, naked except for my socks, and she slid up behind me and cracked an amyl nitrate capsule under my nose. As the fumes set my brain alight, and I slid to the kitchen floor, she reached to the counter and grabbed an egg, which she broke into the pit of my belly. The white and yellow of the egg ran down my naked front, and Sylvia slipped my egg-bathed cock into her mouth and began to show me one Jamaican trick after another. I shared the story with John at a party at a Mayfair flat one night with a handful of blonds and a little Asian girl.

"Go on, go get it, Egg Man," Lennon laughed over the little round glasses perched on the end of his hooklike nose as we tried the all-too-willing girls on for size.

I'll never forget one really painful moment with him. He'd been raised, as has been recounted hundreds of times, by his aunt and had been severely traumatized after his mother was run over and killed by a drunk off-duty cop. I'm sure this had a lot to do with John's attitude toward authority figures. As for his father, he'd abandoned John and his mother when John was about five. Once John became a Beatle, how-ever, some pricks in the media tracked down the old man in Australia and persuaded him to travel to Britain to record a song and capitalize on the celebrity of the famous son he'd discarded.

That night, as John and I stood at the bar of the Scotch with drinks in our hands, the senior Lennon came through the doors with two press scumbags. John immediately tensed up. He swallowed his drink in one gulp but held onto his glass. When the trio reached us, there was an awful silence. The man in the middle put out his hand. John fixed his eyes on the stranger, and an uncomfortable smile came upon his face—always the mark of his nasty, defensive side kicking in. Then, in his nasal accent, John said to his long-lost father so the whole bar could hear: "Well, I guess you found yerself a gig at last, you old cunt." He made a show of wouldn't think of moving to America. For me, it was such a rush. William S. Burroughs lived in the apartment next door to me in London. I never saw him, but I'd notice when he'd pick up his mail and I could hear him shuffling around inside.

I'd come a long way from Newcastle, and I was finally chasing the dream that had haunted me since early teenhood: America. Shit, I wasn't even a teenager when I discovered jazz, courtesy of movies and television. Because of my father's work as an electrician, we were among the lucky few to have a TV early on. Cliché or not, it brought the world into my living room. Clips from America became my obsession, particularly anything to do with jazz or blues. I even took up trombone.

Defining moments are easy to remember. Here's one of mine: I was ten years old, sitting in front of the crackling, fuzzy image of a BBC announcer as he introduced a musician from America. It was my first sight of Louis Armstrong. I'll never forget that image of him, bathed in sweat, wiping his brow with a white handkerchief. He looked so uncomfortable sitting there on that talk show, holding his horn and fretting over his mouthpiece, which one of the show's handlers had taken away to keep Louis from blowing during the interview.

In 1955, a year or so later, the most amazing thing happened. Armstrong came to Newcastle on a European tour as America's Ambassador of Goodwill. I knew his music and had read a lot about the history of the American South, but that wasn't currency enough to get a ticket to his show. So I stood, with dozens of others, outside Newcastle's City Hall and listened through the narrow space between the doors. It was paradise. And, yes, Louis, the whole world was smilin'!

I stood right up against the doors, eyes closed, and sang along. I knew most of the tunes.

When intermission came, two Geordie cops opened the two big doors. Suddenly, right in my face, was Jack Teagarden, The Big T from Texas! The greatest jazz trombonist ever!

I didn't have a pen and paper to ask for an autograph—hadn't even thought of that—but I stammered out a few words. "I play tailgate slide trombone, too!"

Teagarden laughed and motioned for the cops to let me in. As the doors shut behind me, he said, "Wait here, kid. Gimme a minute."

There were all kinds of people milling about, and it was then that I got my first magical whiff of marijuana—a smell I never forgot. Then Teagarden reappeared.

"Hey, kid, come here. I want you to meet somebody."

I followed him down a flight of stairs into another noisy, smoky room that was hot enough to make me sweat almost immediately. A big fat lady with a dish of ice walked toward one corner, set it down, and handed a wet towel to none other than Louis Armstrong himself. He sat quietly among the noise, and behind him sat an open trunk bursting with a circus of pills, balms, and potions.

He looked at me and smiled—a smile as big and as bright as the sun.

"Hey, kid, how's ya doin?" he called out, his voice like dry leaves underfoot. I was speechless and just nodded, frozen where I stood. Some people in the room chuckled at my terror.

Then, from behind me, a voice called out, "Hey, Pops, in five, OK?" As suddenly as it began, it was over. But what a moment! The gates of heaven had opened for me and, in my mind, I was on the next boat to America.

I had to laugh, years later, on the day in 1964 when Louis knocked the Animals, the Beatles and the Stones down the pop chart with "Hello Dolly." Never did it feel so good to be trounced on the charts!

A lot of fans have asked me about "The Story of Bo Diddley," a song the original Animals had on our *In the Beginning* LP, which recounts the tale of the Animals playing with Bo in Newcastle. I confess: The story was pure fabrication. Bo did, indeed, come to Newcastle when we were starting out. His percussionist, Jerome Greene, really did jam with us

Eric Burdon

John Lee Hooker and me on the porch of his Detroit home, 1966.

onstage at the Club A Go Go. Bo himself never appeared, but the fantasy of playing with him was so good we wrote the song.

We did experience the honor of playing with another one of my idols. As a blues-obsessed college student, I had a sweatshirt made which said "John Lee Hooker for President." When John Lee Hooker came to Newcastle to play a couple of years later, the Animals, then just beginning to get notices, were invited to jam with him in honor of his birthday. I felt very protective of Hooker as fans continually asked him to sign his name, and he was very embarrassed by both a stutter and by being barely able to write. I actually forged his autograph several times to help him out.

John Lee and I hit it off wonderfully, and we hooked up again in New York on the Animals' first American tour. At that time he asked me to stay with him at his home in Detroit, which I did as soon as there was a break in the tour. We spent three great days together listening to music in the clubs and just talking. He told me we had a bond thicker than white or black because of where we were born—him from Clarksdale, Mississippi, and me from Newcastle, a gritty, working-class city he always said could have been situated right in the deep American South.

On his second British tour, Hooker wasn't looking forward to New-castle, which made him nervous in general—while the Animals' main haunt, the Club A Go Go, made him specifically nervous!

At the time, he had a new hit, and everywhere he played was filled to capacity (and sometimes beyond). By the time he got to his gig at the Club A Go Go, the place had about eight hundred people packed in it,

John Lee Hooker and I hang out after playing one of his birthday bashes at Humphrey's by the Sea in California.

and Hooker had to be escorted by his handlers—among them Peter Grant and me—through the rowdy crowd to get onstage. Not a tall man, Hooker felt threatened during the ordeal, but felt fine once the show began: The Geordie reaction was incredible.

The John Lee Hooker book *Boogie Man,* by Charles Shaar Murray, recounts a conversation between Hooker and an acquaintance.

"Did you ever hear of Newcastle?" Hooker asked.

"You mean Newcastle, Mississippi?"

"Newcasle in Britain! Boy, that was rough. There was a bar I played in every night. It was rough. It was called the Club A Go Go. . . fightin' outside, fightin' inside. I ain't gonna play there no more. There were little kids carrying knives—it was rough. Everybody says they fight like this all the time."

A bunch of Newcastle Brown-swilling teens had a Detroit ghetto-born John Lee Hooker looking for the exits—Newcastle, Mississippi, indeed!

We were friends ever since those early tours, and every chance I got I joined John Lee on stage for his birthday. Thankfully, our schedules had been in synch over the past few years for that to work out. It was especially painful for me when John Lee died in the summer of 2001. I was on tour in Europe when I heard the news. The timing was upsetting, too. Just a week earlier, I'd been in the studio recording new material.

I was twenty-five and so full of life
John Lee took me by the hand
In a G.T.O. we did go into the fire heart of the ghetto land
Living in a land where a man is no man until he's been to Hell
and back
One thing you must understand you can't kill the Boogieman

It's a new song I'd written about him, a tune called "Can't Kill the

Boogieman"—about how, to me, he made the blues immortal. I miss him already.

The American black experience has always been fascinating to me. On a personal level, I've always found black women among the most alluring. My first serious love affair was with an African girl named Doreen, and I developed an early reputation for having a lot of black friends, particularly displaced Africans in Newcastle, two of whom were members of the first band I was in, the Pagans. I saw what freedom meant to these exiles, and it engendered an even deeper interest in the African experience in America, resulting in a reputation that preceded me to New York.

When the Animals set foot in America for the first time, there was graffiti on the wall of our hotel proclaiming "Eric Burdon is a nigger lover." Well, yeah, he is, I thought. And fuck you for not understanding that you should be, too.

A few weeks into the tour we were in Memphis for the first time. It was great to see this legendary musical city. One of our first social stops was the Stax Volt recording studio, where we hung out and watched Sam and Dave record "Hold On I'm Comin'"—all twenty takes. We were supposed to meet Otis Redding at the studio that afternoon, but he didn't show. Later, I went around to his room at the nearby Holiday Inn. I rapped with Otis while he played. As I kicked back in the room, Big O was stretched out on the bed, playing a white Fender through a little amp on the floor, singing the Beatles' "Day Tripper." The next day I watched him record with guitarist Steve Cropper, Booker T., and drummer Al Jackson, with label owner Jim Stewart engineering and producing.

It was a mixed band with white producers and executives, and they all treated Otis with the respect he deserved; this was surely the New South, I thought that day.

Not long after, Otis and I were on stage together in London,

The Animals in one of our many televised performances on Ready Steady Go!
© michael ochs archives.com

appearing on an episode of "Ready, Steady, Go!" with Chris Farlowe and Mick Jagger, and we talked about what a great time we'd had in Memphis.

The hotel where we'd first met turned out to be the place where James Earl Ray—or some other racist bastard, if you believe that Ray was a patsy—killed America's last great hope, Dr. King. I don't know what effect that had on Otis, but the last time I saw him, backstage at Monterey, he'd become a different person—not friendly, and quite standoffish. He was surrounded by an entourage of black men and was, I was told, embracing his blackness. I couldn't resent the snub, but it made me sad, because those outward, poisonous influences made the sweet Otis—against all odds—a smaller person, at least offstage.

Dr. King's murder had a great effect on me, though it came as a shock, not a surprise. That very first trip to Memphis had been a joy, but it also marked my first encounter with American racists and the Ku Klux Klan. My idea that I was in the "New South" lasted for only those hours I was with Otis in the recording studio. On our way to the coliseum for the Animals' gig, we came across a Klan parade. It was a wonderful balmy southern night, and there they were, gathered under the trees in a public park, a massive cross burning, and a ring of cops protecting them.

Peter Grant, who was on the road with us—and who was Jewish—had less time for those fuckers than I did. He lost his temper easily, but I'd never seen him go off like this. Down went his window and he was bursting with rage, screaming at the Klansmen and threatening to ram every one of their white hoods up their asses. Thankfully, we got out of there before it got too ugly, though secretly I would have enjoyed watching Peter use a burning cross to give every one of those fuckers hot cross buns.

It was the first of several nasty experiences we had with the racist South. On the same tour, we found ourselves in Meridian, Mississippi, which was home of some of America's most active racists.

At the time, we had a black assistant named Sonny who hailed from New York. When we pulled into the motel in Meridian, the guy behind the desk took one look at the group of us and said, "You guys are OK, but the nigger don't get in here."

Peter Grant was huffing in the background, ready to tear this asshole apart, but we managed to keep him out of the fray. This time it was six-foot-two Chas who intervened, telling the motel manager in his best English accent—with a threatening subtext—that, just days prior, racism had been officially ruled illegal. The guy reluctantly gave us rooms but still demanded that Sonny sleep in an annex. The irony was that Sonny had a bunch of sisters from the projects join him, and they partied the night away—while the rest of us were banned from the bar in petty retaliation for our insistence on integrating the place.

The next day, we found that the swimming pool was filled with red-neck families. All it took was for Sonny to dive in and the place cleared, leaving it for us alone.

Before our show that night, we went out for a dinner with the mayor and local dignitaries. In New York, I had scored a Japanese tape recorder, state-of-the-art in those days. I liked to carry it around, and I took it to the dinner, thinking we'd have a laugh down the road, listening back to our conversations with these bozo rednecks. At one point the mayor asked us what we wanted to drink. We'd been warned ahead of time that booze was illegal in the area, so we asked what we *could* drink. He said he'd get the best white lightning there was and sent two of his deputies off into the hills to raid some moonshiner.

Some of the stuff I got on tape was chilling. At one point during the dinner the mayor asked if we wanted to go out hunting with him and offered to let me use his prized, over-under 12-gauge because with both barrels it was able to "sting three or four niggers."

The town of Meridian had been forewarned about the Animals being "nigger lovers." Parents forbade their kids to attend and our gig in the 15,000-seat arena was essentially boycotted. Only about five hundred kids showed up.

Mike Jeffery was with us, and he was furious. There was a meeting backstage between us and the promoter. The sheriff came back and told us that we had to go onstage or there was going to be a riot. Even though there were only a few hundred kids in the hall, he had only twelve deputies to control the situation. Then the promoter pulled out a pistol and pointed it at Jeffery and said, "Get out of town or you're all dead."

The sheriff cooly unlatched his old-style .45, ordered the promoter out of the building, and called for an armored car. The sheriff used it to ferry us to safety outside of town. It was an unbelievable experience. It still staggers me to think that kind of racism has gone on in my lifetime.

One of my favorite haunts - backstage at the Apollo with B.B. King, Rufus
Thomas and others. michael ochs archives.com

I learned a lot—good and bad—from my forays into black America on the early Animals' tours. As a performer nothing benefited me more than hanging out at the Apollo in Harlem—and getting to know the greats like James Brown and B.B. King, Chuck Jackson, Big Maybelle. I was made to feel quite welcome in the dressing rooms and backstage, like color didn't matter. On my second visit, B.B. introduced me to the Apollo audience from the side of the stage. Shit! I was in heaven.

I ran up to Harlem quite often when I was in New York, both to escape my fans and to get a chance to see the artists I'd worshipped from afar for years. I'd made friends with Honi Coles, who was an all-time, tap-dancing great, so I had a permanent backstage pass for the Apollo. The fans would sometimes give chase in taxis or their own cars and then trail off when they reached 110th Street. On my first visit, in fact, I went

In Paris with the Hardest Working Man in Show Business, James Brown, and Georgie Fame. © Charlie Gillett/michael ochs archives.com

to the Hotel Theresa where Malcom X had protested and had met with Fidel Castro in 1960, and they let me see his room. Harlem for me was the great escape, and the source of what I'd come looking for: Black America.

Some of the great black performers' stage antics were rooted, of course, in the Southern churches where the preachers went wild. "The Resurrection" was one little gem I witnessed, and I used it myself. At the climax of Ray Charles' "Talkin' 'Bout You," I would stop in mid-verse, pretend to have a breakdown and collapse to the floor, where I'd stay with the mike held close to my chest. One by one the band members would stop playing until there was a deathly silence.

After a moment I'd cut loose with a ripping scream, my body convulsing as if I were being electrocuted and the band would explode—all of us resurrected. . . yes Lord! The people would go nuts. Then one night, somewhere in white-bread America, in the middle of this routine, I found myself surrounded by paramedics and a couple of cops.

When they found out it was a stunt they were not pleased, and one of the cops said he'd shoot me if I ever did it again. That was the last resurrection of Eric Burdon.

Through the early years I ran wild. Then I fell into the deep brown eyes of Angela King. She was very cool, silly, always giggling, born high and beautiful. Angela was a beautiful Anglo-Indian woman with absolutely perfect breasts. She'd been living with Andy Summers in keyboard player Zoot Money's basement until we started a torrid affair and I stole her away. Soon after, she insisted I marry her or lose her to some old moneybags who had proposed to her and offered to take her to the south of France.

Our wedding was the flower-power marriage of the year. The party the night before became legendary, with me catching free drinks from Jeff Beck, Keith Moon, Chris Farlowe, and just about every other mate of mine in between sessions on my bachelor journey. In the last twelve hours before I got married, one of our roadies had arranged hotel rooms and pads all over town so I could fuck as many of my past girlfriends as possible, including a glorious final egg session with the Jamaican, Sylvia.

Is it an understatement to say the marriage was doomed from the start? Angela and I would meet on the road—Paris, London, New York, Los Angeles. We had some great times together, but it just wasn't sustainable. I saw the end one night as the New Animals were leaving for a gig in Canada after playing a festival in Zürich. It was May 1968, and we'd had a blast playing the Beat Monster Concert with Jimi Hendrix, Traffic, and John Mayall—despite the cops trashing the venue and sparking nearly a decade of youth unrest. As I boarded the plane, Angela and Jimi waved goodbye to me together from behind the glass window of the departure lounge. I didn't have to guess what was going to happen next. Her affairs didn't end with Jimi, and we soon parted. The next time I saw her was at an Andy Warhol cocaine bash with some

The Flower Power wedding of 1967—Angie and I tie the knot. It didn't last, and she'd later be murdered by a boyfriend in Australia.

guy named Eric Love and the core of Andy's circus. He kept taking my picture and, annoyed, I made a quick departure.

I saw her only once more. A few years later, one cold, miserable night, she showed up at my house in L.A. with yet another boyfriend. The two of them looked like drowned cats. They needed to get back to England, she said, but were out of cash. Suddenly, I saw an opportunity that I couldn't miss. I told her I'd buy her two tickets to London if she would sign a piece of paper relinquishing all marital rights. She agreed. The next morning I went to the bank and she was gone, out of my life for good. Over the years, she gave up the coke for heroin. She moved to Australia, where in 1996 she was stabbed to death by her estranged boyfriend while trying to prevent him from taking off with their young son.

It was around the time that I met Angela that the Animals began to fall apart. Bob Dylan came to London, which was quite an event. He had everyone's ear and was surrounded by rock stars, newspaper people, and the intelligentsia of London. Alan Price was one of those seduced by Dylan's spell. Suddenly, we had no keyboard player, at a time when the Animals were booked for Sweden. Several stories made the rounds—he'd developed a fear of flying and would no longer tour; he wanted to do his own thing. It was only when I saw the documentary *Don't Look Back* years later that I saw what happened. There was Alan, sitting around serenading Bob backstage somewhere, with a vodka in one hand and an orange juice in the other, a trick he'd learned from Carl Perkins. Bob asks him, "Hey, where's your band, man?" Alan's answer is unintelligible.

Alan quit the band soon after, when he got the first big check from worldwide royalties on "House of the Rising Sun." Because of that shitty contract we'd signed with Mike Jeffery, the group never saw a dime. Alan's name was the only name on the record, and he took the money and ran. It was doubly frustrating that Alan disappeared just as he and I were beginning our writing career. We were just starting to sit down around the piano, doing stuff like "Inside Looking Out" and "I'm Crying." Alan and I were just starting to stretch out and learn to work together like Mick Jagger and Keith Richards were.

In Pricey's place we brought in Dave Rowberry, a good keyboard player, but with the air of a jazz snob about him. He was a solid musician but lacked the fire on stage. The band soldiered on. We did well in Poland—the first rock band to play behind the Iron Curtain. We did well in France, as we always had. Live gigs were no problem, as Hilton, Chas and I could always jam up a storm. But recording was different.

The critical, unforgiving demands of the studio exposed what the Animals lacked without Alan and John. The spark was gone, and I was soon looking for the exit.

I first suspected the end of the Animals was coming when we somehow found ourselves in a Christmas special called "The Dangerous Christmas of Red Riding Hood" with Vic Damone, Cyril Richard as the big bad wolf, and Liza Minnelli as Little Red Riding Hood—and the band as a group of wolves singing "We're Gonna Be Howlin' Tonight."

We wore little ears and had fake wolf hair stuck on our faces. I hated it. Three hours of makeup each morning—for what? What the fuck did this have to do with music? Mike Jeffery was still trying to disguise a raw blues band as a pop group, stretching our assholes wide to be pummeled by some fucking corporation. At the end of the tour, we all flew down to the Bahamas to stay on a huge yacht, do some recording, and consult the bankers who were guarding our hard-earned millions.

It was great being in the Caribbean for those few weeks, living on a yacht that had once been used by royalty. We cut some tracks there, including "Don't Bring Me Down," which turned out to be one of my favorite Animals tracks. But there was an uneasy feeling and a tension. One night there was a lot of drinking, and a fight broke out between Chas and the road manager, Tappy. Finally, punched out and too drunk to keep fighting, we all crashed for the night.

When I got up in the morning, Tappy was in the galley making breakfast. He was standing over a cutting board with a sharp knife cutting up pieces of bloody steak and throwing them into the bay where Chas was having a swim. Tappy was hoping to attract sharks to finish the job he couldn't do the night before. It was all too much. The bad relations, the bad business deals, and the growing use of alcohol and drugs—LSD had by now become a huge part of our lives—effectively ended the band's short life.

I announced I was breaking the band up, but did honor a short series

Single most embarrassing career moment: the Animals play wolves in The Dangerous Christmas of Red Riding Hood with Liza Minelli and Vic Damone, center.
© michael ochs archives.com

of gigs in North America we were previously committed to, before flying off to San Francisco to dream up what I was going to do with the rest of my life.

What I wouldn't be doing is spending my hard-earned millions. The money the Animals had amassed in two years of constant touring was nowhere to be found. Mike Jeffery was off quietly running several new clubs in Spain that we were allegedly to be part owners of (we weren't). Chas himself flew back to the Bahamas to find the Animals' money. He came back empty-handed. Not only our millions, but the bank—even the building it was in—was gone.

What did we do about it? Nothing. First of all, we didn't have the cash to hire lawyers. Secondly, there is a sort of Geordie code of silence.

Animals accepting an award for House of the Rising Sun. © michael ochs archives.com

There's no way we wanted to go back to Newcastle with the fame but not the money; nobody was going to admit we'd been fucked. That's the sort of way-too-personal thing that any Geordie would rather die than admit. Besides, I think to this day the rest of the band is embarrassed at how innocent we were: All the record needed to have printed on it was "Arr.: The Animals" and the biggest mistake of our lives never would have happened; we simply had been too green to even think of that.

The only settlement we got was that Jeffery ceased to be our manager, and we didn't have to go to court to fire him.

As I've said, it wouldn't surprise me to learn that Jeffery faked his death and ended up with the whole treasure. Very little about the music business surprises me. I once drunkenly broke into the frame of a gold record I'd received and put the gleaming vinyl on a record player. It wasn't a chart-topping Animals album at all -it was an old Connie Francis record. That's how cheap and shallow the record business can be.

CHAPTER 4

clear horizon

S outhern California opened its arms to me in late 1966-67, as I rode a Harley west along Mullholland from Laurel Canyon, all the way into Beverly Hills. It was America's dream factory, and every one of the tall palms called out. I simply knew that California was going to be my home. Compared to London's cold, damp, foggy, asthmatic weather, it was no contest.

Only a few weeks after I disbanded the Animals, I went into a New York studio with a bunch of crack session players and recorded an album, *Eric Is Here*.

But I still wanted English players. I imagined it a cool thing to have an English band based in L.A. I scoured London recruiting good players and found myself ensconced in Beverly Hills in a very large house with a group of Englishmen who would be known first as Eric Burdon and the Animals and then Eric Burdon and the New Animals.

There was Vic Briggs on guitar, Danny McCulloch on bass, John Weider on guitar and violin, Zoot Money on keyboards, and, later,

Andy Summers—who had forgiven me for stealing Angie away from him—on guitar. Barry Jenkins stuck around on drums.

We ate a lot of LSD, performed with our own traveling light show, and preached of a brave new world as we toured England, Japan, Australia, France, Switzerland. We often touched down in New York to cavort with our gang—Derring Howe, Jimi Hendrix, Linda Eastman, and former Animal Hilton Valentine, who soon joined my new band as a roadie. We lived, loved, and tripped together.

I once read that in the early days of LSD, some doctors thought the drug could aid the birthing process by helping a woman in labor dilate more easily. That may or may not be true (I doubt we'll find out any time soon!), but I can say that the compound certainly opens floodgates of a different kind.

I first got involved with acid, courtesy of Beatles manager Brian Epstein. He had a place in Belgravia that was sort of a rock 'n' roll palace, and we used to call at all hours. Despite his Beatles success, he'd always make us welcome and didn't pull any prima donna crap. It was obvious even then that Brian was a man in deep emotional pain. He was the first rich person I'd ever met who was truly lonely. It seemed the pain lessened when he had a place full of partiers and his favorite boys.

Brian was an LSD visionary. He kept his LSD tabs in a little red pill bottle and dispensed his liquid acid generously from a dropper. A lot came out of those little bottles, not the least of which was *Sgt. Pepper.* My first trip transformed me, and, ever since, I have seen the world in a different, liberated light. My acid epiphany was that Fellini movies looked like normal documentaries. And do to this day.

It's not kosher to promote drugs these days, but the truth is that LSD made me aware of the potential of the human mind and the depth of the human spirit. More lately, some drugs have shown themselves to be brilliant liberators, freeing some people from neurosis and depression. With everything, there's a downside, but the near-fascist governments of the twenty-first century forbid even investigating the positive aspects of these chemicals.

Timing is everything. The world I inhabited in the 1960s and 1970s is gone, and I am grateful that I got to use the key to the cosmic lock and have experiences that will stay with me the rest of my life. A historical moment of cultural evolution isn't something that can be repeated.

It was when politics truly entered our music—first, I remember, with the Grateful Dead. That's when I first started documenting the times in many of my songs, songs like "San Franciscan Nights," "Sky Pilot," "Monterey" and "Gratefully Dead." They were my attempt at musical journalism. Later there was "Sandoz" and "White Houses."

Back in '64, on early Animals' tours, John Steel and I were lucky to see San Francisco just prior to the psychedelic explosion. Those were the days of Lenny Bruce doing stand-up routines at the Hungry I, of the cool West Coast jazz and poetry scene. To return in 1967 and see the city's new face was an absolute mind blow. The Vietnam conflict had begun in the early 1960s, but by 1967 the teakettle was shrieking in Hometown U.S.A. There was no middle ground: You had to stand on one side of the line or the other. I felt something in California that was missing in England, something that my friends in England found hard to comprehend. It was just a feeling, an underlying belief that encouraged a new outlook, psychedelic humor, habits, and dress style. I didn't want to become an American, but I did want to become a Californian.

Recording studios were plenty and available, and I was anxious to plug into this new energy. I struck a new record deal with MGM, and Eric Burdon and the New Animals took off.

I found new management in Kevin Deverich, who had worked for the TV show "Dick Clark's American Bandstand." We set up an office in Hollywood, and Kevin began arranging tours.

It was a great time to be English in L.A. I met and became friends with some of the members of Frank Zappa's Mothers of Invention. They had a gang house at the foot of Laurel Canyon, across the street from legendary magician Harry Houdini's place. The yard was covered in Harley parts, and once I'd gotten familiar with the streets in L.A., Frank's drummer, Jimmy Carl Black—known as the "Indian" in the band—loaned me one of the machines to take my first run down Sunset Strip from Hollywood to the Pacific Ocean. It was a Geordie's dream.

"This is to ensure a good ride," he said, laying down two lines of white dust. I carefully weighed the machine between my legs and he gave me a pair of World War II goggles and a leather jacket. I was off. The speed hit me as I cleared the Westwood area. . . a sudden rush through my veins. Leaning into the bends, the machine was hot between my legs, the torque of the bike incredible. I headed up the Pacific Coast Highway, yelling out loud into the wind like a crazy man.

The record company lent Frank Zappa to our new production, and we cut two tracks together: "All Night Long" and "The Other Side of This Life." Frank was brilliant, a musical genius and cultural maverick. He was also, well, weird. It's hard to come up with a better word to describe him. Everyone around Frank was stoned, and he was always straight as an arrow. He showed me some amazing home movies he'd shot, and we really connected talking about film. He liked to call me the "Charlton Heston of rock and roll." (It was funny and flattering then, not so much now that the man who played Moses has turned into a gun-loving freak.) I was sure Frank was going to be a great movie director someday. Seeing him getting into radical experimental movies gave me heart. Maybe this could be my next step, I thought, despite my embarrassing appearance in the nonsense called *Beach Party A-Go-Go.* There was some talk of my involvement in Antonioni's *Zabriskie Point.* I talked with him in New York, and we discussed the film, but nothing came of it. I satisfied my lust for film by making our own 16mm movie. Shot in Laurel Canyon next to the house I'd bought from Elmer Valentine, the owner of the Whisky A Go Go, it was our version of the Crucifixion, with U.S. soldiers nailing Christ to the cross. The son of God was played by drummer Barry Jenkins. We incorporated the film into our light show and managed to upset a few people, though most audiences loved it.

It was in San Francisco at Bill Graham's Fillmore that I first ran into a guy who was, like me, a rocker who was also into movies and was a master at upsetting people. Jim Morrison. . . or Jim Morestoned, as we called him.

It was Jim who helped me make up my mind between Northern and Southern California.

"L.A.'s the place, man," he told me one night as we talked backstage, amongst all the madness and freaks of the dressing room. Jim looked great in those days, and I figured he was going to be the next Marlon Brando. As I got to know him better over the following months, I realized that he was just so out of control all of the time that he could never muster the discipline to complete something as demanding as a film. He was going down and wanted to shout it to the world like some courageous clown.

But he was right about one thing—L.A., it was the place for me, as long as I was able to stay out of the clutches of the infamous LAPD.

I had a house at the top of the hill in Laurel Canyon, and my neighbors were Joni Mitchell, the boys from Canned Heat, Zappa, David Carradine, Alvinia Bridges, John Phillips, Cass Elliot, John Mayall and others. The music scene was amazing. Many of the blues stars had moved west—Lowel Fulsom, Jimmy Witherspoon, Joe Turner, Louis Jordan, Ray Charles. There was a slew of great clubs: the Ashgrove, the Whisky, the Trip, Doug Weston's Troubadour. When I wasn't gigging with the New Animals in Los Angeles or out in the Valley, I enjoyed going to the various clubs where I could see my jazz heroes up close, heroes such as Rahsaan Roland Kirk.

I had first met Rahsaan back in 1965 in New York City, when he was doing a two-week stint at Birdland. I'd been an avid collector of his records and wanted to see him in the flesh. He was something else live— a genius wildman. When I first saw him on stage he looked like a ragged Samurai warrior, festooned with gleaming silver and brass instruments. He was draped in a mess of wires, pickups, and tape machines—a true "sound tree," as he described himself. He played and sounded fantastic, treating us to the "black classical music," as he called it.

A few months later, as John Steel and I were headed for Sam Goody one winter's afternoon to purchase some new releases, we ran into Rahsaan standing on a street corner outside the store, shuffling his feet and playing on penny whistles that he'd hand out to anyone who'd accept. I'd thought at first he was a street musician, perhaps homeless. When I looked closer, I noticed that he had three walking sticks taped together, his black face, blind eyes looking into nowhere. He heard our voices from several feet away as we approached and instantly recognized us. "Hey, it's the Animals," he growled. "How're you doing? What 'cha all doin' here in the Big Apple?"

John stood dead in his tracks, his jaw dropped, and he turned and looked at me. "Hey, it's Roland Kirk. I can't believe it. Roland, how are you?"

"Rahsaan's my name now," he said. "I had a dream one night. This angel came to me in a dream and told me that I should change my name to Rahsaan."

"Rahsaan," I said, "I like it. It's got a nice ring to it."

I pumped his outstretched and we embraced.

"Where y'all goin'?"

"Sam Goody's to buy some records."

The late, great Rahssan Roland Kirk—a huge influence on me.

"I'm on my way there myself."

He took me by one arm and John Steel by the other, and we walked into Sam Goody's.

A black man was coolly playing a tambourine as the store's sound system pumped out a Temptations song. Rahsaan cocked his ear and listened. He leaned over the cash register and said, "I like the way you play that tambourine. You got the touch. Come with me."

We all laughed, except for the tambourine player. His name was Joe Texaco, and he'd just found his vocation in life. He would follow Rahsaan everywhere as his roadie and percussionist.

I had two really strong influences at this time, two really great musical visionaries. They were very different men who both sought to make music a weapon against hypocrisy, hate, ignorance, and fear. One was Rahsaan Roland Kirk, the other was Jimi Hendrix. When they met, they immediately clicked, seeing clearly into each other's souls.

During Jimi's heavy down days, when it was pretty obvious to me that he was going through changes, Rahsaan could feel it. He would take me aside and tell me to tell Jimi not to take so much acid. "He's seeing too much," he said to me. "Jimi sees too much. You gotta tell him to slow down."

Rahsaan had gotten one of his earliest gigs from the great blues singer Jimmy Witherspoon, because Rahsaan was capable of playing one, two, three, or four instruments at once. He had developed unique Yoga breathing techniques which meant he could blow forever. It worked beautifully on his early track "You Did It, You Did It." His approach was looked upon by some myopic musicians and critics as a gimmick. But when Rahsaan blew, everybody listened. Some of us cried and most of us also enjoyed a good laugh with the Great Rahsaan. At one point there was a great jam band put together for a TV show in England: Eric Clapton, Jimi Hendrix, Rahsaan, Ginger Baker, and Jack Bruce. When Rahsaan appeared for a two-week run at Ronnie Scott's club in London, I think I saw almost every show and occasionally we got to play with each other on stage.

Not many musicians can cross the barriers of modern music, which are created by executives ("noncreative garbage" as Monty Python liked to call them) to fit arbitrary and trendy radio formats. But for me this crossing over is where true musical greatness is to be found. Greatness like Billie Holliday, who moved from blues to jazz to pop, and Ray Charles, who traversed the terrains of gospel, blues, soul, jazz—the first black man to really interpret country and western.

Shelly's Mann Hole was a jazz club in Hollywood owned by the great jazz drummer Shelly Mann. He loved Rahsaan so he'd always give him a gig whenever Rahsaan was on the West Coast.

The place was nothing special, and it's gone now; Wally Heider's recording studio now stands in its place. In L.A., nothing's permanent. But memories survive, and there is one night I will always remember. I had a date with a lady who worked in the film industry. She'd been attracted to me, she said, since seeing me the night before, where she poured red wine over my head at the Troubadour club. Hey, whatever works, brother.

I convinced her she should see Rahsaan. We were shown to a table and ordered some wine. The place was quiet and about half full when suddenly there was a demented sound of laughter echoing around the room. Out of the shadows came this walking pile of clothes, this Christmas tree of instruments feeling its way with a white walking stick.

Rahsaan began blowing his tenor sax, and from that point on we were on a trip aboard his ship. The drums, bass, and percussion took our minds to Africa, Egypt, the Mississippi Delta, sometimes by a single note delivered with all the shock value of a Hitchcock moment. At one point Rahsaan got up and left the club—still blowing his sax—got into a cab, went around the block, came back in the club, never missing a beat. My date had never seen such craziness in her life. During the break I took her backstage to meet Rahsaan. I could see his nose flame and his head came up as he guessed her weight and size from the sound of her high-heeled shoes on the stone floor. I'm sure her perfume sparked one of his erotic mind-movies. He would always tell me that when it comes to sex, a non-sighted person has the jump over a sighted person. Rahsaan's heightened sense of smell allowed him to strip a woman naked the very second she entered a room.

When I last saw him in London, in 1976, he had suffered a stroke and a collapsed lung. He was only thirty-nine. I talked to Joe Texaco, the percussionist whom he'd recruited at Sam Goody right before my eyes.

"It's tragic," I said. "How could this happen to such a great man?"

Joe just looked at me and smiled and said, "He's dying from too much living."

After the stroke had rendered his right arm nearly useless, Rahsaan didn't give up. He redesigned a flute and his saxes so he could play with one hand, and he went back out on the road. He could play better with one hand than most sax players do with two!

don't let me be misunderstood

His wife once said that Rahsaan's head "should have blown off his body with all the stuff he held up there." Metaphorically, it did. About a year after I last saw him, Rahsaan suffered another stroke, a fatal one. I was told that he'd requested a final spiritual ritual—to be cremated and have some of his ashes mixed with some really top-drawer Turkish hashish, put in a pipe, and smoked by some of his old friends, including Miles Davis and me. This was my Oscar.

I'll always feel grateful that I was able to thank him for our friendship before he died. I did it in my song "The Vision of Rahsaan," which appeared on my band War's first album. I miss him and his sense of humor. Rahsaan, like many of my friends, liked to tease me about the rarity of warm nights in the Bay area, a phenomenon I'd written about in "San Franciscan Nights," a hit I had with the New Animals at the end of the 1960s.

The song was inspired by one particular night in the city. I was on my way to the Fillmore. Janis Joplin had told me to rap on the side door, and when I did, there she was, ushering me into the club. She shook my hand and I looked down and noticed a little red tab.

"Take it," she said. "It's hot off the press. Owsley's, you'll love it."

I popped it in my mouth and let it rest under my tongue. The sweet smell of pot was in the air as we made our way onto the dance floor and toward the stage door. As we were struggling to make our way through the crowd, we came across a group of men who seemed to be dancing in a circle on a bright red carpet. On their backs were matching patches: "Hell's Angels Oakland Chapter California." But they weren't dancing. Splashes of red were on the floor and on their steel-capped riding boots. Some poor bastard was being kicked from one side of the bikers' circle to the other. Janis grabbed my arm and yelled over the din, "Come on. Don't mess with those fuckers. They'll kill you."

When we got backstage she said that she liked many of the bikers, "but when they're taking care of business, that's their thing, man."

Some of the Grateful Dead were hanging around, as was Janis's band. Then Jim Morrison came up and said hello, handing me a frosty Budweiser. After some small talk, club owner Bill Graham poked his head through the dressing room door and said, "Janis, you got eight minutes, babe. Let's go."

Jim and I rapped about movies and L.A., and then walked out to watch Janis take the stage, bathed in white light. She had on red high-heeled shoes and a very sexy, tight, see-through minidress, against which her nipples strained. Throughout her performance that night I was impressed, as I was every time I saw her or jammed with her onstage. She was never recorded right. No magnetic tape anywhere could properly capture a performer like Janis Joplin. You had to see and hear her in the flesh.

That night, there was a full moon in the sky. It was inspiring. . . and it wasn't a typical cold and rainy San Francisco night, which is how my song ended up the way it did.

Though I settled deeply into California, I maintained my flat in Dalmeny Court, and when I was in London it was back to the old routine, hanging out with old friends and seeing familiar faces. It was in London that Jimi Hendrix and I really became close. He lived with Chas until he got his own place a few blocks away and above a restaurant aptly named Mr. Love's. It was two floors up on the corner adjacent to Grosvenor Square, next to the U.S. Embassy.

One amazing day I was there while a riot was raging right outside, a pitched battle between Vietnam War protesters and mounted policemen. What a change that was! When I was a kid we used to see WWII news on the Pathe pictorials, the weekly events presented just as the government wanted us to see them. By the time the Vietnam War escalated, the public was no longer swallowing what it was being fed, and outrage was spilling out into the streets.

It hadn't taken long. Like the Beatles before us, the original Animals were warned not to mention or discuss Vietnam with American reporters, but by 1967 antiwar sentiment was breaking into the open. In 1968, after my recording of "We Gotta Get Out of This Place" climbed the charts, I was at the airport in Atlanta when two black Marines came up behind me at a newsstand. One of them tapped me on the shoulder and said, "Thanks for the music, man. It helped. It really helped."

Years later, I was grabbing my tambourine off the stage long after a show had ended at a club in Long Island, when I caught a quiet word from someone still out in the audience. It was a Vietnam vet. He hung around after the gig and thanked me for my songs. He told me he'd been stationed at a secret base in Cambodia, where there was supposed to be no war.

"One of the men had a small Spanish guitar," he told me. "It was Christmas night. The stars were out, and the jungle was beginning to come alive, as it always does at night. He started playing "House of the Rising Sun" on that guitar. We were barely into the first verse when the whole lush mountain seemed to come alive in song—even some of the Vietcong on the opposite side of the hill joined in." Over the years there have been many such compliments from veterans—and I always take them to heart.

Jimi was the first American to talk to me about the war, on that day in 1968 in his apartment. As the riot ensued outside the embassy, we smoked a joint and talked.

"So, what do you think of all that's going on down there?"

His answer shook me. "Listen, man, when the Red Chinese come screaming down over the borders of Laos, Cambodia, and North Vietnam, and take over the whole of the Far East and Asia, you'll understand why the U.S. is trying so hard in Vietnam."

I couldn't believe it. In his head, he was still a soldier. He'd just decided to lay down the M-16 and pick up a guitar.

The gun or the guitar: It's an ancient choice. Consider Robert

Johnson and Robert Charles—remarkably similar men in the turn-of-the-century South, born in the same town, in fact, who ended up choosing differently.

When Charles learned of a particularly brutal public lynching and dismemberment of a black man, he called for all black Americans to arm themselves, and followed his own advice. On July 23, 1900, in New Orleans, he and a friend were waiting for two women they had arranged to meet after work, when three white police officers accosted them. As the situation escalated, the cops began beating Charles, then one cop and Charles drew pistols and shot each other, neither fatally. In the ensuing manhunt and gun battle, Charles managed to shoot twenty-seven whites, killing seven of them, including four cops. When he was finally forced out into the streets, cops and civilians alike shot him, hundreds of times, stomping on his body until it was unrecognizable.

Charles picked up a gun. Robert Johnson used a guitar. His demonic songs and licks shared tales of woe and horror, warning his brothers to be wary of the white man.

Like Johnson, Jimi chose the guitar, but he was still a warrior.

One of my striking experiences with Jimi was at the Newport Pop Festival in the San Fernando Valley's Devonshire Downs, back in June, 1969.

As we entered the dusty open field—which looked about as much like a down in Devonshire as Vietnam looked like Normandy—the first thing I saw was a cute little Indian girl by the name of Buffy Sainte-Marie, trying to get her point across to a crowd of about five thousand people baking in the summer heat. A police helicopter hovered overhead, drowning out most of what she had to say and sending exactly the wrong message. That helicopter represented everything the kids hated, and they cursed and waved their fists at it. It was a mess of a fest, bad vibes from the start.

On the first day, Jimi was a mess. The day before, he'd been before a

On stage at Devonshire Downs in California: Me, Jimi Hendrix and Buddy Miles..

judge in Toronto for a preliminary hearing into his heroin bust. Once at Devonshire, someone gave him a heavily spiked drink, and by the time Jimi took the stage he was so out of it he couldn't control his feedback or remember lyrics. The crowd was unforgiving and Jimi staggered off the stage.

I was also playing the festival, but the memorable time came two days later, when Jimi came back rested and straight. He invited me onstage with him for a long jam. At one point Buddy Miles joined in. After I left the stage, I hung around in the wings, watching the action. Suddenly, a girl named Sunshine—who fancied herself another Janis Joplin—somehow got onto the stage and started singing and wouldn't leave. Jimi came over, still playing wildly, and motioned for me to help get her off. She was a big girl, but I went back out and tried to remove her. She tackled me. We both fell to the floor, and Jimi came over and sat on top of us, playing his finale. Seeing the joker side of Jimi, the crowd went wild.

A short while later, we were all in L.A. partying like mad on Sunset.

*Jimi the clown ... sitting on a girl named Sunshine,
who's on top of me after I tried to drag her off stage
at the Devonshire gig.*

The whole place was tripping on acid. Chas, who was managing Jimi at this time, was nowhere to be found, which enraged a girlfriend of his, Violet, who had flown in from New York.

Violet got really weird when somebody spiked her with acid, and she ended up in a nearby strip club, getting completely freaked out by a python in one of the stripper's act.

She stumbled into the coffee shop where I was, and I managed to get her up to my room. I tried to get her to take some Valium and close her eyes, but she said this only made it worse.

don't let me be misunderstood

Outside, I heard Jimi, who was staying in the same hotel. He was on the balcony with two blondes. A Fender strapped over his shoulders, he had just dropped his fifth hit, he said, and was ready to go jam at the Whisky.

"I think I gotta babysit Violet," I told him.

"Oh, come on, man, let's go. She'll be fine," he begged.

The trouble was I was tripping wildly myself, and thought it better to stay in my room. Meanwhile, Violet spun a tale of having seen her past life as a whore in Babylonia—a whore put to death by snakes.

With the help of some Valium, I managed to bring her down.

I was still high the next day when I met Jimi, again out on the balcony. One blonde was asleep in the bed, and the other was in the bathroom. Jimi—never without a guitar—strummed quietly.

"Hey man, how's it goin'?"

"Good."

"We were at the Whisky," he said. "Me, Buddy, some other dudes from Tulsa. And I met some friends of yours from Chicago. They came back here and said they knew you, and I was to give 'em what they wanted."

"What?" I asked.

"Yeah, man, they put ma johnson in white plaster and made an impression for their collection!"

Cynthia and her Plaster Casters had made it to L.A.!

Eric Burdon and the New Animals continued to be successful, and we embarked on our first tour of Japan. I'd enjoyed my first visit to the land of the rising sun with the original Animals, but this one would prove to be a disaster. The promoter turned out to be one of the country's most notorious gangsters, a little five-foot man with gold teeth and sickly skin whom everyone called "Mr. Big." I was in an Austin Powers movie, thirty years ahead of schedule.

We spent our first three days in Japan doing boring interviews with

Japanese media. Then, we took the then-new bullet train to our first gig, in Osaka. The show went like clockwork. The staid Japanese audience applauded politely, but we knew they really enjoyed themselves. For the next week we traveled all over the country from our base in Tokyo to various well-attended gigs.

The whole band was affected by the Japanese sense of decorum, and one night, at the end of our first week, Mr. Big invited us out for dinner at one of Toyko's finest Kobe Beef houses. When we sat down, half a dozen beautiful Japanese girls came into the room carrying everything they needed to prepare our meal. First, they slipped crisp white linen bibs on each of us, and then a girl sat beside each one of us, cooking the beef and feeding us individually. Talk about a man's world!

The next day, however, things soured. Our gig was right in the center of Tokyo, but the venue was unbelievably bad—a tiny club four floors up, and the stage wasn't big enough for the band by half. It turned out that it was a private gangster hangout belonging to Mr. Big, and we were told we had to play twice a night for a week for the mob elite of Tokyo.

"I ain't doin' that," I said to our road manager, Terry McVay, who was trying to placate the other band members. The band's manager, Kevin Deverich, went off to the hotel to try to negotiate with Mr. Big, and I went out for a walk, fuming mad at the situation I blamed him for landing us in.

When I returned to the hotel, Kevin came in and said there was going to be a meeting in a restaurant across the street and we were all to attend. We all walked in and were shown to a long table in a corner, away from the main eating area. Two of Mr. Big's goons were there, and one of them walked over to our table and asked in quite good English, "May I treat you? Drinks are on your honorable promoter. May I suggest Scotch whiskey all round?"

In Japan, Scotch is a symbol of business, of completing or proposing a deal. The waiter returned with six glasses and put one in front of each of us. Then he went around the table and poured scotch into everyone's glass but mine. The other goon then reached into his pocket, held his hand over my glass, and dropped six 9 mm shells into it.

I left immediately for the hotel. Soon after, Kevin was at my door, standing in the corridor, his face white. I thought he was adjusting his tie with his hands, but when he lowered his arms I saw a huge welt across his throat.

"Christ, what happened to you?" I asked.

"After you left," he said, "they took me aside. The band had gone, everybody had gone, and one of the guys took out a sword and stuck it on my neck, running it back and forth."

"Play or die" was the message.

I immediately phoned everyone in the band and ordered them not to leave their rooms, but to pack for the next flight out of the country. None of us slept that night. The next morning we managed to check out of the hotel and load up the taxis before any of Mr. Big's heavies arrived. Just as we were ready to pull out, three of them appeared and tried to bully the taxi drivers into not taking us. After a brief screaming match—and some substantial bribes—we were on our way to the airport.

At the ticket counter we were having a huge problem trying to put all our flights on one credit card when Mr. Big's boys arrived. We explained our predicament to the ticket clerk, who understood well. After seeing the mobsters he immediately began processing our tickets.

Before we made the flight, however, Mr. Big and then *his* boss and a whole group of goons arrived at the airport to stop us.

That's when I lost it, and I screamed at Mr. Big that I had always loved the Japanese and that Japan had been one of my favorite places when the Animals had first played there—but that his gangster antics had ruined it, and that for me the honorable Japan was truly dead, leaving the corpse of the treacherous, cowardly country that had perpetrated Pearl Harbor. It struck home. The old gangster, much to everyone's surprise, started to cry. Fuck him. We still had to write bribes totalling nearly $250,000 before we were allowed to board the plane. Fortunately, we had a stop in Hawaii a few hours later—during business hours—and were able to call our bank and have the checks canceled. Still, we suffered a significant loss: Aside from a few guitars, we had to abandon all our equipment.

I went back to California and rented a great place in Beverly Hills that had been Boris Karloff's longtime home. It was dignified, white, bright, airy, and tastefully decorated in Spanish style. A magnificent garden was offset by a pool and a '30s-style blue-and-white-striped canopy over a barbecue area.

One of the more bizarre features of the house was a little prayer cupboard concealed underneath the staircase that led up to the guest bedroom. I showed it to a girlfriend one night and marveled as she ducked inside. Her high heels managed to pull one of the floor tiles loose. Taking a closer look, we discovered that beneath the tiles was a square patch of wooden floorboard, which seemed strange. The tiles were quite loose, and when we lifted one of them we saw that there was a secret hiding space. Using a flashlight we glimpsed a big metal box.

Boris Karloff's safe!

The next morning I worked with chisels and hammers and took out the remaining tiles and floorboards. There it was, a green metal safe with a big brass dial. I told my girlfriend that we had to keep it a secret, as I was only leasing the house. But we made plans to crack it. I went out and bought a stethoscope and two contact microphones, which I attached to the safe and wired through my stereo so that I could clearly hear every click of the lock. I tried every combination I could think of—Karloff's birthdate, his child's birthdate, the number of films he made, and anything else I could think of, but I couldn't find the combination.

Curiosity really got the best of me, and I called up a buddy who worked as a pyrotechnics expert in the film industry. He rounded up some C4 plastic explosives from the movie he was working on at the time, and we loaded the safe into my truck and took it to a remote area outside of L.A.

The C4 went off with great force and threw the safe up into the air, but it landed intact, with only a few scratches and scorch marks. I never did get it open. Finally, I put it back in its hole in the prayer cupboard, replaced the floorboards, and put the tiles back.

I guess it wasn't for me to discover Boris's secrets.

CHAPTER 5

great escape

When I had some time off in the late '60s, I'd flee L.A. for the mighty desert surrounding Palm Springs. Back then, the clean air and the big, white sand dunes were straight out of *Beau Geste*. The great dunes are gone now, blitzkreiged by the mighty yellow Caterpillars to make way for housing and golf courses, but the area is still spectacular: The mountains of magenta, black, and blue, and the hot sun keeping the skies clear even when it's raining in L.A.

A girlfriend of original Animals guitarist Hilton Valentine settled in the fledgling community of Palm Desert. An accomplished artist who continues to live and work in the area, Ming Lowe, at that time had a little house and studio that became a refuge from the madness of Hollywood. It was a great meeting place for artists and travelers attracted to the desert.

I'd arrive in my old El Camino, rifle in the rack, my collie Geordie, and my dirt bike in the back. Riding the open desert at twilight in the winter, seeing the landscape blur by, was as seductive as anything I've known. Two hours east of L.A., it could have been North Africa, or any of the world's exotic deserts. It was California at its best, and it's where I became a running mate of one of my screen heroes, Steve McQueen.

The first time I ran into Steve I literally almost ran into him. I was on a Harley borrowed from one of Zappa's boys, heading down Sunset toward the beach. I was flying along in Brentwood when a traffic light turned yellow. I didn't want to run the light and started to brake hard, only to encounter a wet patch of pavement in the shade of one of the giant trees. In the left lane there was a green Porsche. The driver was really paying attention. He saw what was about to happen and quickly spun the Porsche out of the left lane, leaving me room to skid by. When I made the corner the pavement was dry, and I came to a stop safely. When I looked back, there was McQueen—a quick flash of white teeth and the Porsche sped away.

When I rented a house at the north end of Palm Springs in 1969, I was thrilled to find out McQueen lived nearby. My secretary had been out for a wild ride with him on the back of a Triumph motorcycle, one that he'd had specially doctored for the sand. She had a blast and encouraged me to connect with McQueen.

We hit it off immediately—like two boys mucking about in a sandbox. McQueen had a smell of gasoline, black powder, and pot that seemed to drift behind him everywhere he went. I told him it made me imagine him as a young Erwin Rommel, and at times he'd adopt a mock-German tone in his place of his American accent.

We always had girlfriends around, fresh from out of town, making their first trip to the desert. We'd run them out into the dunes toward the east end of the valley, me on my 350 Yamaha and Steve on his desert Triumph.

All along the valley, tamarisk trees had been planted as windbreaks. They were a clear mark of where civilization ended and the desert began. "Step this way," I'd say, pushing the branches aside for the girls, their bare feet sliding through warm, silky sand, the black sky above with a billion stars and a thumbnail moon. There must have been a hundred nights like this.

There were two things you didn't ask Steve about, and one was Charles Manson. McQueen had been friends with Sharon Tate and Roman Polanski, and was supposed to visit her on the night the Manson gang entered and slaughtered the home's occupants. Later on, Steve's name was found on the list of celebrities that Manson wanted to kill.

The other thing you didn't ask about was the big motorcycle jump stunt in his terrific war film, *The Great Escape*. Due to insurance restrictions, he'd not been allowed to film the scene himself. Instead, his riding buddy and stunt double, Bud Egans, had done the jump. It was always a sore point with Steve. I had no doubt that he could have done it, however. One time when we went out riding he took me to a large, sandy berm at the edge of a long wooden fence, and told me it was roughly the same kind of jump as in *Great Escape*. He didn't offer any more information, and I didn't ask. As I headed around the berm, Steve hit the throttle open, piloting his Triumph into the air.

It was skill. And it was balls. Bette Davis once asked him, "Why do you ride those motorcycles like that and maybe kill yourself?"

Steve's answer: "So I won't forget that I'm a man and not just an actor."

One of our many trips out to the dunes took place the day of Ike's funeral in April, 1969. As we stood looking at Mount Eisenhower off in the distance, Steve pulled a joint out of his pocket and fired it up. As he exhaled, he said, "You know, there's a rumor that Ike had secret meetings with space aliens. Some people even think he was a space creature himself." I laughed and McQueen said, "No, I'm not joking. Who else could have won the war? Who else could have beat the Germans?"

Steve wasn't given to deep, introspective conversation, but he was a little self-conscious about his image at this time. Despite great reviews and box office, he was concerned about his film, *Bullitt*. He was uneasy about having taken on the role of a cop, thinking it might jeopardize his image as a rebel.

"You got nothing to worry about," I told him. "Bullitt *is* a rebel—he's a hip cop."

A few years later, after he'd married Ali MacGraw, the two of them were out cruising Palm Springs. He told me they'd dropped in at the grand opening of a new restaurant in town, Melvyn's (now a legendary celebrity hangout), and were turned away by the owner without a second glance.

"You really are judged by what you look like," Steve said, somewhat surprised, since at the time he was one of the biggest and highest paid movie stars in the world.

The restaurant's owner, Mel Haber, is truly a gentleman, one of the most charming businessmen in the Palm Springs area, and remembers feeling bad after turning them away, not knowing who they were.

"It was our opening night, and everybody was beautifully dressed, and they came right up on the motorcycle," he remembers. "Later on my parking attendant asked about Steve McQueen and Ali MacGraw, and I said they never showed up. That's when I realized!"

Of course, Steve and Ali seemed to take it in stride and later did dine at Melvyn's, sans motorcycle.

Before we'd met, McQueen and I were big fans of the legendary Von Dutch, and had frequented his San Fernando Valley shop. Von Dutch was a top automotive artist, gunsmith, engineer, innovator whose design ideas influenced great artists such as Robert Williams and

My riding buddy Steve McQueen with our mutual friend, the actor Ted Markland.

formed the basis of the California Kustom Kar Kulture that's still going strong today. His most popular single piece of art was the Flying Eyeball, based on an ancient Middle Eastern icon.

If you're a real cult film fan, you might know that Von Dutch painted all the houses in the way-out film *Angels from Hell,* which starred my longtime buddy Ted Markland, who played the guy in the wheelchair in *One Flew Over the Cuckoo's Nest.* Von Dutch did a great paint job on Markland's personal bike, as well—all gold, covered with Egyptian symbols. Back before I met Steve, he and Ted used to run in the hills off Mullholland Drive in Hollywood.

The more we saw of each other the more I liked McQueen. I was amazed to see that in the late 1960s such an action hero was accepted by people of the hip persuasion as well as the straights. We never talked about Vietnam.

Through his corporation, Solar, he'd developed a plastic specifically for gas tanks, and he wanted to show me his new design. One morning I rode my dirt bike out over the giant dunes and met him and a couple of members of his crew, who were helping with his specially designed dune buggy—powered by a Porsche 911 engine.

I climbed into the bucket seat, a special design that Steve received a patent for. He showed me how to strap down the racing safety harness. As the massive rear tires dug into the white sand, I was pinned backward. It was all I could do to clench my teeth and hang onto the roll bars, screaming, as we headed east toward Indio. A quick turnaround to the left, and we headed back toward the San Jacinto mountains at the west end of the valley, and soon were tearing up the walls of one of the big dunes.

"See," he yelled over the racket of the engine, "we don't need no gas gauge. All I've got to do is look over my shoulder, and I can see how much gas there is in the tank."

"Yeah," I agreed, "it's fantastic."

"So simple. I can adapt these tanks for dirt bikes as well. All you gotta do is glance down, and you know where you're at."

"Cool," I yelled over the din of the engine, hanging on for dear life.

As we reached the crest of the dune, my tongue was stuck on the roof of my mouth. He gunned the engine as we came over the top, and I held on for dear life as we flipped, the roll bar plowing into the sand. He cut the engine, and we came to a screeching halt. I was laughing hysterically. Steve turned to me and through his yellow-tinted glasses, he squinted at me, his mouth open.

"Sshhh. . . quiet."

We both listened—to what, I'm not quite sure. One of the rear wheels was still spinning. He turned to look at the gas tank, the gasoline still slopping around inside. "Hey," he said, "it works."

With that, he unhooked one of the button-down clasps on his blue-jean shirt pocket, pulled out a joint, stuck it in his mouth, and lit up, taking a huge hit before passing it to me. "Now you can laugh," he said.

"What are we going to do now?"

"C'mon. Help me roll it over. It shouldn't be a problem."

Probably the best McQueen story I ever heard was one that occurred years later, when he was dying of cancer. Steve had his massive collection of nearly two hundred motorcycles, fifty-some cars, and five planes stored at the Santa Paula airport north of L.A., the site of Von Dutch's studio. One day near the end of his life, Steve showed up at Von Dutch's place, picked up a .45 automatic, checked to see that it was loaded, stuffed it into his belt and walked out. He got into the cockpit of his PT-17 Stearman biplane, painted red with black crosses on the wings, taxied down the runway, and took off out over the Pacific.

Von Dutch figured that was the last he'd ever see of McQueen—or the plane. Not a bad way for a screen legend to take his leave of the world.

Hours had passed when finally out of the dusk came the sound of a sputtering engine, running on empty. McQueen dropped down out of the sky and landed the biplane, taxying back to its parking space in front of the hanger.

"Chicken shit," Von Dutch said, as McQueen climbed out of the plane and walked toward the workshop.

"Fuck you," McQueen replied. "I just didn't want to scratch your paint job."

In the years since I had the pleasure of running with Steve in the desert, I've been through my share of Harleys. I gave up riding for a few years in the 1990s because of chronic neck pain—and in protest of California's 1992 mandatory helmet law. But by the year 2000, I couldn't resist temptation and got back in the saddle with a new Harley.

The dunes of the desert are a distant memory, but on still evenings, as the sun sets over the west end of the valley and I cruise quiet back roads, the thought of Steve McQueen is never far away.

The New Animals: Zoot Money, me, Barry Jenkins, Andy Summers and John Weider. © michael ochs archives.com

chapter 6

black 'n' blue

Eric Burdon and the New Animals was a great creative period for me. We had several hit records, among them "San Franciscan Nights," "See See Rider," "Sky Pilot," "When I Was Young," and "Monterey."

We had become one of the bands of the late '60s counterculture, and wherever the freak flag flew we were there to make our statement. A war of youth rebellion raged on the home front, and it was a great, exciting time to be alive. The emergence of the Black Panther movement, the American Indian movement, the beginning of the women's movement, the be-ins, the love-ins, the drive-ins, it all seeped into our skins and came back out through our clothes, our language, the music, the drugs—everything.

The "death of the hippie" had been predicted in Haight-Ashbury in San Francisco a couple of years earlier, but it wasn't until '69 that things really began to flatline. The spring holiday weekend in Palm Springs was supposed to be the first of many annual pop festivals in the desert. But it marked the end for me. Steve Miller was playing, as was John Mayall, Taj Mahal, and headliners Canned Heat, who asked me to join them onstage.

A rare studio shot: Me recording the hit song Monterey. © michael ochs archives.com

Lead singer Bob Hite, better known as Bear, was always half naked and smoking joints. He looked like a fat Rasputin. He and the rest of the band had lived in my old haunting grounds in Hollywood, Laurel Canyon. There was always a gathering of blues aficionados hanging around the house, listening to Bear's incredible collection of 78s, swapping porn magazines, and rapping about Harleys.

The day before Canned Heat's performance, Bear had given me a tab of LSD. It was a glorious evening, so I dropped the acid and went to float around the swimming pool as my girlfriend from Pasadena, Carolyn, a *Playboy* model I'd met at the Devonshire Downs Festival with

Hendrix, prepared a barbecue dinner for some friends who were coming for the weekend.

That beautiful night in the California desert, I floated serenely among the inflated kids' toys. I felt blessed, tripping on the best acid I'd had in years. With only my lips, nostrils, and eyes above the water, I was suspended in the darkness, staring at the sky above, weightless, breathing in and out, up and down.

Carolyn ran out to the pool to see if I was all right.

"I'm just meditating. No worries." I was a little irritated that she'd interrupted my reverie.

"OK," she said, and left me to my hallucinations.

I had reached the point in the psychedelic play when one must ask oneself: "Who am I? Where am I? How did I get here? Where do I belong?"

I was floating, totally free. Not even my toes touching the concrete: The water and the warm summer's night surrounded me like a continuous texture. It was a return to the womb. There was only the sound of my breathing.

Out of one corner of my eye, I could see the sliver moon hanging in the sky. Then I saw a big yellow pool toy floating toward me. I didn't want this inflatable monster obscuring my view, but I couldn't move my limbs. I knew that if I moved, I'd sink. I just wanted to stay floating. Slowly, the inflatable toy loomed closer and finally touched my head. That's when I found myself in space. I was out there amongst the stars. My eyes moved down toward my feet, and they appeared to be encased in space boots. I was covered all over in a silver space suit, though still not able to move.

I could only hear my own breathing. There was just me and this massive yellow spaceship which had touched my head. I slowly, and with great effort, managed to open my left hand. The moment I did, a wrench I'd been holding floated away, off into the blackness.

"Someone, please speak to me," I said. "Who am I?"

At first I hoped that Carolyn would reappear and bring me out of it, but soon I understood that the acid was creating this whole drama, and I came out of the panic, relaxed, and just hung there in the dreamspace enjoying the experience.

Was there anyone else out here? If any other creature haunted this realm, could I demand they make an appearance?

I tested the idea. "Come to me, show me your face, let me talk with you."

Then, suddenly, shadows appeared, blocking out the half-moon. Then I saw them—three of them standing by the pool, in conference, each with six arms which rested on their bat-like wings. Their eyes weren't eyes at all, more like a multitude of tiny television lenses. Their bodies were like giant, purple cockroaches.

This vision shook me to the bone and my arms and legs suddenly came alive and I sank to the bottom of the pool, nearly joining the Brian Jones swim club. I bounced off the bottom and rebounded up through the surface and found the steps and ran, in terror, across the lawn and into the house. I was naked, white with fright—and I wasn't aware that our guests had already arrived.

There was plenty of commotion as I burst through.

"Oh, it's nothing," Carolyn assured the guests. "Just Eric freaking out again."

I was guided to the bedroom, and I fell into a slumber.

The next afternoon, I was inside watching a movie, waiting for Andy Summers to show up from L.A., when there was a knock at the door. Carolyn answered it to discover two big Riverside County sheriff's deputies.

"Is this the Burdon residence?"

I came up to Carolyn's side and identified myself.

The older cop sighed as he looked down at a driver's licence.

"Do you know an Andrew Summers?"

"Yeah. Why?"

They stepped aside and in the driveway I could see Andy, his blonde hair down to his shoulders, his small Italian sports car parked behind the cop car.

"You were expecting him?"

"Yes," I said. "What's the problem?"

"No problem," the cop said. "Thank you very much, sir."

And they turned and left.

Andy came up the drive past them, carrying his guitar and an overnight bag.

"Man," he said, "they got the whole town surrounded. Palm Springs is sealed off. They stopped me and demanded to know where I was going. When I told them, they escorted me here. What the fuck's goin' on?"

What was going on was that the Palm Springs cops were heavy-handedly trying to crush the whole spirit of the music festival. Right away, Andy said he wasn't going to go to the show.

"If it's anything like what I saw today, I don't want any part of it," he said. "Too fuckin' redneck around here for me."

After we sat by the pool and had some sandwiches, I still couldn't talk Andy into going. But I'd promised the guys in Canned Heat that I'd jam, and I wanted to thank Bear for the great acid that was still flashing around in my brain, so I headed out across the desert alone on my Yamaha 350. I used some roads, but then hit the sand to avoid the roadblocks and checkpoints that surrounded the area.

As I neared the stadium, there was no avoiding the police. Red and blue lights were flashing everywhere. As I approached the first road-block I saw that there were hundreds of teenagers wandering toward the concert. I slowed to a stop at the checkpoint.

"Where the hell do you think you're going?" a cop asked.

"I'm performing at the show with Canned Heat."

"Nobody's getting through here. We're shutting down this affair. That's our duty, son."

My duty was to sing on stage, so I revved the bike and veered around the cop cars as the deputy screamed after me. There were so many long-hairs wandering around, there was no way they could catch me.

I was able to get the bike to the backstage area, where I stashed it between some of the production trucks. When I meandered out onstage, I took the band by surprise. Drummer Fito looked a little shocked, but Bear came over and handed me the microphone. I ended up being carried around on his back as we kept up a seemingly endless boogie.

We gave it our best, but there was a weird vibe, and neither the band nor the crowd could really settle into the music. Then I saw the problem—a sea of white helmets. Plastic visors. Weapons cradled and gas launchers poised.

Suddenly twenty or so blue-and-white trails shot up from the regiment of police storm troopers. I was directly in front of the band's amplifiers and couldn't hear what was happening, but it was obvious that the cops had begun tear-gassing the kids.

Soon a milky white cloud enveloped the crowd and panic set in. I bounded off the side of the stage without even saying goodbye to the guys in Canned Heat. I hopped onto my bike and tore off before the crowd of eight thousand burst out of the stadium onto the streets, where they were joined by another fifteen hundred kids who hadn't gotten into the show.

It was the cops who unleashed the hellish scene that followed. It spilled out of the stadium onto the streets of Palm Springs and ended with two youths shot and dozens of cops injured. Angry kids chased two cops into a gas station. The owner defended them by firing a shotgun into the air.

An investigation followed, of course, and the American Civil Liberties Union considered filing suit against the Palm Springs cops for abusing the rights of the teens. But it relented when the police promised to abide by ACLU recommendations in the future. Still, it was the last big rock event in the valley for many years.

don't let me be misunderstood

Around this time, I made friends with one of the great old-fashioned marijuana smugglers, known as El Gordo. We'd met when I was doing one of my prison benefit gigs at San Quentin. That day the entertainment was only for the black prisoners. Before the show, I took a walk around the yard. While near a fence segregating the prisoners, I was approached by a man on the other side who told me he was disappointed he couldn't see the show because he was a big Eric Burdon fan. He'd taken a job in the prison laundry with the hopes of at least hearing the music. He didn't realized who he was talking to at first and was pretty surprised to find out. He told me he was a photographer and getting out soon. I passed a note through the wire with a contact number so he could get in touch with me in L.A.

Soon after, he did call. I loved his stories. I loved his smoke even more. We became good friends.

One hot August morning I was at his house, up early watching the thick smog on the valley below, and over the radio came the shocking news that for many people truly marked the end of the hippie era. Right there in our neighborhood, actress Sharon Tate and several friends had been slaughtered. One of the murder weapons had been thrown onto a nearby front lawn.

Charlie Manson and his "family" had struck at the very heart of the straight world and in doing so killed the hippie myth. From then on, it was open season for the L.A. cops on anybody who didn't fit the identikit picture of straight-world California.

I saw Manson in the months before the killings, sitting outside the Experience nightclub on Sunset in the seat of a dune buggy while his girl gang of witches partied inside. Manson refused to go into the club because he would have had to walk through the huge image of Jimi Hendrix's face which adorned the entrance to the club, something the black-hating Manson wasn't about to do.

Manson showed up at Hollywood parties once in awhile. My old friend Ronni Money had a run-in with him at one bash about a year before the murders. She was visiting a friend up in the hills, and Manson was there, trying to get her to take a drink that he'd obviously spiked with LSD. Ronni didn't drink alcohol so didn't fall for the ruse, but that didn't discourage Manson.

"I didn't know who he was until later," Ronni says, "except that he was an offensive little bastard and kept telling me to take this drink."

After the Tate-LaBianca killings, L.A. got ugly. Beverly Hills became an armed camp. According to one news report, hundreds of shotguns were sold in just a week. Adding to the strangeness were new drugs taking over. It was snowing cocaine in L.A. Speed, Quaaludes, and heroin were taking the place of pot and LSD. The press grew extremely negative toward the counterculture, and I took the whole scene as a sign that it was time for me to move on to something different, and I disbanded the New Animals.

I was burned out and kind of losing it, not talking to people and staying inside my own head. For awhile, I attended the Actors' Studio in Hollywood. The acting lessons were a godsend. I didn't do anything musical for a while, just concentrated on trying to become an actor. My friends joked—with some accuracy—that I was using the method actor's system rather than a shrink.

The Actors' Studio was great, like a mental Gold's Gym. Walter Matthau and Jack Lemmon were regulars, helping out the new generation of thespians. For a year, I was happy there, learning the craft of acting, coming away from each session feeling clean. But eventually I had to face the music, so to speak, and return to my world. The night life was in my blood. Besides, friends said, I'd be in a far better position to land good movie gigs if I were back on the charts as a rock star, negotiating from a position of power. So I packed in the Actors' Studio and said goodbye to my peace of mind.

The first step back to music was jamming at the Experience. It was there that I befriended a new guy in town, Lee Oskar. He'd come from Copenhagen and was never without his blues harps, and was always ready to jam. One of our first shows together was, in fact, playing with Jimi Hendrix at the Newport Pop Festival in the summer of '69.

Then I met Jerry Goldstein who, along with his partner Steve Gold, was selling rock and roll posters and paraphernalia out of an office in Beverly Hills. They had a merchandising deal with Jimi Hendrix, Sly and the Family Stone, and others, and approached me with a similar pitch. Then they found out I was between projects and went crazy with plans for me.

Steve Gold convinced me to re-sign with a new regime at MGM. I wasn't sure that was a good idea, but I wanted to broaden my scope, especially with the intent of getting further into the movie business. For that, at least, MGM seemed a logical place to be. Little did I know that they'd soon be bought by Polygram and be history. When the deal with MGM came together, Gold and Goldstein turned me on to the Night Shift, an incredible black band playing in the San Fernando Valley.

Eric Burdon with a black band—now there's a concept, I thought. I asked Lee Oskar to join me in checking them out. They were massive. Four backup singers, trumpet, trombone, tenor sax, bass, percussion, drums, guitar, and keyboards. They were too big to take on the road, but the nucleus, I thought, cooked. What happened between Harold Brown, the drummer, and Papa Dee Allen on percussion, was wonderful. Rhythm guitar player Howard Scott and the sax soloist, known as "Senior Soul" Charles Miller, were both excellent. Lee, of course, had brought his harmonicas with him and wanted to jam instantly.

That's where the magic began to happen. Gold and Goldstein agreed to manage a new band if I was interested in putting it together with the core members of Night Shift, and I knew immediately that it would work like a dream.

Unfortunately, Peter Rosen, the bass player, killed himself before we got the project off the ground. B.B. Dickerson was brought in from Hawaii. He'd been in an earlier band with the Night Shift guys, and his bass playing was deep and funky. B.B. had a steady Buddha glow about him. He seemed to be permanently spaced out and giggled at most everything—except when the band kicked in and he became one serious musician.

The name of our new band, Eric Burdon and War, came from Steve Gold. Steve had a bizarre laugh and wicked sense of humor, which I assume he got from working for Lenny Bruce. Gold was a strange, ugly little man, a veteran of the Korean War, and walked with a limp from a gunshot wound he'd received there. He preached that greed was healthy and that America, and possibly the whole world, was on its last legs. What a groove it was, said Steve, being a part of it all, going down quickly, like a sinking ship. The idea was to take the most negative word we could find and turn it into a positive. Eric Burdon and War, the group, was born.

Eric Burdon and War: From left, me, Charles Miller, Lonnie Jordan, Howard Scott, Harold Brown, B.B. Dickerson, Papa Dee Allen and Lee Oskar. © michael ochs archives.com

don't let me be misunderstood

The final lineup was me, B.B. Dickerson on bass, Lee Oskar on harp, Papa Dee Allen on percussion, Howard Scott on guitar, Lonnie Jordan on keyboards, Harold Brown on drums, and Charles Miller on sax and flute.

We all met one day around a swimming pool in Beverly Hills to talk about rehearsals, decide on an agent, and pick a road manager. We settled on Terry McVay, who had replaced Peter Grant as the Animals' road manager several years before—and who was staying with me in a house at the top of Laurel Canyon in Hollywood.

It was a great time. Planning our first tour, I remember one hot August night we all left our Beverly Hills office to hit an upscale French restaurant next door. Me, a long-haired, overfed, leaping gnome, and a bunch of black studs from Long Beach.

A well-heeled white couple pulled up to the restaurant in a new Mercedes just before we entered. The Mexican guys working for the valet parking service were all busy, so the impatient Mr. Mercedes looked at percussionist Papa Dee and tossed him the keys. Instead of punching the rude fucker's lights out, Papa Dee jumped in the car and drove off. He stashed it on a side street several blocks away, leaving the windows down and the doors unlocked. What a scream.

We began rehearsals three times a week in a space in the Signal Hill area of Long Beach. At first, it was a bit awkward as I wanted to lean toward the blues. The band didn't. They didn't listen to blues and didn't want to play it. American blues meant one thing to a group of black guys from Long Beach and quite another to people like me, Eric Clapton, Jimmy Page, and Keith Richards.

One afternoon, as we wrapped up for the day, Charles Miller asked if I'd like to head back to his place for dinner. Mrs. Miller would love to meet the little white boy in the band, he joked. We loaded up his Chevrolet with his horns and music stands.

"There's no A.C. It's busted," he said as he rolled down the windows.

107

As we drove away, he drummed his long fingers on the steering wheel,

"I'm gonna take the back way," he said.

The sun was sinking as we made our way through Signal Hill toward the coast, the many oil wells in the area thumping away. Suddenly there was a burst of red and blue lights behind us, and a police cruiser's siren started howling.

Charles slowly pulled the car over.

"You clean?"

"Yeah, I think so," I said.

Charles got out with his hands in the air, walked to the hood and assumed the position—without prompting from the cops.

One went directly to him, while the other came to my side of the car. I went to open the door but the cop, hand on his revolver, told me to stay put.

The other officer patted down Charles before hauling him back to the cruiser. The second cop then walked away from me and went back to the cop car.

I couldn't hear what was going on, but I could hear the radio crackling.

It was only minutes, but it seemed like an hour before Charles came back to the car and got in. I was terrified at the whole experience, but it was a regular deal for blacks in Southern California, he told me. I was sickened.

Charles would have another run-in after being pulled over, though this time he lost his temper. He beat the two cops severely before one of them bit part of Charles's left ear off—and the other one clubbed him unconscious with a nightstick.

War drummer Harold Brown, who had known Charles since they were young, said that he was never the same after the police beating.

"He was a good-looking, vibrant man," Harold recalls. "Well-dressed and always well-kept. . . real sharp, you know? After the attack, he started acting weird. A real personality change. He stopped paying attention to how he looked and got all gruffy like. It was brain damage."

In 1980, Charles was murdered in Long Beach—stabbed seven times. He managed to drive himself to Martin Luther King Hospital in south L.A. in his new Corvette, but he'd suffered punctures to many of his major organs, and doctors were unable to keep him alive for more than a few hours.

While the official story was that a sixteen-year-old girl had freaked out on angel dust and stabbed Charles, his friends say that's not true. Brown, in fact, declares that he believes Charles was killed by another brother from the neighborhood, a hunchback named Baybra Nixon who was a real twisted puppy. Two or three years after Charles died, Nixon himself was gunned down—by his own father, whom he was attacking with a knife.

"My auntie saw Baybra with Charles the day he was stabbed," Brown says. "And the next day he went to my auntie's house and warned her not to talk to the police. I mean, that makes a lot more sense than this story about a sixteen-year-old girl."

Either way, I was shocked to hear of Charles's death, and I miss him to this day. It was Charles who helped come up with the idea for War's first gigs, actually. While I had England in mind for the big debut, I looked around L.A. for places to grease the wheels. The Free Clinic, an organization which had helped young people with drug problems, pregnancy problems, health care and the like, was short of money. Charles was one of the guys who suggested we do a series of charity gigs to help the clinic get over its rocky period. We also did a series of prison shows, entertaining convicts up and down the state: Soledad, San Quentin, Chino. We had a captive audience, if you will—a great way to work in a new band!

I was hanging out in the receiving area at the Free Clinic one day with some of the staff and a group of kids seeking treatment. One of the doctors told me how our little publicity campaign had really snowballed from the street to the straight world. People like Frank Sinatra had given generously. Just then, a strange-looking automobile pulled up. It was a Stutz, long, black, and sleek, with huge chrome side-pipes and wire spoke wheels. I couldn't quite believe my eyes as out stepped the man himself, dressed in a purple jumpsuit, a white flowing silk scarf, in high-heel boots. He started across the grass toward the doorway of the clinic. He was sweating bullets in the midday heat. "Fuck me, it's Elvis," I said under my breath.

He stood there in the doorway, sizing up the room from behind his gold-framed sunglasses, then approached the desk where I was sitting next to a white-robed doctor. I sat open-mouthed as Elvis pulled a slip of paper out of his waistband. He signed it with a flourish—a check for $10,000—and mumbled, "Here, this is for the kids, but don't let 'em waste it on drugs."

Elvis spun on his heels and headed for the exit toward the still-idling Stutz. A black kid who was waiting for rehab counseling said, "I wish I had some of the shit he's running on, damn." Everybody in the waiting area cracked up. The doctor stared in disbelief at the check.

A white Brit, left ashore by the British Invasion, together with a black band—how could it fail? All we needed was a record company to back it, and we could crack. Fair exchange is no robbery, I reminded myself, through endless meetings with Gold and Goldstein. Whatever doubts I had about them were soon allayed, and they convinced me that the whole outfit should move in together in a huge house in Bel Air.

It became party central. Jimi Hendrix, when he was in town, was a regular. Jim Morrison became a fixture, sleeping in the hallway with a string of grotty hippie girlfriends. Jim was a glutton for punishment. Many times he'd go off on somebody, not because he was truly mad, but just to provoke a violent reaction and create a scene. This may have been his true art form, and he didn't need a band for it. Creating chaos was his one-man show!

We had a white grand piano in the main hall of the house, and Lonnie Jordan used to announce his arrival by pounding out chords on the keys. One day when he did this it riled Morrison, who was out in the garden. Jim staggered into the house, walked over to the piano and started seriously getting in Lonnie's face, acting like a real asshole. Jordan told him to cut it out but Morrison pushed as far as he could—and ended up getting his nose smashed in.

Soon after, Jim started fucking with me, and it turned into the Asshole of the World Championship. We're lucky nobody got seriously hurt. I grew tired of stepping over the bodies in the morning on my way to the office, so one day I came down with my .44 magnum in hand and one bullet in the chamber. I stepped over one or two inert figures out onto the marble floor and aimed the gun at the chandelier. Jim, half asleep against the wall, opened his heavy eyelids, looked at me, looked at the gun, turned slowly toward his hippie girlfriends and said, "Naa, he's only joking." I pulled the trigger, click, I spun the barrel, aimed, pulled again. Click. Jim looked at the girls around him and smiled, "See, he ain't gonna do it." I pulled the hammer back again and pulled the trigger. Boom! The chandelier pieces rained down on us all. That was the last I ever saw of Jim Morrison. He left for Paris soon after and became a body in a bathtub.

I also had an annoying encounter with Hendrix at the War mansion. It was really late one night and I was alone in the big house, trying to get some rest. My bedroom window looked out over a massive swimming pool in the backyard. Adjacent to it was an area for guests to park cars. First I heard a car out near the street, bottoming out with a screech as it climbed the drive. I didn't think too much of it—probably just Goldstein coming home, I thought.

Then there were car doors slamming and muffled shouts. We never knew who was going to show up at the place at any hour, but the commotion was such that I climbed out of bed and made my way in the darkness to the window. Looking down into the yard, I saw a long Cadillac limo. Every door was open. There were two guys in dark suits, two sexy little Japanese girls waving their arms about and shrieking. . . and the overblown afro and spidery figure of Jimi. I couldn't hear what was being said, but he was clearly fighting with the girls.

I opened the window. "Hey, come on, man, cut it out! Do you know what time it is!"

One of the bodyguards held up his hands and shrugged.

"Hey, man, we're sorry. We didn't mean to. . . you know, disturb you or nothin.' "

The other bodyguard moved toward Jimi and got him in a bear hug.

"Girls, girls, just get in the car. Everything's going to be all right."

Jimi was so out of it he looked up at me but didn't say anything. He was pushed back into the rear of the limo, and they took off, bottoming out again at the foot of the driveway.

A few years later John Lennon and Sly Stone would be among our neighbors. Lennon was on the run from Yoko. She was in New York while he, like a fish out of water, was stuck in Bel Air. I'd see him at night in the clubs, surrounded by a team of strange guys and accompanying a young woman by the name of May Pang. He was in pain, I could tell. And one night he ended up on the wrong side of the waitresses at Doug Weston's Troubadour. The waitresses there were notorious; if they didn't like you they wouldn't serve you. John ran afoul of them and was ejected yelling at the top of his lungs. Another night, Lennon made the papers by coming out of the bathroom with a Kotex on his head. Some weeks later, he and Harry Nilsson would be thrown out together for heckling the Smothers Brothers.

Harry Nilsson. Now there was a mystery man to me. He was the only guy in the music business who never performed on his own. He appeared only a handful of times, always as a guest of others, most notably with Ringo Starr in Vegas in 1992. But socially, in the early '70s, he was appearing everywhere: in L.A., London, New York, Paris—there was Harry with his cocaine and whisky and, often, our buddy John Lennon.

After Harry died in 1994, a strange story began to circulate: Harry had died in his dentist's chair, and his body had slipped through a hole during the massive Northridge earthquake. It had never been recovered. His coffin was lined with stones to make it seem as if there were a body in it. Too bad it's not true. It would have made for a fitting epitaph for a guy as unusual as Harry.

The last time I saw John Lennon was on his so-called Lost Weekend when he and Harry were tearing around L.A. Lennon kept sending his limo driver over to my house to deliver books, always inscribed. One said: "Your mother's the first person you ever screamed at. Doesn't that make you feel like you want to crawl back into the womb?"

Another day, the driver pulled up and delivered Janov's *The Primal Scream*. The inscription said: "Dear Eric, Becoming an American won't ease the pain. Love to you and yours, John and Yoko."

It was just one more chapter in the life of that wild house in Bel Air, War's operational headquarters. We called our company Far Out Productions, and, as Steve Gold would remind me, there was only one rule: There are no rules.

My birthday party coincided with the release of our first record, *Eric Burdon Declares War*. To celebrate, we put a half-pound of Colombian weed into the birthday cake mix. It led to one of the biggest traffic jams in Bel Air's history.

Lee Oskar and I were from Europe, of course, while Howard Scott, our guitar player, was the only other member of the band who had been abroad. When we were in Darmstadt, Germany, where he'd been stationed in the army, Howard went shopping and showed up at the gig that night decked out in knee-high leather riding boots, a combat jacket, and an English riding hat. Draped around his neck were .50, polished machine-gun ammo belts. It was outrageous, and everyone was impressed. Except, perhaps, for the pilot who flew us from Berlin to Copenhagen the next day. He radioed ahead that he had some revolutionary Black Panthers on board. The stewardess made us stay seated until everyone else left the plane.

Lee Oskar's face was beaming as we walked down the ramp, as this was his great homecoming, his first visit home in five years, and he was returning a rock 'n' roll hero. At the end of the ramp I noticed some commotion. At first I thought it was a gathering of ground crew, but as we got closer my heart began to sink. There were about ten soldiers, dressed in serious gear, very menacing. These guys weren't joking. They seemed to fill up the whole waiting area. They formed lines on each side of the band as we filed into the waiting room, the red-tipped live rounds clearly visible in the breeches of their machine pistols. I saw a men's room straight ahead of me and kept walking toward the door. No one stopped me. B.B. fell in behind, and we went into the bathroom and quickly flushed the various incriminating goodies we were carrying. Then I took a deep breath and stepped back out through the doorway. The band was sitting on the floor with their hands on their heads, the soldiers around them with weapons raised. Lee was red-faced, yelling at them in his native tongue. This seemed to only make things much worse.

B.B. and I were directed to join the circle. I turned to Howard Scott and smiled.

"Howard, I think the fashion statement has to go."

"You think so?"

"Yeah, I think so."

From there we went on to Paris, where we had great success. The band had radical chic appeal. During this period, Paris was pretty strongly left-leaning as it had been the place where many communist leaders, including Ho Chi Minh himself, had been educated. So of course a black band called War was there to make a political as well as musical statement.

We were to play at one of my favorite venues, the Olympia, right in the heart of the City of Lights. My old girlfriend Alvenia Bridges had joined us from London. Stunningly attractive, tall, brown, and beautiful, she was an instant hit with the boys in the band, and was invited to come up and dance with us on stage.

Prior to the show I peeked through the curtains at the audience, mostly male college students. They moved restlessly like a turbulent sea of black leather jackets and blue jeans. The moment we hit the stage the crowd went wild. We pumped and funked them up. Some of them were standing on each other's shoulders, waving red scarves in the air. It was supposed to be a seated concert but the sitting was forgotten. . . they danced in the aisles.

At one point an interloper managed to slide down onto the stage from one of the balconies. This caught the attention of the fire depart-

Spilling the Wine with War at the Beat Club in Germany. © michael ochs archives.com

ment, the gendarmes and the road crew. The energy level was so high it was starting to look dangerous. It was time to calm things down, time to bring Alvenia to the stage. The plan was for her to appear from behind one of the amplifiers during a flute solo that Charles Miller played during a song called "Spirit," which was dedicated to Aretha Franklin. As the stage lights went low and we slid into the mid-tempo beat of the song, the fine silhouette of Alvenia emerged. The fabric of the dress she wore made her appear naked, her long legs and arms making synchronized moves like some Egyptian goddess. The crowd was transformed from wild beasts to utterly transfixed, drooling boys.

From that, we segued into "Tobacco Road," and the crowd went nuts. We were playing it at three times the normal speed. It drove them over the edge. One guy managed to stumble his way through the orchestra pit and drag himself up onto the stage. I was close to the audience, and the guy slipped past me. There was a flash of metal, and I turned to see Terry McVay strike him with a microphone stand. Suddenly the crowd turned ugly, ready to lynch us all.

Jesus, I thought. What am I going to do?

Two firemen ran forward and grabbed the guy who had been hit. Before the audience could storm the stage, I ran to the side of the curtains and grabbed Terry. As I dragged him onto the stage, I yelled at him to play along, hoping a little theater would save our sorry asses. Grabbing him by the collar, I pretended to butt him in the face. Bam! He hit the floor, and the audience roared. Terry, playing it to the max, rolled around in fake pain. Then a gendarme stepped in and dragged him off by his collar.

I was never more relieved to get off a stage in my life. We had averted a full-scale riot. Oh yes, I thought, it's going to be fun on the road with War.

The name itself seemed to attract trouble wherever we went. The music did its job and we became a success, giving MGM its first No. 1

single with "Spill the Wine." The song came from a tipped-over bottle in a recording studio and developed out of a jam session. But the spilling of the wine became quite a ceremony with the band. Promoters would leave bottles of red California wine backstage. These wines have improved immensely over the years, but back then we were getting sub-standard stuff. What we never seemed to have was a corkscrew, but I discovered that these bottles were easy to get into if you just plunged your middle finger into the cork. It would pop down into the bottle—spraying wine upward as it did so. The trick was placing your mouth over the bottle to catch the cheap plonk as it erupted. It soon became a backstage event, this "spilling of the wine." I engendered much noto-riety after starting a rumor that I could do it with my tongue.

Things were looking good for us but once more I was suckered by the businessmen. I didn't see that I was being controlled in the worst kind of way by Gold and Goldstein, whom I would later refer to as my Double-Headed Monster. They needed me to make War a success and to make sure I'd continue, they dangled the most enticing carrot imag-inable: the film of the final Experience show that Jimi Hendrix had played at the Royal Albert Hall.

That was the deal. I was to go on the road, work in the band War, get a hit record, attract other talent for Gold and Goldstein to manage (which I did in the form of Jimmy Witherspoon and, later, guitarist Robben Ford), and in return I was to get control of Jimi's movie, which he'd signed away in a contract between his (and my former) manager, Mike Jeffery, and Gold and Goldstein, and their partner Bernie Solomon.

The basic footage was great. Gold had stupidly allowed his girlfriend to cut the original negative, but there was still enough to work with. Jimi Hendrix in a truly spectacular performance, captured on big, bright, colorful, super-16 mm.

I contacted Saul Bass, one the greatest graphic cinema artists of all time. I'd worshiped him since childhood, ever since I'd seen his *Man*

117

with the Golden Arm, Walk on the Wild Side and *Anatomy of a Murder.*
Saul was a native Swiss transplanted to Hollywood, and he had the
brain and the meticulous manners of a Swiss clock. Everything in Saul's
world ran perfectly.

I met with the great man and told him of my ideas for the Hendrix
movie, which we had titled *The Last Experience.* He loved the project
and wanted to know more about the music scene in general.

Once as we left the screening room, Saul said he saw Hendrix as a
"modern-day Spartacus"—an escaped slave who causes a revolution—
which amused me, of course, since he'd worked with Stanley Kubrick
on *Spartacus,* which starred Kirk Douglas.

So I took care of my half of the deal. I toured every hole in the wall
in North America and Europe with War. But it turned out that the contract was structured so that Eric Burdon and War could be considered
separate entities. So when Gold and Goldstein decided to take War
away from MGM and move on to a better deal at United Artists, they
did so—leaving me locked into my contract with MGM, probably the
worst record label in the world at that time.

Whenever I balked, Gold and Goldstein would haul out the promise
of Jimi's movie. I saw working on it as a great way for me to return a
favor to Jimi, to thank him for all the great times he and I had shared.
I viewed the movie repeatedly. Sometimes alone. Sometimes without
sound. It was wild, raw, concert footage of him at his absolute best.

Gold and Goldstein had also screened the footage and constantly
claimed there was studio interest. The golden carrot was dangled often
in front of my nose. But every time I said it was about time we moved
ahead on the movie project, I'd get the reply that they were short of capital. "One more tour, and we'll have enough money to do it," they
always said.

Thirty years later, the film's still never been released. Steve Gold is
dead and Hendrix's estate is handcuffed, unable to do anything with

the material since Solomon's widow, Donna, now owns the original negative.

A lot of people say if you remember the '60s, you weren't really there. That may be. As for the '70s, I've been trying for a long time to forget them.

They began as War was hitting international stardom, winding up our glorious London club debut in a jam at Ronnie Scott's with Jimi Hendrix.

It was the last time he'd ever be on a stage. Two days later, he was dead.

Jimi Hendrix and me jamming backstage at the Olympia Theater in London just before Christmas, 1967. Photo by Linda McCartney.

soul possessions

*The story of life is quicker
than the wink of an eye
The story of love
is hello and goodbye
Until we meet again.*

This is the final stanza of the note I discovered on the dirty shag carpet after they'd taken Jimi Hendrix's body away. The bed in which he'd overdosed still held a deep indentation, the shape of a human who had lain there for hours without moving. Two women were crying uncontrollably: Alvenia Bridges, the black beauty, and Monika Danneman, the blonde German, whom I'd met for the first time earlier that week. My mind was racing. I'd shared the stage with Jimi just forty-eight hours before, the last time he would ever play. I was angry at the world, and very pissed at myself for not getting there early enough. I was told that Jimi was still alive when the ambulance men carried him up the stairs from the basement apartment. The coroner would later say Jimi had been dead for hours. Either way, the world's greatest guitar player had taken his last flight, and there was nothing I had been able to do to stop it.

After reading the note, I folded it and put it in my pocket. Some time later I gave it to Monika, believing that she was the rightful owner. As I glanced around the flat I saw a couple of Jimi's guitars. If Jimi's guitars were there, so was his heart, I thought. But I was hoodwinked—for years, as it turned out—into believing Monika's story that she and Jimi were engaged.

The previous evening, Alvenia had told me that the girl had come from a big-money family in Germany. Good for him, I figured. Maybe he'd found somebody who could help him out of the management and money problems he'd found himself in. I'd tried my best to warn Jimi on a couple of occasions, since he was being handled by Mike Jeffery— the same man who had taken care of my business and who was responsible, I believe, for the disappearance of several million dollars from a Bahamian bank account that had been set up as a tax shelter for the Animals.

Jimi and I saw quite a bit of each other socially between early '67 and 1970. As we both travelled a lot, these meetings would be in different locations. It's in the blood and the makeup of a troubadour and entertainer. You get up, you sing, you play, you move, you keep on moving. Jimi spoke often of his family back in Seattle with fondness—showing me photographs of his half-sister, his brother and his father, Al. I knew he was trying to put something behind him.

He let it slip in conversation that he'd been turned away from church because his clothes weren't good enough. He was wearing the wrong shoes, or something. By the very fact that he'd brought this up, I knew it had hurt him deeply. He could be the wildman of rock guitar, but Jimi was also very spiritual, very searching and inquisitive. It amazes me to this day that a young black dude growing up in Seattle wanted to know what lay behind Mount Rainier badly enough to join the paratroopers at a time when there was a hot war getting hotter in East Asia. Who can explain what goes on in the hearts and heads of young men?

He'd also acquired a massive understanding of American Indian culture and religion, and had the knowledge of a shaman. It didn't take much imagination to see young Jimi being ushered through a local museum on a Seattle school outing and coming face to face with the awesome, wonderful spirits that are so close to the heart of the great Northwestern Indian culture. Or imagine him listening to tales from his full-blooded Cherokee grandmother, Nora. Later in his life, Jimi took counsel from the late, great medicine man Rolling Thunder. As young and as unschooled as Jimi was, he had a crystal-clear vision of international, multi-cultural possibilities. Sadly enough, here we are today in a world where we still have race riots in major cities of the richest nation on earth, and the bullets are still flying in Israel. Changing this is what Jimi's fight was all about.

As performers we both had experienced the nightly thrill of audiences screaming for more. But being a troubadour is a dangerous occupation. You come to view the crowd as one entity, a separate person that you have an ongoing relationship with. You come to believe you owe them everything. You owe them your life. But the reason you're out there underneath the stage lights is also to teach them something, to pass on something of worth. To push them so far that they'll never forget you.

Entertaining thousands of people is an incredible narcotic, and applause junkies are easily made. You feel like a god as you leave the stage. Going back for more? You bet. But in the solitude of your four-cornered room after the cheers have died away and the amplifiers are unplugged, your ears are filled with white noise. You're uncomfortable being alone for anything more than an hour or two. And in the hours alone, you question what it is that makes your fans love you so much. Maybe, you think, it's because they're slaves and you're free out there on that stage under the spotlight, showing them the way, praying that they, too, will someday find the freedom.

When Jimi left the stage, there were plenty of places and faces to run to: Devon and her magic potions in New York; Alan Douglas, when he was around in either New York, L.A., or England; Kathy Etchingham in London; Zoot and Ronni Money over in Fulham. There was lots of tea and sympathy. We all wanted to see him succeed. We knew that jazz greats like Miles Davis, John McLaughlin, and Gil Evans were waiting for Jimi to make his next move, to move beyond the "Star Spangled Banner" and flaming Stratocasters.

But there was something stopping him. It was The Business. When the seats are all empty and the roadies haul off the gear, it's the lawyers and accountants you have to face. Performers get to do the thing they love most, but have to deal with lawyers on a weekly or even daily basis. I can't think of many occupations where that's the case. Shit, I don't think most lawyers have to deal with lawyers as often as I've had to.

In rock and roll, innocence is the first casualty. It was with Jimi. By the time he got to Woodstock, there were no burning guitars. By then the rainbow had faded. That's why the film of Woodstock is so deceiving—Jimi didn't play to the four hundred thousand-strong crowd at prime time. He played early in the morning to the freaks and the garbage-covered hills. His "Star Spangled Banner" was not a battle cry—it was a dirge heralding the death of the dream. He took the illusion of American patriotism and used it to illustrate bombed-out villages and Napalm-scorched children.

Throughout our friendship, from the very first time we met outside a Manhattan hotel, all the way through to London and L.A. and beyond, I was able to stay in a unique position to watch Jimi's mystery unfold.

And to me, Jimi reeked of mystery.

A lot of things set him apart. For one thing, his color—he actually

Hamming it up backstage in Zurich in May, 1968: Me, John Mayall ,Steve Wind-wood, Jimi and Carl Wayne.

had a kind of purple, bluish tone to his skin. For another, he was doing acid. I'd never met another black person doing acid back then. It was a major springboard for Jimi—that, Bob Dylan's lyrics, and being exposed to a white audience early on in his career, in Greenwich Village clubs. He made a quantum leap from being just another starving New York artist to being the toast of London, which hailed him as the Black Elvis. He was not only a brilliant and innovative player, but a riveting performer, and he took the Old World by storm. At social gatherings in London's West End with the well-heeled society folks, from the darkness of the smoky clubs up and down England on the first tour, he was shining. From the first 45 released in Britain, played by pirate radio stations off the coast, he was shining. On television he was shining.

I had an antique military jacket, an officer's coat with wonderful gold braid around the collar and the sleeves. It was an almost velvet weave, with brass buttons. It had been given to me after I performed at the Duke of Bedford's house, a gift from his son Francis. I wore it with pride. When Jimi saw it hanging in the wardrobe of my apartment, he fell in love with it.

"Oh, man, where did you get this?"

"It was a gift," I said. "Ain't it neat?"

"Shit, yeah." He picked it off the hanger. "Oh, yeah, fuckin' great."

He wanted one so bad I would have given it to him had it fit. I directed him toward the flea market in Portabella Road and when I saw him two weeks later, Jimi had scored. He'd found an old Hussar's jacket, possibly dating back to the Crimean War.

One afternoon in a pub, Jimi and I were having a jar when a Chelsea Pensioner, decked out in his standard bright gold, red-braided outfit, looked at the strange black American wearing the Hussars uniform. He sneered at Jimi and asked him who he thought he was. Jimi replied: "101st Airborne... United States of America." The old codger promptly saluted.

That jacket became one of his favorite stage outfits. Whenever we saw him in the jacket, we knew there was going to be some serious jamming going on in town.

After hours one night in the Speakeasy, I recall Jimi on stage alone, playing for a half-dozen friends and the club's amazed owner. Plugged into a stack of Marshalls, his Flying V hanging around his neck, Jimi also had a Fender bass laying at his feet. Wearing high-top white moccasin boots, he was slapping the bass with his feet while the guitar went wild in his hands. He was soaring, from T-Bone Walker, Elmore James to John McLaughlin and back. With his head, he motioned for Jeff Beck to pick up the bass. Jeff, as shy as ever, wouldn't make the move. So I grabbed him and pushed him toward the stage as Jimi slid the bass toward him with his foot. They flew. The volume got louder. The manager got nervous. Picking up a flashlight, he tried to end the jam by flashing it in Jimi's eyes. Jimi took it as his own personal light show.

I can't remember how it ended. Maybe the manager pulled the plug on the microphone. But suddenly something brought Jimi to a stop. He unhooked the Flying V from around his neck, balanced it in the palms of his hands, and as a visual musical crescendo jammed the guitar right into the ceiling above the stage. It stuck there like a giant Indian arrow, pieces of white plaster falling down on the crazy man's head, the strings still howling like a great dying beast. Thank you—and good night! As we left the club, Jimi handed the manager a fistful of money to cover the damage.

There are those times in your life when you know, even as they're happening, that you'll always remember them. Monterey was one of those experiences. My singular defining moment of the '60s: June, 1967.

Monterey was ground zero for the new music movement. It was there that some of the music business executives, accountants, lawyers, and the like turned on for the first time. It was there they decided to grow their hair, lose their ties and embrace rock 'n' roll as more than a passing fad.

It was the birth of the rock press, the birth of rock radio. It was the coda for the Mamas and Papas, and near the end for the Byrds, but it sowed the seeds for the birth of Crosby, Stills, Nash, and Young, and gave enormous boosts to Janis, the Grateful Dead, The Who, Jimi, and me.

Monterey was the only true pop music festival. Everybody else tried to copy Monterey. But you can't copy feelings; like when musicians jam, the magic can't be planned. But if you wait until there's a smile or a nod from the stage, from a musician who has a space open for you to move in and turn the people on, then that's jamming. And that's what happened at Monterey.

In fact, the whole thing had an improv feeling as word spread by mouth amongst musicians. I heard of it in London when somebody said to me, "Hey, man, are you going to Monterey?" The next thing I knew I was in the first-class section of a specially chartered jet on the way to New York. There was Brian Jones and Jimi and the guys from the Experience, Chas Chandler, who was, by this time, guiding Jimi's career full-time and traveling just about everywhere with him. From the minute we took off it was a party. When we landed in New York, the customs officials were pretty suspicious of the whole crew. As we were standing in line, I motioned to Brian Jones, who was dressed like an old lady in his furs, that we'd better go the bathroom and unload our stashes. When we got into a stall, we pooled our pot, hash, LSD and whatever else we were carrying. We didn't want to waste it and didn't want to get busted, so we split the whole load between us and took it all right then and there.

By the time we'd made it through customs and got to our hotel, Brian and I were about 10 feet off the ground. After checking in, we managed to make it to the elevator—but neither one of us made it out. We rode up and down for hours, laughing hysterically at each passenger who was unlucky enough to come through the doors and ride with us. It was Chas who finally rescued us.

After the stopover in New York, we all headed for Monterey.

The poor, the rich, the faithful, the ragged, the runaways, and the lost ones all found themselves at Monterey. I rented a Yamaha dirt bike and on the morning of the show I rode up to the hotel where Jimi and the guys in the Experience were staying. There was a sight to behold: Jimi, out in the morning sun, a couple of Fender guitars resting on a Navaho rug in the gravel, with an array of paints and brushes. The shaman artist preparing the objects of sacrifice.

At the festival there was an open guest space where people who didn't have hotel rooms were allowed to sleep. I remember Jimi showing up there late one night. "Mind if I play?" he asked, and shimmied up one of the poles to an electrical box to plug in his small amplifier. Heads emerged from sleeping bags, and the smoke was passed from hand to hand as Jimi serenaded the throng.

As for my performance at Monterey, I would say that I put on a respectable show on the opening Friday night. It was all right, but it wasn't great in my opinion, despite the glorious press we got. The most applause we drew was for our version of "Ginhouse Blues." The crowd liked us, but it was one of the first gigs for the new Eric Burdon and the Animals band, and we didn't really cut loose like we would in the months to follow. Of course, the festival did bless me with the great song "Monterey," which I wrote in the weeks that followed.

On the Saturday night—June 18, 1967—there was a jam underneath the main festival stage. Plugged into a small amp, a white Stratocaster around his neck, Jimi began playing a riff. Buddy Miles joined in playing on a bottle. I grabbed a nearby tambourine and suddenly we were cooking.

One of my defining moments, performing at Monterey in 1967. © Paul Ryan/ michael ochs archives.com

"I shoulda quit you
A long time ago
I shoulda quit you, baby
A long time a go
Now here I am
Down on the killin' floor."

Yes we were cookin'. And we were too loud. Bill Graham's face appeared at the side.

"Hey, knock it off, you guys! You're killing the Mamas and Papas."

The show itself that night seemed historical even at the time. Three teenage guys stopped me for my autograph and asked who Jimi Hendrix was. "Just stick around and you'll find out," I said.

Later, just before Jimi set his guitar on fire, I looked into the crowd and, six rows back, there the three teens were. I'd never seen such shock—and joy—on any face in any audience anywhere. Jimi was performing a soul sacrifice. As blue-black smoke rose in the air, he straddled the guitar as if he were in a fight to the death, plucking out his rival's still-beating heart. I've come to think that this was Jimi's best and worst night. He became a star on that Monterey stage, but he also put himself in a corner. From then on the crowds wanted to see the maniac perform his sensational stunts. The musician was overshadowed. I asked Jimi about this later, and he confirmed my contention.

For a time after Monterey, Jimi and I were either touring or living on different continents, and our paths crossed only on the road.

Then came the only sour moment in our friendship.

At the point at which I decided to give up the Actors' Studio, I began jamming with the Blues Image, a local L.A. group that had a hit record with "Ride Captain Ride." I thought it would be fun to play a festival in Northern California with them, so I drove up from L.A. in a rented

Cadillac while the guys in Blues Image flew in from a gig in Chicago. They were late, which turned out to be a problem.

The promoter came backstage and said the show was running overtime. We were scheduled to play right before Jimi. Because the Blues Image was arriving late, Jimi would have to trim ten minutes from his show to give us at least twenty minutes on stage. Mike Jeffery stepped up and said, "No."

It was the only time in my performance life that I'd lost the chance to go onstage. I walked around, stewing. Noel Redding walked with me, trying to console me, but I was pissed off. Out of the show? I went to Jimi's tent, but Jeffery faced me down at the entrance. Jimi was sitting in the corner on an iron chair, bent down low over one of his axes, cigarette smoke slowly drifting toward the roof. A couple of roadies stood behind Jeffery to make sure I didn't get through to Jimi, who ignored me.

A few months later, I got a phone call from Jimi, who was in Hawaii, acting like the blues festival fiasco never happened. He was bursting

Goofing off at one of our performances together in Europe, Jimi, me and Noel Redding.

131

with excitement about the islands. He'd found his paradise—the place where he wanted to build his dream studio, Electric Ladyland. The Hawaiian Islands, he told me, were the center of all the planet's positive energy, and he was going to leave dreary London for them.

In Jimi's world, conflict between artist and management was inevitable. Hendrix only wanted to expand his music and wasn't interested in the business side of things. He wanted double albums, which record companies hated because it meant less than half the sales of a regular album. Jimi was an artist born in the studio, and that's probably where his best stuff came out. But there was a lot of fighting going on because he wanted to spend so much time recording and experimenting. He also wanted the right to develop or choose his own cover art.

His dream of building the studio in Hawaii was short-lived as Jeffery wouldn't allow it; the studio was built in New York, and opened just weeks before Jimi died.

During the sessions for *Electric Ladyland,* Jimi's third album, Chas had finally had enough of trying to rein in Jimi and the band while also dealing with Mike Jeffery. Chas quit and sold his twelve-and-a-half percent interest to Jeffery, who from then on owned a full quarter of everything Jimi Hendrix.

The remainder of Jimi's life was a cascade of accidents, screw-ups, and bad decisions, and he'd often phone me for advice, saying he was sorry he hadn't listened to my warnings about Jeffery and that he wanted Chas back as his manager.

He and the Experience broke up in late 1968, playing two farewell gigs at the Albert Hall the following February. The shows were filmed for the aborted movie that I was promised by Gold and Goldstein, *The Last Experience.*

It was at this time, also, that Jimi lost a lawsuit brought against him by his first manager, Ed Chalpin. Hendrix had signed with Chalpin when he was in Curtis Knight's band and was still under contract when he left for Britain with Chas after the death of the Animals. I thought it was a shitty deal but under the law, Chalpin had Jimi's name on a piece of paper, and although he had nothing to do with his career or success, he ended up making a fortune off an album, *Band of Gypsies,* which was compiled and released solely to pay off the lawsuit.

Chas stayed out of the picture. Life was much easier by then for him, and he had new plans, new bands—such as Slade—and a family to think about. Alan Douglas would show up in New York on the production end of things, helping with the sessions. The sad thing was that Hendrix was standing at the threshold at this moment and couldn't see it. America's finest players were waiting for him to step up and take his place along with the jazz greats. But there was so much shit in the way, And it just kept coming. In Canada, Jimi was busted at the airport packing heroin. Only a girlfriend—L.A. music journalist Sharon Lawrence—kept it from getting messier when she took the blame.

After breaking War in on the road in the U.S. and Europe, I decided to take the band to London. The target was Ronnie Scott's jazz club. I figured that an interracial L.A. funk street band with a white boy fronting in a jazz club would be an immediate hit with the press. I was right. I was nervous going into the date, but all fears were dispelled by the second set of the first night. The black boys from L.A. and I were going to cause a disturbance in the old town. I'd heard that Jimi was around, and got a call from his friend Eric Barrett, who told me that Jimi had been hiding out in the Cumberland Hotel and at some new girlfriend's flat.

"Eric," he told me, "he wants to see you."

Jimi was clearly at his most troubled crossroads. Everything had gone to shit: He had legal and management troubles and, in the previous weeks, had lost his band. His latest tour, which began at the Isle of Wight, wiped out in a mess of confusion in Europe. Bass player Billy Cox had been badly dosed, and returned to America as Jimi retreated to London.

"If he wants to talk to me, he can come and see me," I told Barrett, figuring it would draw Jimi out of his lair. The ruse worked. On that Tuesday night he emerged, and word spread quickly that Jimi was on the town. He made his entrance with a string of babes, including my ex-wife, Angie, Alvenia Bridges, and Monika Danneman, a new neat little blonde whom I'd never met before. Kathy Etchingham, Devon from New York, and Jeannette Jacobs—each in her own head believing she was Jimi's special girl—were also tagging along.

When I finally saw him I was devastated. Jimi was a mess—dirty, out of control like I'd never seen him and, for the first time, without his guitar. He had a head full of something—heroin, ludes, or the German sleeping pills that would take his life a couple of days later. I didn't know what he was on, but I sent him away.

"Come back tomorrow night and bring your ax. Then maybe we can talk."

"Sure," he mumbled, and wandered off with Monika in tow.

The guys in War finished off the audience in great style. I walked away from the club satisfied, arm-in-arm with Alvenia, who ended up back in my hotel room.

Thursday night the house was full. Things were hot. There was expectation in the air, and sure enough, Hendrix made his entrance during the second set. There was a crack in the air. I introduced Jimi to the audience. "Ladies and gentlemen, a very special guest. . . a friend of mine. . . Jimi Hendrix." He took the stage. The typical London jazz crowd tried to show indifference as he took the stage, but a ripple of applause greeted the greatest guitar player in the world. They continued to drink, clinking their glasses and making small talk.

Jimi's presence was intimidating, but the guys in War held their ground as we launched into a triple-time version of "Tobacco Road."

Howard Scott's guitar playing was inspired. Having Hendrix on stage made him play better than he ever had before. We slid into "Mother Earth," a beautiful blues written by Memphis Slim. We ended the set with a burning jam. Jimi was flying. And then it was over.

Jimi and I embraced backstage, but he didn't stick around too long. Before he left, a reporter by the name of Roy Carr pinned him down for a couple of minutes and Jimi explained how he wanted to create a new kind of music.

"Maybe it's not jazz," he said. "Maybe it's. . . I know in my head how it sounds. It doesn't sound like the music I've already recorded, or music like we were playing tonight."

But Jimi seemed deeply fatigued, and he complained about his management and legal troubles.

"Too many things keep getting in the way of the music, too many lawyers. I'm getting very tired. Sometimes, like tonight, I'd rather play in a band just like I'm doing with Eric, like I used to do a few years back in the States around the clubs."

Jimi left Ronnie Scotts before I did.

The next thing I remember was the telephone call. It was Monika, the German girlfriend I'd met the day before, telling me she was having problems waking Jimi up. I'd answered the phone in a sort of dream state and told her to slap his face and give him some coffee. I lay back down, but quickly was shocked into wakefulness by a deep, bad feeling. I asked Alvinia for Monika's number, and she found it in her handbag. I called Monika and told her to call an ambulance if she couldn't wake Jimi. She didn't want to, as there were drugs in the apartment.

"Call a fucking ambulance," I screamed at her. "I don't care what's in the flat!"

Picking up the sense of urgency, Alvenia slipped on her jeans, warned me that the press would soon be all over the place, and ran on ahead.

I'd been at the center of the so-called drug culture. Taking acid and going up to the Joshua Tree monument in Southern California on magical starry nights to look for UFOs. . . that was the essence of the drug experience to me. I never imagined that Jimi, a guy with so much light around him, could slip into the abyss. I instantly thought it was heroin, since Jimi had narrowly avoided doing time for smack possession in Toronto. But as we raced to get him on the morning of September 18, 1970, none of that mattered.

I saw the flashing blue lights of the ambulance as my cab rounded the corner. Even from outside the flat I could hear the moans of Monika and Alvinia. I knew the cops would be there shortly, so to help calm the girls down, I gave them something to do.

"Come on, let's clean this place up," I told them. "Let's get rid of everything we don't want the cops to take. They'll be here any minute now."

The three of us moved back and forth throughout the apartment, gathering the essentials. The girls brought out two guitars. I found the cases, and packed them and stashed them in some bushes in the back garden. Monika gathered documents, photographs, and Jimi's U.S. passport.

I was acting on automatic. Sheer instinct. Soon there were uniforms and big black boots all over the place, notebooks were extended and pencils were poised.

I could hear other people arriving upstairs. I recognized the voice of Gerry Stickles, Jimi's roadie. I stepped outside, climbed the iron staircase to escape the massing cigarette smoke within the tiny room. I found myself standing next to Monika's little yellow Opel sports car, which was like a mini-Corvette. A few clouds had broken, and the rain had stopped, and the sun was beating down on the pavement of the wet street. The word "Love" was scrawled on the window of the Opel. I was sure Jimi's hand had written it there the night before.

For a long time to come, I believed that if I'd insisted Monika call an ambulance immediately when she first called, Jimi might have had a chance. For a long time I felt guilty that I hadn't acted immediately, that

I hadn't raced to the flat the instant Monika said she couldn't wake Jimi. I was mad at myself and everyone else. I felt we were all guilty for letting him slip through our hands.

It eventually became clear, as the various doctors and pathologists involved were interviewed over the years, that Jimi had been dead for hours even before Monika called me.

Dr. John Bannister, the first doctor to see Jimi, has publicly said that Jimi wasn't even admitted to the hospital, since he was so clearly gone.

"He was obviously dead," Dr. Bannister wrote in a 1993 letter to the London *Times* newspaper. "He had no pulse, no heartbeat. . . his hair was matted. He was completely cold."

That morning in 1970, however, I didn't know that. I sat on the curb, my feet in the gutter, watching cars arriving and leaving. Curious neighbors were wondering what the hell was going on. My mind was still back there, downstairs in the basement flat, before it filled with policemen and investigators and friends and press. I kept thinking of how it must have been only twelve hours or so earlier.

I'm not quite sure of what happened next. I found myself at King's Cross Station, on the platform, holding one of Jimi's guitars with one arm and a weeping Monika with the other.

We headed north to my parents' house in Newcastle to escape the press. My mother did the motherly thing, and made a space for Monika across the street in my Aunt Nora's. "Let the girl be alone with her sorrow."

My old man had taken the car out for his nightly drink. I walked to catch up with him. It gave me something to do. The bar was almost empty. My old man was alone in a corner. I waved to him and pointed. "Want another drink?"

"No thanks. One's enough," he said.

I got myself a large scotch and sat down next to him. After a long silence, he said: "Can someone tell me what's going on here? What in heaven's name are you people up to?" There was a long silence. "You still doin' them drugs? Are you on drugs now?"

"No, no I'm not," I said.

"Haven't you had enough?" he went on. "Aren't you ever going to grow up? I warned you. I warned you before you went to London. Now you see what it's led to. Didn't I bring you up properly?"

What could I say? I was living in a different world by then. It cost me more each month to park my precious Corvette in London than what my parents paid every two months in rent. My sister Irene and I had always fought and were never close, even at this time of crisis in my life.

"How do you think that lad's parents are going to feel?" my old man asked. "Is anyone trying to contact them?"

In the whirl of events, I hadn't thought of this.

"No," I said. "I guess Chas will take care of it. He's down in London. He's got their telephone number, I'm sure."

I remembered that Jimi once told me he'd like to be buried in London, but the thought was shattered by the force with which my old man stared at me.

"I remember the last time you came home, smashed out of your brain on whatever it is you take. Driving that bloody sports car of yours. Do you remember what you said?"

"No," I said, looking at my glass.

"You and that bloody Hilton told me that you were going to save the world. That you were going to speak through your music to the people of the world and bring peace. Now don't you think that if you're going to take on a job that important, you'd better do it straight for once in your life?"

He stood up, leaving his unfinished drink on the table, and walked away. The bar door flew open and my old man was silhouetted against the Newcastle night. He motioned toward me.

"Come on, then, let's go home."

Reporters hunted me, but I managed to avoid them for almost a week. I arranged for Monika to be flown back to Germany, but Jimi's death was too big for me to escape. A black rock star. Narcotics. A white woman. It was explosive material and was plastered all over the pages of the popular press.

Finally, my mother told me that there had been a call from the BBC, that the respected reporter Kenneth Allsop had wanted to interview me. I should have said no. But back then, when the BBC called, it was like being summoned to the highest court in the land. Unfortunately I believed that Allsop, whom I'd watched many times on television, was a fair and compassionate individual who loved music. Maybe there was a chance, I thought, that I could explain that all was not as it appeared in the papers. But in retrospect, I had no business going anywhere near the media.

Kenneth looked different in the flesh. Under the harsh lights in the BBC studio, the flaky makeup and the glaring eyes left no doubt he was the hanging judge. His job, for which he was well-prepared, was to take my wretched little soul and, in a quick four-and-a-half minutes, place it in the stocks for the collective national village to throw rotten eggs at. I can't even remember what I said. I felt I was alone with the impossible task of explaining what had happened to Jimi to those people who just didn't get it. Before going on camera, I went into the bathroom just outside the studio, closed the door and stood on a toilet seat to light up. And just as countless men have raised a glass to salute their fallen comrades, I raised a joint in honor of my departed friend. Leaning against the wall, I smoked slowly, the blue fumes coiling toward the overhead fan. Then I retired to the green room to await my fate.

Allsop took me apart. Sure, I was stoned and shouldn't have been there in the first place, but I thought he *understood*. When I said Jimi had killed himself because of the evils in the record business, that he was being killed artistically by his manager and all the accountants and lawyers, Allsop went for my jugular. Hypocritical bastard. He'd be dead of a drug overdose himself a couple of years later.

Back then it was easy to believe the future was ours. But as I left the BBC studios through the huge brass-handled glass doorways and stepped out into the cool night, a face I recognized as a record company executive said, "You'll never work in England again for what you just said." This turned out to be true.

It was time for me to head back to Southern California, where I could heal myself in the warm sun.

Over the next decade, less and less was said about Hendrix—Jimi Hendrix the person. As the years went on, the man I knew was replaced by the legend. It was painful to see that a dead rock star is worth far more than a live one. Jimi's Royal Albert Hall footage was sold off in bits to the highest bidders. His unfinished works were bootlegged and pawned off as new, original, finished music.

Jimi had often phoned me to play new songs he was working on. When I heard some new Jimi track on the radio and recognized it from a sketch Jimi had shared with me, I would be haunted for weeks. The fighting over Hendrix went on for years. One morning, twenty years after his death, my telephone rang at six o'clock. I instantly recognized the voice of Kathy Etchingham, who had been fighting for years with Monika Danneman over the official title of Jimi's "True Love."

"How ya doing?"

"I'm OK," I said, half asleep. "What's going on?"

"Listen, a High Court judge is going to reopen Jimi's case."

"Oh really," I said. "Why not just let the guy rest in peace?"

Kathy rambled on before ending the conversation with, "You just better get your story straight, because we're going to go through this with a fine-tooth comb, and if you haven't got all the answers to the questions, you could be looking at doing time."

And she hung up.

don't let me be misunderstood

Some months later, *Rolling Stone* magazine published a book—a sort of encyclopedia of rock history—which credited me, instead of Kathy, with requesting that the inquiry into Jimi's death be reopened. It's a falsehood that follows me to this day.

As the years passed, Jimi's spirit continued to have a great effect. Sure, in Francis Ford Coppola's *Apocalypse Now,* it was Jim Morrison singing "This is the end" as the chopper blades whop and a tree line is toasted by napalm. But among the doomed characters in the film, the one soldier who survives is the crazy acid-head—the one with the little white puppy dog in his arms—the one with the music of Jimi Hendrix flowing through his mind.

After many years of court battles, Jimi's family finally won the right to his catalogue. His father, Al, got what was left of his boy, though It took twenty-five years.

"Some justice at last," I thought.

The family planned a joyful victory celebration in Seattle and invited me. I agreed to appear at the Bumbershoot International Jimi Hendrix Electric Guitar Festival, even though I was a bit apprehensive because I wasn't allowed to bring my own band.

To make sure there wouldn't be any problems, I went out of my way to use the talents of Dean Restum, a guitarist who's been with me for years. He helped me demo a piece of music—a combination of "Third Stone from the Sun," one of my favorite Hendrix tunes, and the note that I'd found by his bedside that final, fateful morning many years before.

I wasn't sure I could do the material justice, but I spent a day in the studio, and we finally agreed that the track worked. I drove back home to Palm Springs and copied the tape so my secretary, Jeri, could send it up to Jimi's half-sister, Janie, in Seattle. She was then to hand it over to Nada Walden, who had been given the roll of musical director.

On the plane to Seattle, I listened to the track. No reason it wouldn't work. All the musicians needed to do was play "Third Stone." All I had to do was remember those farewell words—something that was a breeze: They were tattooed upon my soul.

I was met by Janie's husband, a cool, respectable, well-heeled dude. I followed him to the limo. As we approached the car he turned to me. "We have a bit of a problem," he said. "This is the only car we've got, and several groups are coming in at the same time. We're going to use a taxi as well. Just squeeze in as best you can."

"That's fine," I said and opened the limo door. Inside, it was so packed with bodies and amps I had to jam myself behind a keyboard rig and recline. There wasn't enough room for me to sit upright. Then I noticed guitar player Stanley Jordan.

"Hey, how you doing, Stanley?"

As more bodies and equipment were stuffed into the already packed limo, Stanley smiled and nodded. "I'm good, man, and you?"

"Did you get my demo?" I asked.

"What demo, man?"

"I sent a demo that was supposed to be given to you with a piece of music I wanted to do with you today."

"No, man, I don't know what happened. I didn't get no demo."

"Well, listen," I said as the city streaked past the limo's tinted windows. "As soon as we get there and settle in, we'll find a space and walk through this. It's not that difficult. You know the lick 'Third Stone from the Sun'?"

"Yeah, sure," Stanley said.

As we entered the Bumbershoot festival grounds, fans surrounded us, causing the limo to drive at a snail's pace. There were thousands of kids. My spirit soared. Hendrix, exposed to a younger generation full tilt. This was great. At the end of a large, green playing field, there was a covered stage area, and a sea of percussion equipment, drums, amps, and guitars. The unpredictable Seattle weather seemed to be behaving itself. As we pulled up in the backstage area, my eyes focussed on a truly recognizable face, that of AIM Native American leader Dennis Banks. I saw many colorful, young bright-eyed faces— a running stream of kids decked out in pseudo-hippie paraphernalia and costumes. I myself dressed in a conservative black suit, white shirt, and turquoise bolo tie and sported my Texas purple-and-black boots, dyed especially for the occasion.

My urgent objective was to find my dressing room, dump my overnight bag, find Stanley and see what we could work out. I made my way through the crowd slowly, and I ran into Janie Hendrix. "Welcome," she said. "We're glad you're here. This is going to be fun."

Evening was coming on, and it was getting cool. I was still really nervous about what I was going to be singing. I wanted something a little more certain before walking on stage before ten thousand people. Then I saw the familiar face of Mitch Mitchell, looking exactly as he had years before.

"Hey man, how ya doing?" he said in his exaggerated West End accent.

"Great, how are you? You look good, man."

"Yeah, we're going to jam this afternoon."

"Looking forward to it."

"If you got any music question, you just ask Nada," Mitch said. "That's his office there. Come on, man, I'll introduce you."

I followed Mitch up a flight of iron stairs into a prefab office. The interior was filled with tables and chairs, a bank of telephones and computers, and the walls were covered with stickers and phone numbers. A muscular, good-looking, bald-headed dude was sitting at a desk humming to himself as he looked at a musical chart.

"Yo, Mitch, what's going on?" he said.

"I wanted to introduce you to Eric Burdon. He's here to sing a couple of tunes."

We shook hands, smiles around.

"Did you get my demo?"

"No, we didn't get no demo."

"But it's me and Stanley Jordan?"

"Yeah, that's right, man. Check the schedule. Looks like we're running on time. You'll go on about 8:30."

Nada had everything in the world on his computer, but he didn't have my demo. Oh, well, I was here, I might as well enjoy the evening, I thought. There's no way my plan of jamming "Third Stone" to Jimi's last note was going to come down.

I walked to the backstage area where there was a fence that separated the stage from the crowd. The second band of the night was playing. Once I could persuade security to let me through into the crowd, I walked around to the front of the stage. The backdrop was a massive portrait of Jimi's face. This is what he really wanted, I thought to myself. Here it was, the face of a black man who wasn't black. A red man who was a leader. A dead man who was still alive. The young kid from Seattle with the gift from God.

When I reached backstage, I immediately ran into another familiar face—Noel Redding.

"Hallo, ya cunt!"

"How are ya, you bastard!"

"What are you up to?"

"Bad suit, man."

"Ya, thanks."

"Come here," he said. "I want to talk to ya."

Noel took me by the arm and pulled me over toward the office. "What's the deal here? Who are you playing with?"

"I had a piece of music together, but nobody's heard it," I said.

"Well, we'll work something out."

"They already have. Stanley Jordan and I are gonna do 'Little Wing.'"

"Cool."

"Well, yeah, but I wanted to do something really special," I said.

"It'll work out, man. Listen, you know that fucking bitch Monika Danneman is around here somewhere? Watch out for her, mate. You know what that cunt did to me?"

"No."

"I was going to publish a book on Jimi, and she put a stop to it."

"What a drag."

With that, Monika approached. Noel grabbed me and pulled me into a space between two portable offices. I watched as she strolled by. Her white face seemed powdered, making her look like death. Her once blonde hair was totally silver, and she was dressed in a long, blue velvet dress. She looked neither to the right nor the left, but walked straight. Her eyes were fixed.

"She gives me the fucking creeps," Noel whispered,

"So where are you living these days?" I asked, making more small talk.

"Oh, over in Ireland. Got a house there. It's great man, you should come check it out."

"I will, yeah."

"Yeah."

And he was off. I found a place to sit backstage. I couldn't find Stanley. As the night wore on I joined people standing on the stage. It ended up there were more people onstage partying than playing. Then I heard my name announced, and on the far end of the stage I could see Stanley putting the last bits of his rig together with a roadie. He waved at me. I waved back. I walked onto the stage and someone handed me a cordless microphone. Somewhere off in the distance I could hear the chimes beginning, the opening chords of "Little Wing."

I sang the song and left the stage with a dry mouth, and an empty feeling. There was applause, sure. But what did that mean? I'd come here with a mission, and I'd failed miserably. As I walked down the stairs to the backstage area, one of the roadies looked at me and said "Nice, man."

"Yeah, right," I thought to myself. I'd come to deliver Jimi's final words and had failed.

At that point, a couple of drum kits were set up alongside each other with a percussion rig and amplifiers. The drummers were taking over. For the rest of the night, Buddy Miles and Walden pounded on, while several Jimi-wanna-be guitar players thrashed away. Amongst a sea of people, I was lucky enough to stumble across Donovan and his missus, and we settled in to reminisce about the old days. Then the jam band on the stage slid into the "Third Stone From the Sun" riff, the tune that I had planned to recite Jimi's final words over. As if to prove to myself that it would have worked, I leaned over to Donovan and his wife and sang Jimi's parting words. Nobody heard me sing it except those two. When I finished, I shook Donovan's hand.

"Well, I came and did what I set out to do. I'll see you guys around." I walked away.

Then the skies opened up and it began to rain heavily. People were suddenly running for cover. Kids streaked by, wrapped in plastic. The infield of the stadium emptied quickly. I figured the quickest way out would be to avoid the main road, so I circled around backstage and wandered out into the field as roadies were trying to gather equipment. I turned to look back at the giant mural of Jimi's face. As the colors melted in the downpour it looked like he was crying.

Monika killed herself in 1996 by inhaling fumes from her idling Mercedes. For the longest time I wondered if Jimi had decided to put himself to sleep for good that night in 1970. The note I found beside his deathbed made me wonder.

No one alive knows what really happened in that London flat. But the years have brought clarity to the story.

I'd long been a supporter of Monika, believing her assertion that she and Jimi were living together at her flat, and that they were engaged. That turned out not to be true.

don't let me be misunderstood

Monika's story changed nearly every time she told it. She even claimed to have been in the ambulance with Jimi. She charged that the paramedics had caused Jimi to choke to death by sitting him up rather than laying him prone. Neither is true.

The Final Days of Jimi Hendrix, by British writer Tony Brown, put that September week in 1970 into focus for me.

My critics will be scornful once more, but here it is: Privately, some of Jimi's friends suspect that Monika seriously dosed Jimi with her powerful German sleeping pills to keep him from returning to America—and accidentally killed him. He was booked on a flight back to America the very next day, and Monika had thrown a jealous tantrum at a party the night before, hugely embarrassing Jimi.

Jimi knew his drugs, which is why I was always reluctant to believe he accidentally overdosed. If he wasn't trying to kill himself, what experienced drug user would take nine strong sleeping pills and wash it down with a bottle or two of wine? If Monika dosed him, he would have had no control. Maybe the pills were ground up in the tunafish sandwich Monika said she made him just before he went to sleep.

In hindsight, I think Monika was what is now known as a stalker. Ronni Money, whose flat Jimi stayed at when Chas first took him to London—and who knew all the London girls in Jimi's life—firmly believes that Monika was an obsessed fan that Jimi fucked a few times. She had followed Jimi around Europe, and they'd met on a couple of previous occasions before hooking up in London. Once she had him in her flat, and she didn't want to let him go.

Ronni recalled, years later: "That bird, that girl, she believed they were having an ongoing affair. Oh, he saw her a couple of times, but she wasn't his old lady. He was with Kathy (Etchingham)."

It's undoubtedly time for me to forget Jimi's death, speculating on how it might have happened, fantasizing that I might have been able to prevent it; it's time to remember his life. There was a great deal of magic to Jimi, but the legend was once a man, a fact best illustrated by one of my first meetings with him in London, in November 1966. Jimi was new in town, a stranger in a strange land. Standing next to a roaring fire in an elegant Chelsea apartment, he and I were among the first to arrive at a party. I asked him if he wanted a drink and he said, "Yea, a scotch and coke."

I wandered into the kitchen and got us a couple of drinks, but when I returned, Jimi was gone. I figured this was a great chance to sneak a joint before anyone else showed up, so I wandered out through some French doors into a garden patio and sat down. As my eyes adjusted to the dark, I noticed the outline of Jimi's afro on the far side of the garden. I walked over and whispered, "Hey! Wanna hit?" and Jimi turned around, surprised and somewhat embarrassed. He kept his back turned to me as he finished jerking off.

And here's what he said, swear to God: "S'cuse me while I kiss the sky."

Every so often, fans and musicians on the road ask me: "Hey, man, you knew Jimi. What was he really like?"

He was human. Warm, loving, brilliant and the best electric guitar player the world has ever known. And did I mention funny? That's probably the one thing people don't realize about Jimi—he was hilarious. One night in September 1968, after a huge show at the Hollywood Bowl, he came to my house at the top of Laurel Canyon in Hollywood. He had a bunch of reel-to-reel tapes to play for me, stuff he was working on. On top of one of my speakers was a human skull that somebody had given me. When Jimi cranked the volume on the stereo, the bass shook the house.

It shook the speaker.

It shook the skull, right onto the floor.

And it kept right on shaking, baby—rolling past me and Jimi and

After many years, I finally had the chance to spend time with Jimi Hendrix's father, Al, at his home in Seattle.

out an open door to the balcony and off the edge, down into the hills below. Never did find it. But we laughed our asses off.

In the summer of 2000, I finally spent some time with Jimi's father, Al, at his Seattle home. He seemed genuinely thrilled to connect, and he grabbed an old camera someone had given him years before so that he'd have a picture of the two of us. The film had to be seven or eight years old, but he got his picture, which has a sort of sepia quality to it. He kindly sent me a copy with a handwritten note.

It was a sweet gesture befitting the gentle father of Jimi, whom I think about almost daily even thirty years after his death.

CHAPTER 8

"lungs" full of blues

As a teenager, despite my best efforts and all the influences and inspirations in the world, I came to realize that Eric Burdon was never going to make it as a trombone player.

Instead of being half-assed on a horn or harmonica or guitar, I concentrated on singing, and as time went on I gravitated away from my beloved jazz to the blues, which were at that time beginning to rattle the English music scene to its core.

In the Newcastle clubs, jazz was still the standard. But I managed, as a young teen, to slide into a few establishments and get guest spots. The most influential outfit I got to play with was Mighty Joe Young's Jazzmen. Joe was a true gent, and was cool enough to allow me to sit in on a few songs each Saturday night.

One such evening, a music critic for the local Newcastle *Evening Chronicle* was in the club. I made the local press, got my first write-up, and was both amazed and disturbed by what he wrote. He called me Eric "Lungs" Burdon and said me singing in front of a jazz band was proof of the "White Negro."

A kinder word has never been written about me.

don't let me be misunderstood

Alexis Korner is usually perceived as the guy who gave birth to the English blues, but I'll never forget Muddy Waters's second appearance at Newcastle's City Hall. On his first visit, with Chris Barber's band, Muddy had played only his acoustic guitar. The second time, he plugged in. I remember that gig like it was yesterday. I was blessed to be able to listen to him live. His voice was like the howling wind.

The blues became my passion, and I looked upon my nights in the clubs as sacred. It didn't matter where the gig took place: local halls, social clubs, student common rooms—they were all part of the new church.

Then the fever hit: Elvis, Jerry Lee Lewis, Carl Perkins, Roy Orbison, Gene Vincent, Buddy Holly, Eddie Cochrane. It was the singers who excited me the most. I remember seeing Jimmy Witherspoon with the Buck Clayton Band in 1959. The way Witherspoon got the band to groove was a pleasure to witness. He was a man who could really show off the power of the solo human voice.

Another of my heroes, the great Jimmy Witherspoon, left, with my daughter Alex.

151

My life in the blues came full circle quite by chance in the early 1970s, when I met Witherspoon.

One night, coming in from London, I arrived at LAX tired and in a bad mood. I told the cabbie, "Just stop at the nearest bar you can find. You can join me if you want, but I need to get a shot of something."

"No problem," said the driver.

He pulled into the parking lot of the Club Carousel. I entered the darkened room where a jazz band was playing on a small stage. The place wasn't that full. As my eyes adjusted to the dark, my heart skipped a beat. Standing at the bar drinking were two of the greatest blues singers of all times, Jimmy Witherspoon and Big Joe Turner. Big Joe was so huge, the stool underneath him seemed to disappear right up the back of his jacket. He had crutches leaning against the bar next to the drink he was nursing. Witherspoon had his arm over the great man's shoulder and was whispering in his ear. I couldn't believe my good fortune. Two of the greatest blues vocalists of all time leaning against the bar next to me, talking. It was now time to behave like a record executive rather than a performer. I approached Jimmy, introduced myself.

"I've heard of you, yeah," he said. I told him about War, and the company, Far Out Productions, and our plans for future recording.

At that moment, someone passed a huge silver Shure microphone over to the bar. Jimmy grinned at me, his big, wide face filled with pleasure. He took the microphone in his huge hands and passed it over to the even bigger Joe Turner. Joe, without moving from the bar, began to jam with the band.

"Ooh, weeh, weeh, baby, you sure look good to me.
Ooh, weeh, weeh, baby, you sure look good to me.
Now tell me, baby, who can your good man be?"

Before I knew it, I was pulled into the vocal fray. I couldn't believe it. I was in heaven. Two of the greatest blues singers of all time, and me stuck in the middle. The mike was passed to me. I did what I could. Big Joe smiled on me like the huge California sun on a golden day. He put his huge arms around me.

"Well, hell, hi," he yelled.

These two mighty voices on each side of me. Now the whole place was rocking. Even the taxi driver who had been sitting outside came in. After one of the best hours of my life, I made sure Jimmy had my telephone number, and left for home. These guys, I thought to myself as the car wound its way up toward the Hollywood Hills, are two good reasons to be settling in California.

There was one element that worried me, however: The treatment of blacks, particularly in the state's prisons. To my experience, it began in earnest with the three athletes defiantly raising their fists in the air at the Mexico City Olympics, but the black power movement spread like wildfire into the formation of a political militant group calling themselves the Black Panthers. Blacks had been clashing with California law enforcement both inside and outside of the jails. There had been beatings and shootings on both sides—most markedly with the informal executions of the Jackson brothers in the yard of Soledad.

While the popular press turned a blind eye, the Panthers themselves tried to expose the conditions American blacks were subjected to in the nation's prisons. Beyond the obvious ill treatment, the Panthers discovered that the authorities had adopted a "policy of weeding out and identifying prisoners who show either leadership qualities or capacities for political analysis," or those whom they thought would join a revolutionary struggle once released from prison.

Many of the prisoners who showed such promise "were murdered either by guards or by other prisoners who became lackeys for the authorities in return for special favors, bribes, or in response to threats, pressures, or fear," the Panthers declared.

The situation was also coming to a head in the U.S. military, of course, where young blacks were being forced to put their lives on the line to protect the so-called democracy that has been oppressing and abusing their people for hundreds of years.

When tensions cooled off slightly following the Jackson killings, authorites attempted to soften the perceptions of the public and the press by opening some prisons for entertainers and journalists to visit.

The first prison I visited was Soledad—the appearance of which shocked me: the barbed-wire fencing and high gun towers revealed it as more of a concentration camp than an American jail. The Panthers themselves made this analogy, describing many of the jailed blacks as concentration camp victims of the struggle against the "fascist-imperialist Babylon" that was intent on repressing anything and anyone in the world that wasn't white.

The emotionally troubling sight inspired me to write and record a song about what I'd witnessed, "Soledad," on the album *Guilty!* that Spoon and I released shortly after.

On the same record was material that Spoon and I recorded in the big yard at San Quentin's infamous Bastile by the Bay.

That day I felt like I'd been dropped into the center of history. There I was with black royalty at the top of a concrete ramp underneath the barred windows of death row: I was between Spoon, Muhammad Ali, his beautiful wife, and Curtis Mayfield. We were among the twenty or so dignitaries who had been invited to inspect the conditions at the prison. As we walked down the huge ramp toward the big yard, I was surprised to find that I was the only white guy in a yard full of about 500 black prisoners, all with their fists raised in the air. I had left California and entered Amerika.

It was wonderful to see Ali again. I had met him on one of the first Animals' trips to New York in 1964, shortly before he converted to Islam and changed his name from Cassius Clay. We were all staying at the Holiday Inn on 57th Street and there was a group of great-looking black girls running around the hotel. Hilton and I struck up a conversation with a couple of them and offered to take them downtown to some Village clubs.

After a great night, I left the last club early, getting back to the hotel around two in the morning. The lobby was empty, but as I got to the elevator, I was followed. The man nodded a greeting, but I didn't really pay attention. He leaned casually against the fake leather padding inside the elevator and asked me if I was in a group called the Animals.

"Yes," I replied.

"I heard you took two of my cousins out tonight. Where are they?"

I looked into what I realized was the face of the newly crowned heavyweight boxing champion of the world and pleaded innocence.

"No, wasn't me." I said. "It was Hilton Valentine. . . I think he's in room 1503."

When we got to my floor, I exited the elevator quickly and made it to my room.

The next morning I was in the hotel restaurant having breakfast alone. As I dug into my eggs benedict, the two gals from the night before came up and asked what happened to me—why I disappeared from the club. I told them the truth, that I was tired and it seemed they were having a good time so I just cut out.

They sat down with me, but, before they ordered, a huge hand descended upon my shoulder. I turned and looked into Clay's face. He said, "I told you once, boy, I ain't gonna tell you again! This is the heavyweight champion of the world talkin' to ya! I could crush your head with one hand!"

He was kidding. I think. We met again backstage during one of our visits to "The Ed Sullivan Show," and he was a gentleman, though constantly teasing me. I was sorry I never took him up on his invitation to visit his training camp in Florida.

155

At San Quentin, there was so much going on and so many people around that Ali and I just exchanged greetings and didn't get much of a chance to talk. One thing that did strike me, however, was that it was Spoon who really had the deep street credibility with the black prisoners—he lived and worked on the streets of South Central L.A., where many of the prisoners came from. Ali, meanwhile, wasn't from California, and he had fully embraced Islam, leaving the jive-ass boxer persona behind. While he was the highest-profile black to refuse the Vietnam draft, he wasn't an outspoken participant in the protests; that didn't mean he wasn't keenly interested in helping his fellow black Americans, however.

I made an effort to connect with some of the inmates.

"What you holdin'?" one whispered as we walked around the prison.

I was wearing a big turquoise ring, under which I'd stashed three hits of acid and one tab of mescaline—for a lucky inmate to be chosen at random.

I made a motion with my head and was escorted off into a shower facility. As several inmates guarded the door, I took off my ring and gave my drugs to the boys—who proceeded to add them to their own stash of speed. They crushed it up into a big blue pile, and then the prisoners came by one by one for a hit. One inmate came up to me after imbibing and tapped his fingers against his forehead.

"Thanks," he smiled, "this is my first time over the wall in six years."

Once onstage, Spoon and I had a great time together. We invited an inmate by the name of Ike White to sing and play guitar. White performed like a man possessed—and he was, possessed by the thought that this was his chance to project himself beyond the prison walls, something that finally came to pass. Luckily, we'd arranged to record that day and had been given permission to bring our own mobile recording unit along with our stage equipment into the yard—something the prison guards, the local sheriff's deputies, and a flank of Green

Berets brought in just for the occassion searched down to the last nut and bolt for contraband and weapons.

After the show, I wandered down to the recording unit, being helmed by Jerry Goldstein, to listen to the playback. The truck's side door was open, and several inmates had already gathered to hear the rough tracks. As I descended the stairs, I was surrounded by black men in identical blue prison uniforms, several wearing red bandanas. They were surprised that we'd been given permission to bring the recording truck into the yard itself, and for them this was a vision of the outside world that they'd been shut off from for years. As I got to the bottom of the stairs, they crowded around and stopped me. One man whispered that if I could get a recording truck in the yard, I could probably get a film crew in as well—and that if I pulled that off, the prisoners would provide a show for the whole world to see—something far beyond what Hollywood could envision.

In a word: revolution. The inmates told me that they had, for years, been hiding guns and ammo in various places throughout the prison and buried in the ground, waiting for the right opportunity to break out.

The prospect of what these men were capable of in retaliation for the way they'd been treated was frightening. With a dry mouth, I said that I'd be back to San Quentin, that there was more recording to be done. . . and that performers such as myself were using our celebrity in an effort to bring change to the system, if not secure the release of the thousands of political prisoners in California jails.

As the small gang parted and let me through, I turned and looked back. I thrust my fist into the air and yelled, "I'm black, and I'm proud!"

Not without a sense of humor about what I'd done, the guys returned the gesture with a chorus of hoots.

Later on, as the sun was sinking and most people were beginning to leave, I was waiting for my escort from the big yard toward the outer perimeter wires. I watched a frustrated redneck state official, his dark

glasses hiding his eyes, an ear piece giving away who he really was, con-
front a black man and woman who were making the most of the day.
The cop glared down at the man, who was lying on his back with his
head near the wire fence. His female companion was sitting astride his
groin, her flowery summer skirt spread out over the dirt. "You can't do
that on prison property," barked the cop in a mixture of embarrassment
and officiousness.

The woman looked up and sneered at the white officer. "Hell, this is
open day, isn't it?"

"Yeah, you're right, it is open day," the cop replied and stalked off.

Jimmy and I drove back down to L.A. in his big, old Cadillac. It was
great making friends with one of the people that I'd hero-worshiped for
so long, but it remains a stain on the American soul that the conditions
in the prisons, and the treatment of inmates, only got worse in the
months after our San Quentin visit—culminating, of course, with the
shameful slaughter of prisoners at Attica in upstate New York.

When Spoon and I finished our blues record and released it, we
called it *Guilty!* I dedicated the album to all California prison inmates.
In recent years, it's been re-released on CD as *Black and White Blues*.

Eric Burdon and War had given the new regime at MGM the company's first hit record and single, but things did not go well for me. I was
signed to a watertight contract with MGM, War was not, and they
moved to United Artists. With Jimi's death in September of 1970, I slid
into a deep depression. By January I was emotionally and physically
exhausted. During a War show on January 30th, I collapsed. I rallied to
do a February 5th show, but couldn't make it through the set. An
asthma attack led to pneumonia, and I had no choice but to pack it in
for America and let the band go on without me.

While War went on to continued success with their new deal at UA, I
was left stranded at MGM. Gold and Goldstein told me that my only
recourse was to become a one-man picket line outside MGM's Hollywood

Not one of my better career decisions, protesting my own record company in Los Angeles..

offices, an act of defiance that would surely convince them to release me from my contract.

It didn't work. When I hit the sidewalk, an MGM executive said this: "If the birdie don't sing, the birdie don't get no seed." My checks from MGM stopped coming.

I was forced to go to battle against my own company, Far Out Productions, and Gold and Goldstein, who had put me in this precarious situation in the first place. We were supposed to be three-way partners, but after they'd locked me out of the office they cut off the salary to the band. When I launched legal proceedings, I was also cut off from my only source of income, as the company had control of my performance rights in America. From 1972 to 1974, I concentrated on healing myself, while quietly working on what I considered to be some of my best work—a high-concept album and illustrated book on the blues and Hendrix, called *Mirage*.

But my protracted legal battle with Far Out and Gold and Goldstein had made me a tainted entity, and after all the work and investment, the record company pulled the plug on *Mirage*. It has never been finished or released. Creatively, another couple of years had been wasted.

Then came the worst blow: Gold dropped a dime on me to the IRS, which promptly pounced, claiming hundreds of thousands in back taxes—on royalties that Gold and Goldstein never paid me! As a result of the IRS attack, I was prohibited from leaving the U.S. And at the same time I wasn't allowed to work in the U.S.! I had a knife at my back and a gun in my face.

The IRS did a thorough investigation and discovered that I'd been telling the truth about the situation, and I was soon given clearance to leave the country.

Before I left for a six-month stay in England and Europe, I ran into my old pal El Gordo, the pot dealer I'd hung out with before. He had just gotten out of prison and looked trim and slim, suntanned, with a mustache on his lip and a big smile on his face.

"Things are going to be different from now on," he said. "I'm going straight."

For awhile I believed him. But cocaine was now the drug of choice, and El Gordo starting dealing, a little bit at first, but then he moved up to kilos. Worse, he started using his own shit. Paranoia was rife. One night, I was up at his house trying to convince him to get away from the coke. His eyes were wild, wide open. His teeth clicked together as he spoke. "I heard about your problems with the Double-Headed Monster."

"Yeah. I don't have any recourse. My band split, they're with U.A.,

don't let me be misunderstood

I'm stuck with a record company that don't want me and don't care for me. I have no other choice."

"Oh, yes, you do," he smiled. He bent down and pulled a long cardboard box from underneath his bed.

"This," he said, smiling as he opened the box, "is just an investment to protect my investments, you know what I mean?"

It appeared to be a machine gun. There was white powder caked on his mustache as he fondled the ugly-looking weapon. As he screwed in a silencer he smiled at me and said, "Look, for ten grand I'll get you out of your dilemma overnight, no questions asked. I can make this happen, believe me. If you go to court it will not only cost you money and time, but it's going to cost you your nerves. You won't be able to sing. They'll stop you from recording. This way, I'd take out the beast."

I got out of there as fast as I could. "Buenas tardes," I said to the Colombian gentlemen who were on their way in.

CHAPTER 9

gotta get out of this place

Because of my legal problems, I couldn't work as a rock star, but that didn't mean I couldn't act like one. Fresh from my European vacation I moved in with three girls, seven dogs, one kid, and two cats.

Not only could I not perform in the States, but to further frustrate me, Gold and Goldstein began selling off the precious Jimi Hendrix movie in bits and pieces. Then everything I'd recorded for my own Far Out Productions was released as new and original Eric Burdon material. The bad joke continued. Gold and Goldstein sold some tapes to Capitol. I came into town from Palm Springs one weekend to be confronted by a massive billboard: *Stop! Eric Burdon.* It was a whole album of material I had never intended the public to hear. Rehearsals, outtakes. . . just me in the studio writing. I felt raped.

I had nights of pure erotic heaven living with those three girls, but I knew it couldn't last. I then met Rose, another girl whom I thought was sympathetic. We hit it off. She was very nurturing and attentive and it wasn't long before we were on our way to Vegas to get married. Maybe I was just cold and alone and needed someone on my side—it seemed like a good idea at the time. We got a house out in the desert near Palm Springs. It seemed far away from Hollywood, which was what I needed.

Rose got pregnant, and I tricked myself into believing that I could settle into a somewhat normal life.

One Saturday morning there was a knock upon my door. Standing there was a young black kid, 21 years of age, a drummer. Alvin Taylor had been born and raised in the Palm Springs area. He was anxious to let me know that he had played drums for Frank Sinatra at private parties. I liked Alvin. He was a powerful drummer. He had plenty of ego which, when pushed in the right direction, made for good showbiz. He introduced me to a young black guitar player called Aalon Butler. They

A short-lived domestic life: Me, my second wife Rose and our daughter Alex at our home in Palm Springs. © michael ochs archives.com

163

brought in a bass player by the name of Randy Rice. We rehearsed in L.A., and our sessions proved to me the band had potential. I committed myself to the project and we were soon off to tour in the U.K. and Europe.

Everything went well at first. We got good reviews, did some great club dates, had good audiences. Then one reviewer unfortunately mentioned the similarity between guitarist Aalon Butler and Jimi Hendrix. The review was published with a photograph that made Aalon look slightly like Jimi. From that moment on, things took a tragic turn as Aalon believed he had been endowed with the spirit of Hendrix. Before my very eyes he turned into a faux Jimi. It seemed like Hendrix's ghost was tagging me everywhere I went. He just wouldn't lie down. I'd hear his voice coming at me from the grave over the radio airwaves. I felt him pointing his long freaky fingers at me, letting me know he was watching. I returned to the quiet of the desert. Emotionally, I was so bent out of shape I would just start crying for no reason at all. Rose tried her best to console me.

The first in a long series of Eric Burdon Band: From left, Aalon Butler, Randy Rice, me and Alvin Taylor. © michael ochs archives.com.

Then Capitol fucked me and released the L.A. rehearsal tapes as an album called *Sun Secrets*. I couldn't afford to do a thing about it. I revamped the band and hit the road again. During this period there were lots of changes in the Eric Burdon Band. Aalon wasn't the last guitar player who turned into Jimi Hendrix. As I as getting ready to leave for one tour, Rose hit me with this: "Look, Eric, if you're going to leave again, and you're going to continue to be on the road, then I want something from you, something to make me feel good about our marriage."

"Like what?" I asked.

"I want a new house."

She wanted to raise our daughter closer to a better school, somewhere she'd have other kids to play with.

"Okay."

Two days before I left for a major tour, we went searching for a new house, and found one on Palo Verde Avenue in Palm Springs under the shadow of Mount San Jacinto. It was a beautiful place, small but old, one of the original Palm Springs homes. It bought the family some time—me, my wife Rose, and my daughter, Alex, whom I was able to grow closer to when I wasn't working.

But to pay for it all, I had to be on the road a lot. In the middle of a smooth, successful tour in Germany, I got a telephone call from Rose. "You've go to come home. I'm in trouble. I'm in deep trouble."

"Well, what is it, baby?"

"I can't tell you on the phone, you have to come immediately."

"I'm in the middle of the tour!"

"It's a matter of life and death."

It was an impossible thing she was asking, but she sounded desperate so I told the guys in the band and the agency that I had to go. There was an emergency at home. I caught the next trans-Atlantic flight.

A day later, I arrived at the house in Palm Springs. As I put my key in the door, I knew something was strange. The place was empty, dark, cold. Dirty dishes were piled high in the sink. I sat down, relaxed, made myself tea. Three days later, Rose showed up with Alex and said she'd forgotten that she'd called me in Germany. That sealed my decision. I couldn't live this way any longer, torn between the duties of marriage on the home front and the only thing that I knew how to do to make a living. I knew it would get worse before it got better. There would be more fights, more finger pointing, more mental suffering and the biggest tragedy of all, damage to my daughter's emotional health.

One weekend I took her alone for a ride across the wide open desert in the Mercedes. She was sitting up front listening to her favorite tape, Mose Allison's *I Love the Life I Live and I Live the Life I Love*. She was four years old. I turned down the volume, turned to her and said, "You know, baby, I have to tell you one thing, something about your daddy and your mommy. You know, we don't quite see eye to eye. . . ."

She broke in, looked at me and said, "Everybody knows that." As far as I was concerned, that was another good indication that the end was near.

Rose then started getting meaner and meaner. At one point she got rid of my beloved collie, Geordie. She didn't say anything in advance—I came home from a road gig and was greeted at the front gate by a Doberman. It was hell. Cold and lonely nights, bad drugs, guitar players who turned into Jimi before my very eyes. I seemed to be sliding into a dark pit.

One cold winter night violence erupted at the end of a gig in Wyoming. It was our roadies against the drunken remains of a group of pissed-off cowboys with nothing better to do. I was ushered through the room to the front office as chairs flew through the air. I was sitting with the owner of the club as he counted the take for the night. Suddenly there was a loud thump at the door, and a guy rushed in holding a severed ear on a table napkin. I immediately put it on ice and sat there waiting for the paramedics. When they arrived, they slapped me on the back and said, "Hey, you did the right thing."

When I got home, the house was empty again. Rose was not to be found, and neither was my daughter. A few days later, the two of them showed up, as if nothing had happened. "Oh, hi! What's going on?"

What had been going on was cocaine. One night when Rose thought I had a gig, I followed her to L.A. Through a bedroom window, I saw our daughter hanging on to Rose's dress as she's scoring coke from some dealer I'd never seen before. My poor, lost, lonely daughter.

It had been two years since the start of my lawsuit with Far Out, and the money was gone. A million bucks in lawyer's fees, taxes, and trying to buy stability at home with the cars, furnishings, and a new house. When we did finally settle the Far Out suit, I got $400,000, which didn't cover my taxes or legal bills. What's more is that my own lawyer fucked me by agreeing to sign away my publishing royalties in exchange for the shitty settlement in the first place.

I went back on the road to try to pay for this better life for the family, but soon after arriving in Germany, I got yet another panicked call from the desert. This time, it was to tell me that the Palm Springs house had gone up in flames. No one was hurt, thank God, but I'd lost everything. On a radio talk show, some kid called in and offered to sell me some of my own memorabilia that had been stolen by looters from the smoldering remains.

I never said so before but in my heart I accused Rose of setting the fire—shit, she got rid of my dog while I was out on the road. It summed up my life at this point. . . burned. There was more.

I had been trying to collect unpaid royalties from MGM, now the label's New York office went up in flames, taking all the books with it and eliminating any possibility that I'd ever get my money. As a last resort, I went to the German headquarters of Polygram in Hamburg, where I'd befriended a young executive. He told me that officially he couldn't help me—but off the record he offered to find out how much money the company owed me. He left the office and came back a few minutes later with a computer printout. On a scrap of paper he wrote the figure DM 250,000 and showed it to me. Then, quickly, he took his brass Zippo lighter and sent the flaming piece of paper into his wastebasket.

"I didn't show you that."

A quarter of a million deutch Marks. About a hundred grand, I guess. I couldn't afford more lawyers and another lawsuit, so the money went uncollected.

My marriage to Rose was over, so I decided to stay in Germany. There, I was able to put together a great touring band that attracted solid attention, and I was able to earn decent money. After awhile, I decided to take the group to Ireland to record a new album. Ireland was attractive because it was away from the glare of the press in Germany, the tax situation was favorable, and the country vibe was so positive.

I'd been in Ireland only once before, when the original Animals did a gig in Belfast. That had been a shocker for me, a kid from Newcastle—seeing cops with guns. It was at that gig that we ran into a quiet lad who was the lead singer for a band called Them. He seemed to carry the weight of the world on his shoulders and needed cheering up, the Animals thought. So we pinned him down on the dressing room floor and snapped an amyl nitrate cap under his face, which reddened immediately from the blast.

"Jesus!" Van Morrison cried out.

"Don't worry," Chas told him, "it only lasts for six hours."

We were Animals, all right.

About fifteen years later I was back in the Irish countryside, this time outside of Dublin, on the eighteenth-century estate of Brian Malloy, called Roundwood House.

Waking up there the first morning will always be one of my favorite memories: greeting the day in the thick, white sheets of the feather bed, so high off the floor that I felt as if I were hovering in the room.

The band I'd assembled for the session included guitarist Henry McCulloch and keyboardist Mick Weaver from Joe Cocker's band; Chris Stewart from Spooky Tooth on bass; Brian Robertson from Thin Lizzy on guitar; Greg Penniston on drums; King Crimson horn player Mel Collins; and Bobby Tench on lead guitar. Our road manager was Robbie Wilson, a Scottish Protestant, and the album's producer was Tony Meehan, an Irish Catholic. Quite a mix, when you consider that Glen was a black vegetarian karate expert from Aruba and Bobby a Trinidad-born Londoner.

The whole lower floor of the manor was to be used as the studio recording space, while we awaited Ronnie Lane's mobile recording unit to arrive from England.

The first night, we all gathered at the local pub—called, hilariously, El Pasco—complete with New Mexican-themed decorations.

We celebrated our arrival with the first round of the spiritual black brew, Guinness. We listened in awe as the one old gent, a direct descendent of the original Fitzgeralds, told us tales of mortal combat in far away India. His waxed face glowing in the flames of the fire, he recounted what it was like to run a man through with a sabre. He continued telling his tales until he finally fell silent in a rush of emotional tears. The only sound in the room was the cracking fire. . . and McCulloch sucking on a joint he'd just rolled.

As our sessions got under way, we were generously fed from the manor's kitchen—satisfying lamb and potato dishes, courtesy the cook, Camilla, and the matriarch of the household, Henrietta, and her daughter Caroline. Tony Meehan had brought the wine—cases of it— and we consumed copious amounts in the weeks that followed as we settled in to record what would eventually be my album *Darkness, Darkness*.

This mixture was stirred up with cocaine, red wine, white heroin, black hash, and last, but not least, the Irish air. It was an explosive blend.

The first morning of work was spent checking out the acoustics of the main recording room. Meehan said the place was too dry and needed some acoustic shoring up. Finally, he decided on hay bales. My vocal booth was like a manger with a peep hole. Meehan used the hallway as the drum booth. By the time the mobile recording unit arrived, there were wires and hay bales everywhere in the lower half of the house.

In the Irish countryside, the arrival of the recording unit, built into a silver Airstream trailer, was like a UFO landing. As word spread of our presence at Roundwood, people came out of the hills, including Chieftains Paddy Moloney and Derek Bell, who came down one night for an evening of carousing and playing. Paddy and Derek appeared on the title track, their arrangement of the song testament to their status as the world's premiere Celtic musicians.

At times, the explosive, unlikely mix of personalities got a little tense, but things didn't get unruly until we began running out of money. I had to send for $15,000 of my own cash from an American bank account.

As we waited for nearly two weeks for the money to clear the Irish bank, the recording went on and on. And so did the fun, at high cost.

After one drinking session at El Paseo, I drove back with a gang of people in my Range Rover, which I'd shipped over from England. Pissed drunk, I missed a turn just a few miles from Roundwood and went over an old stone wall, destroying both it and my vehicle. We escaped unharmed, luckily. But another drunken stunt in a VW van resulted in a deep gash to my face, just missing my left eye.

After the sessions, I discovered that the armed guard I'd hired to go with me to the accounting firm to pick up the much-needed cash had been, in a previous career, one of Ireland's most notorious bank robbers.

As the sessions continued, the master tapes also briefly disappeared. Once retrieved, they had to be locked up at the local police station each day after recording was completed.

It was a magical, insane time. I've loved Ireland ever since.

CHAPTER 10

The Istanbul Express

I come from a background of great family strength—I never even heard my mother and father have a serious fight. Our home was a place of warmth and love. Actually, I remember taking Carl Perkins back to my parents' house, and he was so blown away by my mum's great fish and chips that he said he was going to open a chain of fish restaurants all over the U.S.! My mother and father made home life look so easy. But by the end of my second marriage I needed to run—to get away before I slipped into a deep depression. That's why I stayed in Germany.

The touring and the *Darkness, Darkness* album were all positive creative experiences, but I was still unfulfilled. Rescue came in the form of Frau Christel Buschmann, who approached me about shooting a musical movie based loosely on my own experiences. It was called *Comeback*.

I would play the lead and have input into the script; I would have some say in casting, and I would do the music for the film. It seemed like a golden opportunity to learn the process of movie making. From what I had seen personally of the German post-war film industry, I figured it would be an exciting adventure with new people.

A publicity still from the semi-autobiographical film Comeback.

The plot called for two separate bands in which I would be the frontman. One band was needed for the Los Angeles shoot and another was needed for the German shoot, which would take place in Berlin. There were plenty of musicians in L.A. I could choose from. Among the great players were Snuffy Walden on guitar, Terry Wilson on bass, Tony Braunagel on drums, and Ronnie Barron on piano.

The plan was to complete the movie, then choose one group, head for Europe to tour and promote the film. For my leading lady, I chose Julie Carmen, a beautiful New Yorker living in L.A., just beginning her movie career. She seemed thrilled to be involved in a foreign production.

The filming in L.A. went extremely well, I thought, and we were soon off to Germany to film the second part of the movie. I was looking forward to an extended stay in Berlin. The place always seemed to excite me. There was no place like it in the world in those days—an island of capitalism in a sea of communism, with the bloody great Wall running through the heart of the city. It was still jointly occupied by Great Britain, the U.S., the U.S.S.R., and France. It was the spy capital of the world and the place reeked of erotic intrigue.

On one of our first nights there, some of the crew and I were walking toward the Kurdamm, the Broadway of Berlin. There was a chill in the night air. Suddenly there was a hum among the people on the street, and everyone was moving in one direction—away from the Kurdamm toward the zoo. We were going against the stream of people.

Looking up at the massive glass store fronts and office buildings, I saw blue flashing lights. A formation of police armored vehicles, water cannons at the ready, were escorting hundreds of marchers away from the Kurdamm. We couldn't tell what the protest was about. Everyone in silence carrying flaming torches. It was the orderly silence that got to me. No sound but the marching feet. Some of the banners bore the acronym RAF. It sent shivers up my spine to see Germany on the march

On the set of the German production of Comeback

again, but the faces of the marchers looked young, innocent. They were mostly males, bearded, like guys I went to art school with. I had no idea what it was all about, nor was I anxious to find out. In those days I assumed most demonstrations were against America. But it was more dangerous and complicated than that, as I was to find out soon enough.

Seeing "RAF" seemed perversely funny, as it made me think, naturally, of the Royal Air Force, those brave men who had knocked the Germans out of the skies around the time I was born. But now RAF stood for something entirely different: Red Army Faction. And what it really meant was the Baader-Meinhof gang—in a word, terrorism!

The next morning I heard from a member of the crew that the marchers the night before had gone around in circles until the early hours, when a full-scale riot erupted. That morning, as we drove to the location shoot, we passed the scene. There was a wall of Plexiglass screens, riot shields, and helmets. Officers in green uniforms were taking a coffee break after the night's rioting. The odor of CS gas still hung in the air and stayed there for the next month. There were riots all summer long during the whole time we were filming, and we had to move our locations several times because of the unrest.

To me it just added more excitement. I was fascinated by the place. There was a high-rise club where we would sit and drink martinis, looking down from the sixteenth floor overlooking the Wall that divided West and East. From the bar we watched the East German border guards on their nightly rounds, machine guns hanging from their necks, with bullet-proof jackets and guard dogs, smoothing out the barrier of white sand that existed between the massive blocks of the Wall.

An important part of the screenplay called for us to do a live show at the Metropole Theater, one of my favorite places to play. I told Christel I was afraid there wouldn't be a big enough crowd because people were so caught up in street politics, and it seemed nobody had any money. She assured me that everything would be all right.

When I did a radio interview before the gig, I was asked how I felt about the political climate. I said I knew little of what was going on, but if I had my way I would open the doors of the Métropole and let the concert be a free one—let the street people come in and enjoy the show. How does that saying go, "The road to Hell is paved with good intentions?" I'm sure my name went into an official dossier in an office somewhere, as I was stopped by a cop as soon as I left the radio station. He warned me that I was being influenced by the left movement, and that I could find myself in some trouble if I didn't watch out.

We finished the film after several weeks, and I left the editing in the hands of Christel and her crew and flew back to the United States. I had hoped that my return wouldn't be too painful, but my daughter Alex and her mother had disappeared. All I could determine was that they were living with some new man on a boat in some Southern California marina.

The heartbreak of missing my daughter was dulled by the impending distraction of the road. It wasn't long before I had to return to Germany for a tour and to begin publicity for the film. The first gig was at an outdoor festival at Lorelei in the beautiful green hills above the River Rhine, near the city of Koblenz. We played to an outdoor capacity crowd and a television audience of millions. We rocked! The band was in great form, and I left the stage covered in sweat, totally exhausted but glowing.

We dried ourselves off and changed quickly because we had to hit the road immediately after the show, driving down the winding hill away from Lorelei for our gig the next night in Vienna. We caught a train to Munich where we were to make a connection at Munich Central Station, boarding a train that would take us across country through the mountains and on to Vienna.

As we stood on the cold, windswept station in Munich, I looked up at the signpost that announced the departing train we were to catch. It

175

was the Istanbul Express via Budapest, heading off into another world—the Far East. As I boarded I had flashes of the movie *Midnight Express*. I now wondered about the wisdom of making this trip by train. Why, I don't know. I wasn't carrying anything illegal, but I was nervous. As we neared the German-Austrian border, the border police boarded the train to check passports and tickets. A few moments later I was looking into the dead-fish eyes of a very young, uniformed, human German shepherd. He looked at my passport, then looked at me.

"Ah, you're Eric Burdon, ja?"

"That's right," I said.

"Herr Burdon, do you have any trouble with drugs?" he asked.

"No, the only trouble I have with drugs is I can't find any right now," I quipped, trying to lighten the situation.

He laughed. "I think you have the face of Che Guevara."

We both laughed at our little jokes, and then he snapped shiny cold steel handcuffs on me.

"Follow me."

There I was, standing cuffed in the freezing cold of the station.

The band had no choice but to leave me in the hands of the German border police, and the train disappeared down the tracks toward some nice warm hotel rooms in Vienna, while I was locked in a sort of dog pound next to some railroad tracks.

I couldn't quite grasp what had happened to me. I had no food, no warmth, nobody—and no information. It was very scary and very surreal. There was hardly a soul around, and I didn't sleep.

At sunrise, I was given a mug of tea and a sandwich by a sympathetic rail worker. Soon after, a police car arrived, a dark green Audi. Out stepped a cop in civilian clothes. A detective. As I was let out of the dog pound, he put a new pair of handcuffs on me, this time from the rear— most uncomfortable, as I was then put into the back of the Audi. We sped off into the countryside. In the warmth of the car, with the morning sun shining through the window, I nodded off to a fitful sleep. When I awoke we were deep in the Black Forest of Bavaria. We stopped, and the detective opened the door.

"Step out. Do you want to take a piss?"

He uncuffed me. I walked toward some bushes as he stood there smoking a cigarette.

"You see the beautiful Bavarian hills, ja?"

"Yeah," I said. "Very beautiful."

He then unbuttoned his jacket and showed off a mean-looking Glock in a shoulder holster.

"Well, you run, I shoot, you got it?" He patted the Glock.

"Yeah, I got it."

I was cuffed again and thrust back into the car. We sped off. Out on the autobahn, I caught a glimpse of a sign: Stuttgart 200 km.

I managed to fall asleep again and didn't wake until the car came to a stop. I opened my bleary eyes. The sun was blazing against a long, high white wall, which began to move. It was an automatic gate. The Audi moved forward and came to a stop in a yard. I looked out to see gun towers, surveillance cameras, massive lights, and barbed wire. The cop leaned into the car and said to me with a smile, "Welcome to Stammheim Maximum Security Prison."

Stammheim was about as hard as they came in West Germany. The cops moved me forward through the metal mesh gate, and I was pushed into the noisy reception area. The detective who brought me in signed me off, a big grin on his red, Bavarian face.

"Well," he laughed, "you can be on television all the time now."

Everyone else in the reception area was smiling broadly. A grinning blonde girl behind an ancient wooden table handed me a brown paper bag and a plastic bucket for my personal effects. I was shown to a changing room. They took my street clothes, and I was taken naked into a huge, hard, cold, concrete cell. A line of naked men stood before me, and others fell in behind. Before I had a chance to realize what was happening, I was positioned in front of a huge lead wall and X-rayed— an efficient way of saving both prisoners and guards the indignity of a cavity search. This was Deutsche efficiency at its best.

I was told to put on massive prison clothes: a blue overall that was at least two sizes too big and wooden clogs that made it impossible to walk normally. This would demean and degrade anyone. I was led by a screw in a green uniform down a long, brightly lit white corridor. I was going from one wing of the prison into another. We passed a clock whose hands were running backward. Could it get any worse? As the door slammed behind me, I was surprised to find I had a cell to myself. At least I could be alone, undisturbed.

Several hours passed as I checked out my new surrounding. There was a toilet in one corner. The cell had a high ceiling. A small window admitted daylight, but it was too high to reach, and the inward-curving walls made climbing impossible. The steel door had a flip-down round inspection hole. The bed was basically a steel slab with a thin mattress upon it. There was graffiti on the walls. My favorite showed an inmate in his cell, lying naked upon the steel bed, a ray of sunlight shining on his genitals, while a jailer, peeking through the hole, masturbated. "Der Wachtel's Traum," read the caption—"the screw's dream," I guessed at the translation.

Sometime in the afternoon, I heard voices outside, doors opening and slamming, feet moving along the stone hallway, and my cell door was thrust open.

"Hofgang!" yelled an officer. "Hofgang!" he indicated with his hands that I should come out.

I slipped my feet into the awful clogs and shuffled toward the door. The inmates were led out into a small, high-walled yard. At the far end of it was a workshop—owned, I was told, by BMW. There, some prisoners worked and got paid for it. Beyond that, I could see a small spire with a cross on it—the prison chapel.

don't let me be misunderstood

My walking pace in the clogs was so slow that people were over-taking me in the counterclockwise walk around the yard. One guy, as he passed, said, "Saw ya on TV the other day, man. You was great!"

Before I could say anything he disappeared into the line ahead of me. Then another older guy slid up from behind me. His hand moved toward mine, and he pushed something into my fist. I looked down. Cigarettes.

"Thanks! Danke! Danke! But, nein, kein rauchen, I don't smoke," I said to him.

"Never refuse cigarettes in prison," he said. "I'm giving you money, don't you realize that, boy?" He turned and smiled at me and walked on. I stuffed the cigarettes, three of them, into my overall pocket and kept walking. I saw the guy who'd given them to me passing along the other side of the circle, and soon he caught up with me again.

"So what are you doing here, man? You don't look like you belong here."

"Well, thanks," I said. "I truly have got no idea."

"Look," he said, "don't worry about that. One thing you find out for sure is—everybody in here is innocent, everyone!"

"Yeah, I get the picture," I said.

"Well, judging by the wing you're in, your politics are slightly to the left of red."

"No, nein, my politics are zero," I said. "I don't have any politics, I've got no idea why I'm here."

"You know you are in the prison of the Baader-Meinhof gang? They're held for many years in solitary, in what we call the 'dead wing.'"

"No," I said, "I didn't know. What's the deal with Baader-Meinhof?"

"You mean you really have no idea?" he asked.

"No."

"They're in here for many things—political actions, forgery, theft, kidnap, murder—they're media stars. The very symbol of the chic radical left. They've done bank robberies, they have set fire to buildings, they are out to bring down the government. There's a war going on here, didn't you know? You think it stopped in 1945?"

Then he was off again, continuing his walk around the yard until the whistle blew and we were sent back to our cells.

I was to find out later that my wing of the prison had been condemned as inhumane by Amnesty International. At the time, of course, I was just grateful not to be stuck with four or five others, which I'd seen in some of the other cells down the corridor.

With time alone, I ended up smoking a cigarette. Just for something to do, to watch the smoke drift.

My head was filled with conspiracy theories of how and why I'd ended up in this place. The next morning in the exercise yard I learned more about the Baader-Meinhof gang. And the more I learned, the more I realized what deep shit I was in. They had links to organized terrorism, had trained in Libya. Some of them had died on hunger strikes within the prison, while others had kidnapped and killed some of the country's top financial brains. The gang was basically Marxist but it was said that Andrea Baader, the Clyde to Ulrike Meinhof's Bonnie, just loved to drive fast cars and shoot machine guns. I remembered that in every airport and railroad station there were wanted posters with the gang's faces and the prices on their heads—DM 10 million for the arrest of Ulrike Meinhof. As each gang member had been caught, a red stripe was drawn across his or her face on the poster.

I picked up the most important piece of information when the old man told me that the gang were heroes in the eyes of the left-wing press and particularly admired by many filmmakers. My mind went back to the time I was in Munich before we'd shot the movie *Comeback*.

I'd been told by the director, Christel, that it would be the thing to do to be seen in the German cinema social circuit. So there I was one night in a club in Munich, hanging out with the famous faces of modern-day German cinema, Rainer Werner Fassbinder among the many notables.

Fassbinder had made more movies in his short life than John Huston did in his seventy-odd years, and was the ultimate German media star. Movie director extraordinaire, his films were loved by the intelligentsia of modern Germany. Tragically, he was to die of a cocaine overdose.

Unfortunately for me, some judge was so intent on crushing sympathy for the Baader-Meinhof gang that he was having everyone with any association, however passing, rounded up. That meant me. I was being made an example. And I suspected that the film company wasn't too distressed about my arrest as it made for great publicity for the film. Who knows, maybe it was someone connected with the movie that told the German authorities that I had ties—or at least sympathies—with Baader-Meinhof.

I was allowed no outside contact, and as the days passed I spent my time trying to remember fact and events, wondering who did what and who said what when I was out in the Munich clubs.

Then one day I was startled by a metallic rattling sound. Something was banging against the bars on the window high above my head. A tin cup on a makeshift rope clattered its way between the bars, and I managed to reach it. The guy upstairs had made contact. Inside the tin was a stone to weigh it down, some rolling papers, and a plug of tobacco. I dropped some rolling papers that I had into the tin cup, placed the stone on top of the papers, and banged on the cup once. It disappeared through the cell window.

At night the voices of the boys in the Islamic wing would kick in. The din was tremendous. Lovers sending messages to each other, yelling from one end of the quadrangle outside to the other, the prayers of Islam echoing out into the night.

One morning a jailer came to the door. "Raus," he bellowed with his big, red face. I slipped into my clogs, and I followed him down the corridor. He swung open a door and there were half a dozen barbers' chairs—they wanted to cut my hair. I stood in the doorway, refusing to move. I expected to be clubbed in the guts or hit from behind or something, but nothing happened. The screw simply led me back to my cell, and the door was shut once more. For a moment I felt a sense of triumph.

Next came a visit by a man from the British embassy, a ministry man to the max with his pin-striped suit, balding head, moustache, round-rimmed wire glasses, and weathered briefcase.

"Well, Mr. Burdon," he said, "we have got ourselves into a fine mess, haven't we?"

We were in an interview room. It was an opportunity to slip out of the clogs and walk barefoot around the room. He sat there gazing at me, then continued.

"I heard that you refused to take a haircut. First of all, it's for your own good. Health really does matter in such a place, and secondly, it's not very good to refuse these people. Look," he said, reaching into his briefcase, "I brought you some reading material, and I suggest you get a job as you're probably going to be here for awhile. There's a shop. You can work and get paid by the state for it. Also there's the garden—that would be what I would choose. I have to remind you that if you get anywhere within, say, three feet of the fence, they will shoot you from the towers. Normally they shoot to maim, but I wouldn't want to count on that, would you?"

"Listen, man," I said, "would you just please explain what's going on here, what I've been charged with?"

"You've been charged, Mr. Burdon, under the Emergency Powers Act."

The embassy man said he could be of no further help at that moment, and he wasn't too helpful in explaining the Emergency Powers Act, though it was pretty clear that it meant I didn't have any rights.

By nighttime I found myself singing with the Islamic boys, "Allah-u-Akbar, Allah-u-Akbar, God is great, yes, He is." Later, I tried meditation. Finally, I slept without dreaming.

The next morning, the fat screw was at the door again.

"Raus quickly! Raus schnell!"

As I trailed along behind him. "What is going on?" I asked.

"Rechtsanwalt."

I'd heard that word before, I understood it to mean lawyer. My prayers had been answered at last. Someone on the outside had sent some help. The cavalry had come!

After walking the length of the corridor and going past the clock that went backward, I was directed to a transportation room. I sat there for fifteen minutes alone, then was taken to stand with my toes on a white line outside an office window.

Inside I could see two people. One was obviously a woman, the other, a man. I could hear their voices and a typewriter clattering away. A red light went on, and a buzzer went off. The door swung open, and I stepped forward from the white line. I sat down at a table, on one side of me a good-looking blonde, and, on the other, a middle-aged, cigarette-smoking civil service type. They immediately launched into questions about my personal life.

"Eric, you have a daughter, Alexandria, this is right?" the woman cooed.

"Yeah, that's right."

"She must be almost a teenager now, this is correct?"

"Correct."

"And you have been divorced from your wife in California, this is true?"

"Eh, wait a minute," I said, "What's all this about? All I want to know is when you guys are going to get me out of here? You are lawyers aren't you?"

Silence fell over the room.

"No, nein, we are not lawyers. We are sent from the judge to make a psychological profile of the subject he will sentence in the coming week."

I stood up and walked out of the room.

"Nein, verboten, you must. . . ."

I slammed the door. Screw it. I'd take the consequences. I was surprised, once again, that nothing happened to me. No reprimand. And when the tin can made its daily descent from the cell above, it was empty. I took one of my cigarettes, dropped it in and yelled as the tin cup disappeared.

"Allah-u-Akbar, good on you, mate!"

"Yeah, what's happening up there?" I was feeling like one of the boys.

The next day at walkabout I was approached by two blue-eyed blonde prisoners who looked like twins. I'd seen them before in a transportation cell and wondered what they were all about. Walking on either side of me, Hans and Fritz informed me that on weekends it's permissible to share a cell with fellow inmates and indicated that they had some good—wink, wink—shit.

"What kind of shit are you taking about?" I said under my breath.

"Coke, man. Snow. We got some of the best you've ever tasted, so if you want to, come to our cell on Saturday afternoon. We also have a guitar, man. We got the works, you wanna join us?"

"Ah, well, I'll see what happens when Saturday comes around. Thanks for the invitation." They walked on ahead of me.

I wondered about those two. But by the time the weekend rolled around and my door was opened, I strolled down the length of the corridor. There they were, Fritz, Hans, and two other inmates.

"See here," Fritz said, "we have good shit. Have you ever seen such a glint in the dust?"

I'd lost my wife and, by association, my daughter, to the horrors of cocaine, so I wasn't immediately thrilled at the prospect, but. . . . What the hell, I thought, there's nothing else to do, and nosed a couple of lines. It was as though a gleaming angel had dropped in, down through the ceiling, and wrapped her white wings around me. I felt totally elated. One of the German boys helped me climb up to the high window with the slanted sill. I could feel the sun shining and I hung there for as long as I could, looking out into the garden with its vegetables and flowers, and beyond that the wire and the gun towers.

For a moment I felt relief, I was comfortable. I felt silly. As one of the Germans strummed on a guitar the opening notes to "House of the Rising Sun," I sang my ass off. But the afternoon of pleasantness was soon over, the cell door swung open, the jailers were back rattling their keys, and I was returned to my little private hell.

Toward the end of the long, boring week, I heard that I had visitors, and that I was now allowed to communicate with the outside world. My girlfriend from Hamburg had gotten her family to assist her in finding a good lawyer, who told me in no uncertain terms that he would get results immediately if I hired him for the sum of DM 5,000.

"And ze proof will be," he said, "I vill have your own clothes returned to you immediately, Zen you will know you can trust me. Zen you know I can make the moves to get you out of this mess and I vill represent you in court."

"OK."

We shook hands. Deal.

That same evening the screw with the big, red Bavarian face swung open the door and unceremoniously dumped a brown paper bag on the floor. He was gone in a flash. The cell door locked, and I looked in the bag. My heart leapt as I caressed the fabric—my blue jeans! My leather jacket! Quickly, I took off the prison overalls, slipped into my own clothes, and walked the length of the cell as if I were free. Soon I would be.

That Saturday morning, the sun shining brightly, I was led out into the courtyard and transported with other prisoners to a courthouse somewhere in the city of Stuttgart. The handcuffs were removed, and I was placed in a holding cell with a Turkish boy, who stood making graffiti on the wall with a sharp-edged instrument. I think it read "Fuck the pigs." I couldn't figure it out with assurance, but he caught my interest. I thought it was a pretty bold act. He didn't seem to give a damn. I grinned at him, he laughed back at me, scraping away intensely at the wall with what looked like a 9 mm bullet.

"Ja," he said as he pointed to his leg. "Dey shoot me! Bang! I take de bullet as souvenir."

My name was called, the door opened, and I was led into a conference room to meet my well-dressed, rosy-faced lawyer from Munich.

"Well," he said, "I have you out, that's what we want, but there's a price."

"How much," I asked.

"DM 60,000, plus my fee, which is DM 5,000, and you must also make a plea to the court and admit you use cocaine."

"But I don't use cocaine," I said.

"You're associated with people who use cocaine. You use cocaine."

"No," I said. "I associate with people that I know use cocaine, but I don't."

"Let me ask you something," said my lawyer, standing up, his thumbs in his waistband. "Do you remember last week, the two young boys, they invited you to their cell?"

"Yes, I do."

"Well, there, on that afternoon, you used cocaine."

"How did you. . . .?"

"Listen, my friend, the whole of Stammheim is wired, audio and video. They have you on film, and we have to deal with that. You must admit to using cocaine."

Jesus, I thought to myself, feeling like I'd been hit with a lead fist. "You mean those two guys were. . . .?"

"My friend, this is serious business that you're involved with. The state wishes an end to this activity. Let me point out, if you want to argue it they will have to bring in witnesses, and they will keep you here until those witnesses make an appearance. That could be months—you have no choice."

I stood in front of the judge a few moments later, my lawyer at my side, smiling proudly as if he'd just solved the crime of the century. The judge in his black robes looked too young to be judging anything about anybody, but as he passed the sentence in German there was a round of laughter and some applause in the court.

"What did he say?" I whispered to my lawyer.

"The judge made the remark that you should be grateful that due to the state of West Germany you have received the best free publicity that anyone in the music business could receive."

So there it was. Between the court fine and my legal costs, the tour's profits went down the drain. Somehow I controlled my anger. Then, as I walked out into the free fresh air toward an awaiting Mercedes Benz limousine, I found all of the guards and other prison staff lined up for me to autograph their Animals and Eric Burdon albums, as if nothing had happened over the past 10 days. I made a half-hearted attempt to be pleasant. Outwardly, I smiled; inside I was fuming.

As I was about to step into the car, I heard someone call me and turned around. It was the detective who originally brought me down from the Austrian-German border to the prison the day I was arrested.

"Remember me, Ja? Ze great Bavarian woods, ja?" He stuck out his hand. I hesitated but I shook hands with him.

"Come on," he said, "Smile, it's not so bad. At least you held on to your hair. Goodbye. I'll be seeing you again in the future. You can count on it. We are everywhere!" Laughing, he turned away.

The limo pulled away from the courthouse at high speed to avoid the photographers who had suddenly appeared. I couldn't wait to get back to my friends in Hamburg.

CHAPTER 11

hamburg

Many of my friends in California were horrified that I would return to Hamburg in the wake of the bust, but they didn't know the Germans like I did. If I'd been busted in Mexico I would have had reservations about returning. But the Germans abide by the law. To them, paperwork is the most important thing. I'd been caught in a trap, found guilty by association. But the matter had been settled, and I didn't expect German officials to hold a grudge, so I tried not to either.

I'd found more reasonable people than unreasonable in Germany, which is more than I can say for most places I've been. The former group included the photographer Gunther Zint, whom I'd met years earlier.

In Hamburg, I tried to forget the dismal past few years. While I started to sink deeply into drugs and alcohol, I managed to put together a new band, called the Fire Department. The group grew out of late-night jams that began at 3 A.M. We played for the working girls and their pimps, prominent politicians, writers, newsos, and, of course, the police, some of whom became big fans.

One night in southern Germany, after a show, I was upstairs in my penthouse suite with a gorgeous local girl named Karen, who owned a leather-and-lace shop. We were out on the balcony, smoking hash, when the phone rang.

"Mr. Burdon?"

"Yes."

"This is the police. We are downstairs in the lobby and we want to talk with you. We will meet you in the bar."

Shit, I thought. Here we go again.

I took the elevator down to the ground floor and entered the bar. The place was packed with a huge crowd that included the band and our crew. The barmaid was pulling steins and pouring vodka shots. The noise was unreal. Over in a corner, I spotted the three cops. Two were bearded. One had a leather jacket and dark glasses.

"Hello, Herr Burdon, comenze sitz! Would you like some fine local beer?"

"Sure," I said.

"We are the three musketeers," said one. "We are also big Eric Burdon fans."

"No, really. . . that's nice," I said.

A beer and a shot of Russian vodka appeared for me.

"Prost! Prost!"

I sat, forcing a smile and praying the dark light of the bar would conceal my bloodshot eyes.

"Ja! We are special police. Look—no weapons! We only observe, then pass on information to our superiors. Our only weapons are radio phones and field glasses. But we can be anywhere in six hours."

"I was wondering who the three musketeers were," I said. "So, tell me, who do you report to?"

"Well, I could tell you but then I'd have to kill you," joked the one in dark glasses.

"Come on," I said, "who pays your wages?"

The cop in the leather jacket pointed upward and said, "De Chancellor."
Then the guy in the leather jacket changed the subject.

"Did you vote for George Bush?" he asked.

"Sure," I answered, lying.

"Ja! Mister Bush is good for America. Good for the vorld. So, when Mr. Bush, your president, arrives in the country, we. . . look at the overall picture of security. We see the holes in the Secret Service protection units and report to our boss. We then report to your president."

"Wow," I said. "That's really interesting."

Meanwhile, Karen joined us, wearing a tight rubber dress that showed off her stark white breasts like two fried eggs.

I introduced her to the cops, thinking it would surely loosen things up a bit.

"Ja! We are policemen but don't hold it against us!" said one to Karen.

"Nein! Alles Klar," she answered.

"We wanted an autograph from Mister Burdon. We saw the show, it was great."

Karen talked in German to the boys and then stood up, telling me she would go and get some photos for me to sign for the policemen. As she left, the leather jacket leaned forward and said, "We know about your little problem at the border. These are tough times for Germany. There are some who really want to ruin our recovery."

I thought it was best to keep my mouth shut, drink my beer and vodka, and listen.

"Sometimes we make mistakes but not very often. But we are getting better. There are some new techniques we are developing that your FBI is interested in. We are catching some terrorists before they are able to commit their acts."

I nodded with interest.

"For example, you are following someone. Possibly to a high rise apartment in the better part of the city. You notice apartment number

5008. . . only sees his wife four hours in a whole week. The both of them own high speed cars and lead separate lives. They dine well, and the woman always parks on the street even though they have a secure parking space in the basement. We send this into HQ with the profile of the people and run checks through our computers. What does this tell you? They are probably terrorists."

All three cops smiled as Karen returned with the photographs and copies of my latest album. I signed them all and we shook hands.

The leather jacket cop said, "Ja! Mr. Bush good for America."

These cops aside, I was making a lot of friends in Germany at this time. I loved spending time with photographer Gunther Zint. He was in every political demo, filming pitched battles between uniformed police and the ever-present turbulent left. It was like a great game, and Gunther with his camera was in the middle of the action, like a referee. It was a dangerous position to be in. He was also making a photo record of the people of St. Pauli, Hamburg's red light district. He photographed the whores, hookers, rockers, and cops. There were thousands of legal prostitutes. Gunther helped me understand for the first time that there was nothing glamorous about the world of a prostitute.

With the gig money now coming in steadily, I bought myself a new 'Vette and had it shipped over from California. I now had some status again: I had a flash car, and a young girlfriend who introduced me to her family. They took me into their home and helped me pull through this period. I was flirting with danger and I knew it, but I really didn't care. As the distances between the gigs got greater and greater I drove faster and faster. Early one morning I crashed. Luckily, I didn't burn. The car was a write-off and, guess what, I didn't have any insurance. Not very smart, Eric.

The morning after the crash, I received some mail from California, from a girlfriend who was studying sociology at the University of Southern California. It was her final paper, which had been on Speed and the Egomaniac. As I placed that on the coffee table next to the newspaper with the headline, "English Rock Star in 150 MPH Crash," I realized that my lead foot days had to come to an end. Otherwise, they would bring me to my end.

It was at this time that my mother, Rene, was diagnosed with cancer. It would prove to be a slow death. From Hamburg I could get to England in hours. Visits to Newcastle to sit by her bedside and talk her through the night became a regular occurrence.

Then, during an airport stopover in Amsterdam I got a message. My father Matt had died of a heart attack, suddenly, in his sleep. A piece of us floats away and drifts off into the infinite when we lose a parent. I headed back to Newcastle, went to my old man's favorite pub, and drank several pints of his favorite beer, tears rolling down my cheek. Everyone stayed away from me; everyone seemed to sympathize. That's what home is for.

The German winter, though, chilled my soul, and I went south in search of the sun. The village of Deja on the Spanish island of Palma de Mallorca had always held a special place in my heart. I'd made my first visit there when I was just a kid. It was the perfect village, my first taste of the exotic.

Rene was going down slowly. Every time we thought the end had come, she would rebound, her mind still intact, her body falling apart. I bought her a radio Walkman. She said she loved it, and kept it tuned to BBC 4 for the classical music. Her ward in the hospice was almost empty. There was just one other woman, in a coma, near her. The staff were angels, and their care was wonderful.

There she was, the soul of the family, battered and beaten by life. She was draining away, living on her own body fat, sleeping most of the time. I walked over to the window and looked out. There was a China garden, a pond with ducks, partly iced over. There was a crisp frost on the green lawn. I wished I could slip her something quietly and send her on her way. The only thing she was getting was a liquid morphine drip. But then I heard her voice.

I turned to her. "Hello, Rene, how are you?"

"Ho! Smashing!" she said. "It's just that that bugger over there makes so much noise." Her hand was raised, shakily indicating the woman in the coma.

Rene then slipped back into her morphine haze. I held her hand for an hour, until the clock said it was time to go to the airport again. As I got up to leave, the voice returned.

"Now you just sing that song proper next time, you hear?"

"Yes, Mom," I said, waving goodbye for what would turn out to be the last time.

spanish retreat

My sister Irene had been holding down the fort with my ailing mother while I moved from Germany to one of my favorite Spanish islands.

Carlos Moysie, one of the top Spanish promoters, and I became good friends during this period. Carlos's face was full of smiles. He drove his BMW like a maniac. Carlos had been wheelchair-bound since he was a child, but his sense of humor and his love of life were as big as the man himself. With his massive arms, no one in all of Spain could beat him at arm wrestling, although many tried. And he was good with a shotgun—unsurpassed as a skeet shooter. He was the best on Menorca, where I bought a house.

Menorca is a tiny little island, one of four in the chain known as the Balearic, off the coast of mainland Spain, forty-five minutes by air from Barcelona. Buying a house there seemed a smart move. I would have really liked to buy a place on the bigger island of Mallorca, but the price of real estate there had gone through the roof. A short ferry trip would get me to Palma, and I could visit all my haunts yet still live more quietly, away from the madness.

don't let me be misunderstood

Why did I buy a house on Menorca? Maybe it was because it reminded me of California and, for the time being I couldn't be there. I had to be close to Rene, and a jet flight from anywhere in Europe could put me into Newcastle within three hours at the most.

I met Anna-Lena Karlsson when one of my tours of Europe took me through Gothenburg, Sweden, her hometown. She was a striking, natural beauty with a great sense of humor, and we became close. At the time, had I believed I could ever get married again, it would have been to Anna-Lena. Together we travelled the world—London, L.A., Spain, the south of France. I loved her and I loved the friends that she had back home.

By the end of my '82 tour the band was in the Austrian countryside and my bad-boy antics were at an all-time high. On the final night, we

An end-of-tour prank gone wrong in Austria - I end up with a broken leg.

195

were all wild, fired up on barack, a Hungarian traditional drink made from apricots. We had planned to play a joke on the crew while the end-of-tour photo was being taken. The crew assembled on the front of the stage, the band behind them holding steins of beer. Just as the camera flashed, we were to pour the ale on the crew members' heads. But before the plan went into full effect, someone in the crew saw it coming, and they scrambled. The band pushed forward, and I fell off the stage onto the concrete below, several members of the group landing on top of me. Snap went the leg.

I was in a world of pain, but once it was set in a cast I was able to hobble around on my crutches and retreated to my Spanish island as soon as I was able. Anna-Lena arrived soon after to nurse me. While I had the house in Villa Carlos, Menorca, I decided to spend the summer in a rented casita in Deja on the big island of Mallorca so I could revisit old haunts and friends from my visits there as a youth.

I had a Willys Jeep there, which I had restored to its original 1941 military state. I'm sure we were quite a sight as the Jeep made its way up the old road toward the village. Unfortunately, on the ferry trip, Anna-Lena had consumed some unrighteous seafood and began slowly losing her color. We managed to reach our small casita, unload the Jeep and stagger tired to our bed. I sat beside her, feeling her brow for temperature, which was slowly rising. Anna-Lena was as tough as she was attractive and told me not to worry. She knew it wouldn't be easy for me to go in search of help while I was on crutches. Deja is built on a very steep hill, and much of it is inaccessible to automobiles. She convinced me to wait until morning.

I awoke to feel the sun on my face, streaking in through the curtains. But my girlfriend was turning green. I reached for my crutches, staggered to the door and shouldered my leather pouch. I made my way painfully, slowly up the stone stairs. I stopped to rest as I made my way to where the Jeep was parked, and realized I was standing in the shadow of the house of Robert Graves, the great English writer known to me and my friends as "Don Roberto."

The basement shutters of the house were open, revealing the massive printing machine, imported from Germany, on which Roberto printed his books. The massive Heidelberg printing block was silent. Indeed, the whole house was silent.

I continued on my way painfully up the ancient stone stairs, past ancient Christian images carved into the walls. About twenty hurtful minutes later, I arrived at a place known as the "German bar," which seemed devoid of life. A Volkswagen pulled up outside and a middle-aged woman entered the bar.

"Ola, buenos dias," I said.

She looked at me and stuttered something in German.

"Sprechen Sie Deutsch?" I asked.

"Ja," she replied.

Then in English I asked her if she'd known my old friend, the song-writer Kevin Ayers.

"Yes," she said in her thickly accented English. "I know Kevin very well, but he is not here today. He's gone to the city of Palma shopping."

"Well, I'm a friend of his from England, and I have a girlfriend who is sick and I'm needing a doctor."

"You need a doctor?"

"Yes, she's sick with food poisoning."

"All right. Come. Jump in the Volkswagen. We'll go."

We left the village heading north and then began to descend toward the water on a narrow, winding road. Soon, we reached the house of Dr. Javier Dominguez. It was Sunday and Dr. Dominguez was at home, sitting at a wooden table repairing a lobster net. After making a quick introduction, my newfound German friend departed.

"Please sit down," said Dr. Dominguez. "So tell me, how long has your girlfriend been ill?"

"Oh, this is the third day, I think."

"Three days, huh. Is she having a period?"

"No, I don't think so"

"Hmmm, then sit down, relax. If she's been ill for three days she can wait a few hours longer. Would you like some wine? I just rolled a joint."

He opened a bottle of Torros Sangre and passed me a large spliff. As we began to talk and explore each other's past, I told him that I was no stranger to the village, that I'd first been there in 1958. He told me of his lifelong friendship with Don Roberto. We used to see Graves, tall, graying hair, his gangly frame underneath his black hat and cape, his walking stick in hand, making his way slowly up the cobblestone streets of the village—the perfect village, Deja.

As it turned out, Anna-Lena simply needed bed rest and plenty of water—there was really nothing else that could be done for her food poisoning. Thankfully, a few days later she was feeling better, and we decided to go exploring together. She had a nose for wild mushrooms, and we'd been told that the pickings were good, if the weather was right. I pointed out to her that the great Robert Graves was responsible for keeping the idea of the mushroom cult alive. The roots of the cult could be traced all the way back to ancient Greece. During the psychedelic '60s, the cult had a great revival. People like Tim Leary picked up the baton handed down from Aleister Crowley, Aldous Huxley, and others.

That morning, Anna-Lena stood in the kitchen frying bacon, eggs, and sliced tomatoes. "Eric, how many pieces of toast do you want?" she called out over the noise of the splattering fat and the singing kettle.

"Two will do," I yelled back from the living room, grabbing my crutches and hobbling toward the kitchen. Anna-Lena had been really excited about the prospect of meeting old man Graves, but there was sad news. He was dying. The whole village seemed aware of it. Daily bulletins would be passed from mouth to mouth in the German bar every lunchtime tracking his declining health.

This particular day we had an appointment at the stables to go riding. We had made friends with an American cowboy who had sailed all the way from Boston on a small sloop. He and a buddy had settled there, looking after a wonderful stable of horses on the north side of the island. Anna-Lena and the cowboy would ride over the hills while I relaxed at the American's house and read.

I was alone, and the morning had turned hot. Picking up my crutches I headed for the door and hobbled down toward the stables, looking in on several of the horses. The cowboy looked after these animals for rich Europeans who would come here and ride one month out of the year. The rest of the year he had all these wonderful animals to himself, and for a guy who loved horses this was paradise. A large pile of horse manure had been shoveled up against the white wall at the end of the two rows of stalls and something caught my eye. Growing out of the manure were several white-stemmed mushrooms. I made a mental note as I headed back toward the house.

The cowboy and Anna-Lena returned and I watched her dismount. She was suntanned and gorgeous.

"You guys have a good time?"

"Yes, it was wonderful," she said, stroking the beautiful animal.

The American took the reins and led both horses back to the stables. I grabbed Anna-Lena by the arm. "Listen, babe, I've got something I want you to look at right at the end of the stables, just around the corner, there's a pile of horseshit."

"Hmmm, interesting," she said. "Horseshit, I love horseshit."

"No, no, I'm serious," I said, "just go take a look. Check out the mushrooms."

"Oh yeah," she smiled. "Just my cup of tea." She walked off, down the row of stables, laughing.

She returned with her riding hat filled with those milk white stems. She sat down next to me. Putting one of the stems of the mushrooms between her forefinger and thumb, she pressed. "Look," she said. "We have magic." A bluing effect on the stem of the white mushroom was the proof. "I think we scored." We both laughed.

We climbed into the Jeep, me with my broken leg dangling over the side onto the fender, she at the wheel. We couldn't wait to get home and put these little 'shrooms to the test.

Back at base camp in the village, around 4:30 in the afternoon, Anna-Lena made a strong pot of mushroom tea. I lay in the bedroom, the frame of the iron bed propping up my injured limb.

The white goddess entered the room with a tea pot, two cups, and some honey. "It's a pity darling, we couldn't invite Mr. Graves over for a spot of tea," she laughed, putting the tray down on the bed.

"It is indeed."

She made a fluttering motion with her hands over the teapot and said, "We make this tea in honor of Robert Graves."

I lifted the teacup to my mouth: "I drink this tea in the hope that we will find a new world."

She added, "A world of wonder, a world of happiness and peace."

We laughed, clinked our cups and drank the acrid-smelling tea. From the German bar on the other side of the valley, I could hear a rock band cranking up—a guitar that could only be my old friend Olly Halsel's screaming into the night. Another hot jam session in the crowded little bar.

Anna-Lena called from the bathroom where she was fixing her hair, "You should head over to the bar, they're probably all wondering why you're not there."

"They don't have to wonder, they know where I am," I said. "They've all seen you, they know I'm busy. Do you feel anything from the tea yet?"

"Yes, I do feel a little flutter in my stomach," she said. "Let's just go back to bed and relax a while and then we can think about going to the bar for the late set."

"That's a good idea," I said. "Should I pour you another cup?"

"Why not?" she laughed.

The humid night turned to rain and then there was a crash of thunder. Lightening struck out across the mountains.

"Ooooh," cooed Anna-Lena.

"Yes, isn't this wonderful?" I said.

There was no doubt we were both coming on. She came rushing out of the bathroom, "Don't, don't look in the mirror," she said urgently.

"What are you talking about?" I said.

"My face just fused with the glass, don't look in the mirror."

"Are you okay?" I inquired.

"Yeah, I feel fine, but I think I look horrible."

I took her in my arms. "Don't, don't say that. You look beautiful," I said, kissing the back of her neck.

"No, don't get me wrong," she said. "I want to tell you something." She looked in my eyes and said, "I'll never, ever be afraid of anything again, especially death."

I knew at that point that the little mushrooms were working full tilt. We were both now hearing the same music in our ears, seeing the same explosion of flowers on the ceiling, feeling the same trembling strength running through our systems, and hearing Olle's guitar screeching out across the valley.

Anna-Lena staggered to her feet. Her hands grabbed mine and she dragged me the length of the bed, forcing my crippled body to its upright position, "We can go, baby, we can go, we can make it."

"No," I said, "don't even try. If you try you go against it. Just go with it, enjoy, enjoy the visions that are going to come to us. We don't have to go to anyone. We just stay here in the warm, safe bed, screw everybody else."

Giggling, we fell arm-in-arm back into the sack. The jam had ended and the music subsided. We could hear voices as people left the bar. I saw the lights going out. I figured it must be three or four in the morning. No one could be more in love than she and I were at that moment.

"Let's go out," she said.

"What do you mean 'out'?" I asked. "I can't drive with my leg in this condition, you know I can't handle the Jeep."

"I can," she said. "Come on, there'll be no one else on the roads. We'll have the roads to ourselves, I can handle it."

"Are you sure?" I said.

"Yes, come on. Let's go to the point and watch the sky, the stars, and the clouds."

Convinced that I'd be a spoilsport if I didn't, I managed to get the crutches under my armpits and somehow swing my legs, wobbling toward the Jeep. The engine coughed to life and we set off slowly through the deserted village. The night was warm and balmy. There were still clouds and the rain threatened, but we threw all caution to the wind. Driving down ancient roads that had been built by the Romans using Arabic slaves centuries ago, we made our way to the point. Never had I felt more alive. And now that I saw that Anna-Lena could handle the Jeep, I relaxed. My crippled leg once again hung over the side, resting on the mudguard, we headed up the winding road, the elevated, winding, ancient road toward the point. It was early in the pre-dawn. I saw headlights coming down the hill toward us.

I could make out a delivery-type van coming down, slowing at the hairpin bends, then speeding up again, then slowing at the next curve. He was still far above us, but I leaned over and said in her ear, "Be careful now, babe, there's a vehicle coming on the road up there, you see him?"

"Yes," she said, gunning the engine as she shifted down.

I took a look behind us to see if there was any other traffic on the road, but we were the only ones—us and the oncoming truck. Then my heart sank as I saw something I couldn't believe. As it came to one of the hairpin bends, the truck simply drove right off the elevated road, crashing down into the bushes below.

My God," I said, "he went off the road."

As we neared the wreck site, I imagined the terrifying picture of what we were about to encounter, the driver with rain and blood running down his face, the crashed vehicle on fire, us stoned on mushrooms having to deal with it all. Police cars, blue lights flashing, emergency vehicles, the Guardia Seville, police investigations, late night at the hospital. My God, could I handle this? I doubted it. We pulled to a stop near the skid marks where the vehicle had left the road. Down below I could see the crashed vehicle on its side, its wheels still spinning.

Then, surprisingly, out of the wrecked vehicle's door, a head appeared. A small, wiry Spaniard with a large moustache looked up at us and waved his arms, a huge smile on his face, "Señor, Señorita, everything is okay. There's no problemo! I have just called the airport on my radio, they are sending a truck. Everything is OK, carry on. I'm fine, is no problem, I can assure you!"

Was I imagining this? Was it real or a hallucination? We both sat in stunned silence as the little man disappeared back into the vehicle. We looked at each other for a moment, then Anna-Lena put the Jeep into gear and we took off up the road as if this thing had never happened.

"Well," said Anna-Lena, breaking the silence, "All's well that ends well," and laughed hysterically.

We reached the point, parked the Jeep, and she helped me down. As I stood there looking out at the sea, I was still trembling. "I can't believe it," I said, "pinch me."

"Everything's fine," she said. "Look at the clouds racing across the sky." Behind the clouds were twinkling stars and, hanging in the sky, a half moon.

"This is just wonderful," I said, "wonderful." I felt alive and close to God, and I held one of his most beautiful creations in my arms. We kissed, our heads in the sky. We walked together slowly over to a fence. Beyond it was a farmer's field sloping down to the valley below. "Don Roberto, I love you," she said, her arms open, her head toward the starlit sky. And then we both saw something truly magnificent, a white stallion slowly walking up the hill toward us. He came up to the fence and put his huge white head between ours. We both laughed hysterically as the animal's head moved up and down between us, nodding a welcome.

The next day Don Roberto died, and I couldn't help feeling that the village was about to die with him. I returned there in the late 1980s, about five years after his death, and television, the great killer of cultures, was loose on the island. An MTV video was being filmed in one of the little casitas next to the new parking lots which had been provided for the local people.

A member of the Graves family told me that Don Roberto's dying wish was that the Love Walk, a path which led from near his house down the mountainside, be left in its original state. But soon after his death the local government paved it over with tarmac, and these days the Love Walk is crowded with terribly out-of-place SUVs and noisy tourists who come and go, leaving their garbage behind.

I gave up my rented house and moved full time to the Menorca house I'd bought. The locals called the place the House of the Rising Sun, and had done so long before I ever visited the island. They told me it was haunted. It seemed like a good buy, perched on top of a hill over the port. Every morning when the sun rose over Africa, the house caught the first light. Built of limestone, it had once been a gin mill, and before that had been owned by a white Russian princess who, legend had it, committed suicide there.

It was a magical place, but one winter there would nearly take my life. The sea, the salt, the dampness, the whiskey, and the hashish brought my asthma back with a near-deadly vengeance.

A local merchant, Frank, a black Jamaican, had a small night club called the Colibri, which I frequented. I became friends with him and his English wife, and one night they invited me to a dinner party. It was a hot August night, and the rich food and wine were the last things I should have been indulging in. I'd been fooling myself into denying the seriousness of my asthma. But at that party, as I stood near the fireplace, a full-blown attack grabbed me like an iron fist. I plunged my inhaler several times but there was no relief—I couldn't breathe. I stumbled out into the courtyard where several guests were standing with drinks in their hands, and collapsed on the ground and hugged the cold cobblestones praying for relief. I could hear and see but could not speak. I really believed I was going to die right there on that Spanish courtyard.

Fortunately, the lady of the house was a quick thinker—and an avid scuba diver. She grabbed an air tank and blasted some oxygen into my desperate lungs. After nearly an hour, the local medics arrived and took me to a local hospital where sad-eyed nuns and their beautiful young assistants nursed me. As they drifted silently in and out of my little white room over four or five days, I was slowly healed by the Spanish sun coming through my open window, ancient palms outside blowing in the breeze. The cortisone they'd used against my asthma had made me balloon up, and when I got out I swore I needed some radical changes in my life. I loved those Spanish islands, but it was not the climate for me. I'd had seven attacks in a row and the only thing that could bring me out of it was cortisone. I had to move or die.

My body hungered for the desert, the arid desert of Southern California, but before I headed back to the States, I had one more adventure in mind: I wanted to experience the Sahara.

I teamed up with two friends and we hired two Toyota 4 x 4s, two drivers, and two cooks, and headed out south from the North African city of Algiers. I was still moving slowly and was often moody from my long illness and recovery, but it was a wonderful journey.

At the time, the U.S. was battling with Libya's Colonel Gadhafi, and we were warned that there could be air attacks in the region without notice. It gave the trip that added dangerous edge I've always loved. But we forgot about politics once we made it out to the huge red dunes. Each night we'd set camp, unload the stoves and have dinner under the desert sky. Unfortunately the food all tastes the same, as the locals cook exclusively with some sort of cooking oil that tastes slightly like gasoline.

Small communities were crawling with mercenaries and arms dealers. I thought at the time that I was experiencing a place where peace wasn't going to last, a place that wouldn't be open to strangers much longer. We headed for the nearest place of civilization, the motel that is the halfway stop for the Paris-Dakar run. Praying for the comforts of a modern facility, we were sorely disappointed to arrive and find no wine, no beer, and no bathing water: There was a country-wide shortage, and we were allowed only one small cup of water to drink. We were told we'd have to wait until we returned to Algiers to bathe. Despite the discomforts, our journey was well worth it, seeing much of the wildlife of the northern plains.

I had one final adventure before I got out of the country. I was accused by the local authorities of trying to smuggle currency out of Algeria. Forced to miss my plane, I was held in a small, unventilated room. When I was finally allowed to use a phone, I called a connection in Algiers who promptly came to my rescue and got me on a Saudi Airways jet to London. Being detained had cost me the opportunity to bathe, so there I was, sitting in the cool, green-and-gold-trimmed first-class section, not having seen, let alone taken, a shower in two weeks. A true infidel, no doubt.

A few years later, the whole area would erupt in religious and political violence. . . just one more addition to the growing list of places where white men fear to tread.

CHAPTER 13

"fuck me, i thought he was dead"

If there's one question I get sick of being asked it's this: When are the original Animals getting back together?

We're not. Believe me.

We tried that already—several times. The last attempt was such a fuck up that I hope most people don't remember. I know I'd like to forget it.

Our first reunion was in 1975. Producer Mickie Most had re-released "House of the Rising Sun," "I'm Crying," and "Don't Let Me Be Misunderstood," and they again soared up the charts. The following summer, we gathered to record our first new music in more than a decade, *Before We Were So Rudely Interrupted*. On that occasion, we camped out at Chas's house in Surrey, east of London. The place was fabulous and had, in fact, been the home of legendary seaman, Captain Cook. Chas bought crates of wine, a huge quantity of pot, and we started recording with the Stones' mobile unit.

The sessions went well, even though Chas was sort of re-learning the bass as we went—for more than ten years he'd been a manager, not a musician. We were off to a good start, all in a good mood, and cranked out two songs after a few days of rehearsals.

And then one day I got a telephone call from Alan saying he couldn't make it. His house was surrounded by armed police and SAS (the elite British military commandos) because the IRA had kidnapped two old-age pensioners after a shootout in the West End and were holding them hostage next door. It took several days before Alan was able to leave his house.

All in all, this recording reunion wasn't an unpleasant experience, partly because we never had plans to tour. Our thought was—and this was before MTV—that we could make a little promotional film and break the record without going on the road. This also meant we didn't have to face living day in and day out with Alan Price over a year on the road—something that would have been pretty difficult considering how angry we all still were over his keeping all the "House of the Rising Sun" money.

The glitch came when we were done recording, and Gold and Goldstein came back into the picture and slapped an injunction on the album's release until my suit with them was settled. It took two more years before our new album *Before We Were So Rudely Interrupted* was released. Please think about that: A release from a reunited '60s band in 1975 was highly anticipated; the same release two years later, in the thick of the punk revolution, was laughable. The Stones, Led Zeppelin, and the original Animals were the "boring old farts" that the Sex Pistols savaged. And Johnny Rotten told me so himself one night when he saw me in a London pub, shortly before the fists started flying.

Ultimately, the Animals' reunion record got great reviews—some critics called it among our best work ever. It sank like a stone when it came to sales.

Eight years later the rock scene had changed, and there was a friendly embrace of pioneering rock groups. When it looked like there was serious cash to be made by putting the Animals back together and taking them around the world, Chas Chandler, Hilton Valentine, John Steel, and Alan Price—got together and hatched a plan. They found financial backing and even a two-album record deal.

All they needed was me.

Unfortunately, it was the last thing I wanted to do. I had run off to Europe to escape such madness. I lived between Hamburg, the south of France, and Spain—I was having a difficult time finding myself, and at that point that's all I was interested in doing. Going back to the Animals seemed like it would only hinder the process. I'd spent more than fifteen years trying to distance myself from them, but all my friends said: Do the tour. Take the money and run.

"After all we've done for you," grumbled Chas and Alan. "After all the bullshit we had to put up with from you."

I was without a manager at the time and was lying low in Spain. But I immediately hired a representative just to protect me from their plans. Finally a meeting was called at the office of a financier, Colin Newman.

I was told that Miles Copeland at IRS records would take two new Animals recordings sight unseen—one studio, one live. At the conclusion of the meeting, I said I'd think about it. I gathered my stuff and began to leave the room. Just then Colin's secretary came through the doors with a tray of hot coffee, Chas hit me from behind, and I crashed into the tray, the hot coffee scalding my chest and face.

As always with the Animals, we were able to cool things down, and apologies were made. Several days later I agreed, on the condition that I be able to shoot a documentary of the reunion tour. So I signed up and the Animals were back together—after I insisted on an augmented band, since I didn't believe the original band members were polished enough to hit the road without assistance. After all, I'd never stopped performing while they essentially hadn't played in a decade. I demanded there be two horns, a second keyboard player and a percussionist. We brought my friend Nippy Noya, a percussionist from Amsterdam; Zoot Money, on keyboards; Steve Grant on second guitar; Dave Crumley on saxophone and veteran road manager Tappy Wright.

As Alan himself told one reporter, "Nobody can accuse us of getting back together out of nostalgia. Our memories are horrible, abysmal. We're doing this to remove those memories."

Nice sentiment, but the rehearsals and all the logistics of actually putting the band back on the road were a terrible strain, and things didn't go smoothly from the start. The first problem—the one that told me I was in for a hellish year—erupted shortly after we'd finished rehearsals and hit the road. As part of my participation, extensive filming had begun at the start. But soon, the rest of the band backed off and stopped participating. I began financing it myself and spent about $15,000 before I deciding I couldn't afford to continue on my own. Despite their earlier promises the others refused to help, and filming was stopped. Somewhere there's about fourteen hours of footage.

The original Animals gather to sign our 1983 reunion deal: John Steel, Alan Price, me, Chas Chandler and Hilton Valentine.

On stage, the reunited Animals were a crowd-pleaser. This was me on stage during an outdoor show in Manhattan.

To add insult to injury, I was given less-than-professional quality on-stage sound equipment to work with, and was constantly in danger of losing my voice because the P.A. was so bad. During the tour, I threw a lot of abuse at the monitor man, although the substandard equipment was really to blame. But when you're out there straining to get your voice across while everyone else is jamming with their amps on 11, you gotta take it out on somebody. One night I lost it and hurled a beer can at the sound guy. He got the message and from that point on wore a steel army helmet.

I had T-shirts made up with the slogan "Eric Burdon. . . Fuck Me, I Thought He Was Dead!" and passed them out to the crew. They loved them. As the tour wore on, and my patience diminished further, the crew banded together and made up their own T-shirts, which read: "Fuck Me, I Wish He Was Dead!"

But I temporarily forgot all the hassles when we made it to Austin,

Eric Burdon

Texas, where the local dignitaries threw the band a special welcome. I'd been through Austin on tour with my own band just a few months earlier, and now found myself on a podium with the other original Animals, next to the deputy mayor and a huge police officer. I was having a silent giggle. As the city dignitaries welcomed us and keys to the city were presented, I thought back to my previous visit, during which I was set upon by a young rock 'n' roll gypsy by the name of Janie Palomino. She was Texas wild. She was loaded. She had a wonderful, animated mouth, brown marble eyes and a tight body. A young girl in flames, standing naked at the end of my bed, twirling my handcuffs (which I used to chain my personal case to radiators while I was onstage). We had a whale of a time.

I was snapped back to reality when the cop tapped me on the shoulder. A mountain of a man in the light tan colors of the city police, he greeted me, smiling, "Hey there, Mr. Burdon."

I turned.

"Yes, sir."

"I saw yer show last time you was in Austin."

"You did!?"

"Yes sir, I did." His long arm gestured toward the staircase, and we headed up toward the champagne and sandwiches as he continued, "Do you recall a little ol' gal by the name of Janie Palomino?"

I wondered what the food was going to be like on the prison farm, with this guy's buddies sitting on horses with western saddles, straw Stetsons and 12-gauges while I dug a ditch in a striped suit.

I looked up into his big, blue eyes.

"Well sir," he went on, "those were not regular police cuffs, and we had to take her to the station to remove 'em after we got a phone call from the front desk telling us about a maid finding Ms. Palomino the following morning after your party." He leaned forward and said in my ear, "She was engaged to one of my friends. So since you saved him from making a dreadful mistake, we'll just keep quiet about it, OK? The Animals are one of my favorite bands," he said as he walked away.

"OK, Sir—thanks," I said.

Back on the bus, our next stop was Houston. Unfortunately, it was also the next for Hurricane Alicia. Why, I wondered, would we head there when everybody else was headed in the opposite direction, responding to a statewide storm alert?

"Because," said Chas, standing up in the front of the bus like Captain Bligh at the helm. "Because it's an act of God, and according to the contract, we have to make an appearance at the venue to collect the money if an Act of God shuts down the show."

"Okay," I said, "but is it worth risking life and limb to get the money from this gig? Surely it's not that much?"

"I'll be the judge of that," Chas said.

Everybody else seemed to agree. It would be great fun, they thought, driving into a hurricane. I wasn't so sure, but I was outvoted, and there

A sign of things to come on the Animals reunion tour: Me outside our Houston hotel the morning after Hurricane Alicia hit.

we were on an empty freeway hurtling toward Houston and Hurricane Alicia. The sky was blue and black, the winds were picking up, the temperature around 95°. At around 4:30 in the afternoon we pulled into town.

As soon as we checked in to the hotel, I was downstairs and into a taxi with Nippy Noya, looking for a Mexican cantina that I'd discovered on a previous visit.

"Shit," laughed the cab driver, "there ain't no restaurants opening up. The hurricane's coming."

"But why are you here?" said Nippy.

"Well," said the black driver, "anything's better than going home to my ol' lady." He laughed.

He hit the meter and we took off into downtown Houston. The taxi driver was right. The streets were deserted, and when we found my restaurant it was closed and boarded up. Deflated, defeated, and deprived of a great Mexican meal, we headed back toward the hotel, a massive, towering block of reflective glass. By the time I got back to my room on the twenty-second floor, the wind was rattling the windows. This is fucking madness, I thought, but I would make myself as ready as possible. The telephone rang. "Hello, this is the front desk. We are warning everybody not to use the elevators."

"Thank you." I put the phone down, realizing that this was serious stuff. I didn't unpack a thing except for my medicine bag so I could clean my teeth. I took off my jeans and laid them over the top of my cowboy boots, and laid them at the foot of the bed with my baggage, ready to bolt for the door if I had to. I switched on the TV; a movie channel was showing *The Exorcist*. I took two Valium, propped myself up with pillows and watched Linda Blair turn green as her head began to spin. There was a knock at the door.

It was Alan. "Listen, Eric," he said, "Chas is really upset. He thinks that you put out a Mafia hit on him because of the things that you said in the English press before we left. Would you come down to his room and straighten it out now?"

I couldn't believe this nonsense. Me putting out a Mob contract on the Animals' bass player? Fucking ridiculous. This hurricane was making everyone nuts. I followed Pricey down the stairs and we met with Chas in the corridor on the nineteenth floor. I couldn't believe what I saw. Chas was crying and so was Alan. John emerged from his room with an unbelievable smirk on his face, trying not to break out into laughter.

"Would you do this to me?" said Chas through tears. "Would you threaten my wife and kids?"

"No," I said, "come on, Chas, it's just the newspapers, it's just bullshit. You know what the fucking British press is like."

"No, I don't know what you mean, and I want an apology."

"All right," I said, "if that's the way you guys want it, I quit."

Alan turned and looked at me. "You can't quit," he said, "you can't quit because I quit first."

What a bunch of babies! Other doors began opening and people started asking what was going on.

"What's going on?" John asked.

"I don't know," I said, "fucking silliness, I think. Listen, I'm going back to my room. I mean, the weather conditions, the way things are goin', we gotta be ready to move any minute."

"I agree with you, we can't go on like this, this is madness."

"Well, as far as I'm concerned," I said, "we shouldn't have come anywhere near Houston. If we had turned around and gone in the other direction we could have driven out of this shit." What I was really thinking was that I shouldn't have come anywhere near the Animals' reunion tour.

"Well, it's too late now."

"I'm going back to my room." I left the huddle that had gathered in

215

the corridor and headed back to bed, now really drowsy from the Valium. Linda Blair's head wasn't the only one spinning.

The local TV news broke in on the movie. A map came on the screen. Hurricane Alicia had made landfall.

I leaped up and out of the bed, slid into my blue jeans, stomped into my boots and headed for the door. Just as I grabbed the door handle the window behind began to crack. A huge sliver of glass flew across the room and missed my head by inches, smashing into the door as I headed out. They're using the fucking elevators, I realized. The pressure caused by the elevators was sucking in the windows.

But there was nowhere for us to go. For three days and nights we were stuck there in that hotel. The food ran out, and the bar was drunk dry. Because of the wind and broken windows, we had to camp out in the hallway. I made myself a little place in one corner with blankets and pillows and was mostly left alone. By now, my only contact in the band was Nippy. Everyone else steered clear of me. I could not have cared less. I had my Walkman, extra batteries, a good book, and a bottle of Jack Daniels. Chas and John set up a makeshift office on the first floor. At one point, a television crew arrived. They were the first people we'd seen, aside from police, in about forty-eight hours.

As I read Frances Fitzgerald's great book on Vietnam, *Fire Over the Lake,* Alan came over to my corner. He must have been bored and in a shit-stirring mood. He made some snide remark about my divorce, and told me that I should get married again.

"You can give someone else all your pain and make it easier on the rest of us."

As he walked away I threw the book at him and, lucky shot, nailed him square in the back of his head. Alan didn't come to my corner and bother me any more.

On the third day we ventured out to score some grass. We found a connection in the old part of downtown. A large tree had crashed through the house next door and killed the occupant. Oddly, her name, like the hurricane, was Alicia, and she was the only local fatality of the storm.

When we finally made it out of Texas and onto the sunny California coast, things looked a little brighter. We found ourselves back on the *Billboard* charts with the release of "The Night," a song I'd written a couple of years earlier. Our last U.S. date was Honolulu. From there we'd head to Japan.

I was looking forward to Hawaii, but I'd been to Japan recently with my own band and didn't think there'd be much enthusiasm for an Animals' reunion there. I suggested we just cancel those dates and hang in Hawaii for a week, soaking up the sun. At this point we had our girlfriends and families with us. My daughter had flown in from California, and Chas had his wife and son with him. It was a great time, I thought, to happily relax by the poolside.

But Hilton would have none of it. He had his heart set on going to Japan. He'd recently become a Buddhist and wanted to visit a particular temple. "Besides," Chas told me in all seriousness, "the T-shirts have already been printed and this is supposed to be a worldwide tour."

Percussionist Nippy Noya also wanted desperately to go to Japan since he was searching for his father, a Japanese soldier during World War II who had coupled with his American mother.

I gave in, again, and we hit Japan just in time for more hurricane weather. We had three weeks of steady rain and in that time played only three shows, to half-filled halls. Most of the time we just consumed the tour's profits in hotel bills.

I drank myself silly every night and went out of my way to be as nasty as I could possibly be to everyone around me in retaliation. It was hell. As Chas himself told a reporter: "It was as if Eric had set out to make it as unpleasant as possible. It was sheer bloody-mindedness. As if he wanted to settle as many old scores as possible."

217

It was in Japan that the road crew got new T-shirts printed up. They said "Fuck Me, I Wish They Were All Dead!" Chas was amused until he found out the "Fuck Me" T-shirts throughout the tour had come out of the operating expenses of his company, which was producing the tour.

When we reached England, we did a gig at the City Hall in Bristol. As I left the stage for a breather while Alan Price sang his song "Oh, Lucky Man," a regular feature in the set, I was set upon by several of Bristol's finest. They threw me up against the side of the wall, ripped off my shirt, and pulled down my pants. Two of the police officers searched for drugs as Alan sat primly on the stage in his white jumpsuit singing.

Fortunately, the cops were wasting their time. I was clean.

As the tour wound down, we were at each other's throats. Nippy quit, and we pulled the plug on dates in Hungary and Poland.

We still had to fulfill the contract with IRS records for a live album, but the breakdown in the band was so severe that nobody would go into the studio to do the mixing. Besides, we didn't have enough material.

With the intent of heading off yet another serious legal problem in my life, I teamed up with guitarist Steve Grant. Steve had been on the road with us and helped write material for the studio album. We went to IRS boss Miles Copeland and got clearance to use MTV tapes from a New Year's Eve bash we'd played with The Police. Steve and I and an engineer hunkered down in a small London studio and combined the live material we had with the MTV tracks and some outtakes from the studio album sessions (mixing in fake audience cheers), and came up with our live album, *Rip It To Shreds.* I was so pissed off. I wanted to do a definitive, live Animals album, and this is what we ended up with. Steve did a good job, and we delivered the master. The record company was happy, and the whole hellish experience of the Animals' reunion was over.

The Rolling Stones have been together for more than thirty-five years and continue to mount massive world tours. Yes, it's a huge money machine, but ultimately, it comes down to the fact that with Mick and Keith and Charlie Watts and Ronnie Wood, it's all about the music. And that's why the Animals could never stay together and should never have even attempted to reunite: With our personalities, it could never just be about the music.

Alan and I don't speak.

John and Hilton still play together, and two or three times a year I hear from one or both of them. In fact, with Dave Rowberry, they joined me onstage for some classic Animals tunes at my 60th birthday concert in Los Angeles in the spring of 2001. It was a blast, a pleasure to be making music with them again for the first time in nearly twenty years. I wouldn't rule out playing with the three of them again—but it won't be the original Animals. That's impossible. Besides my desire never to have anything to do with Alan again, the Animals ended forever in the summer of 1996 when Big Chas Chandler died of a heart attack. Aside from the end of any Animals future, it marked the far-too-early conclusion of a wonderful life. He did so much—not only for his family and, all those years ago, for Jimi Hendrix and other artists, but for our hometown of Newcastle as well. There his memory continues to be revered. One of his last projects was spearheading the New-castle Arena, a 10,000-seat entertainment and sports center.

We had our differences, and I know now that Chas had to be the bad guy on the reunion tour because he was in charge of the money and the logistics. But I'll remember him for the sweet soul underneath the towering, gruff exterior.

With Chas forever gone, so too is the once-great band that was the original Animals.

CHAPTER 14

into the holy badlands

We were somewhere near the Jordanian Border. It was August, 1985. He knelt down to look at the dust alongside the idling Jeep. I was behind the wheel. "I don't know how good these maps are," he said. "They're from the '72 Campaign; but these bootprints are Israeli issue so let's keep going."

He was an ex-Mossad agent who told me to call him Morty—but he warned that I couldn't photograph him. He was my guide on a Jeep tour of Israel and its wondrous Negev Desert.

After the Animals' reunion tour, remnants of the augmented section of the band stayed on with me as I went out as the Eric Burdon Band once more. London agent Rod Weinberg found me work in areas that were new to me, one of which was Israel. I jumped at the chance to go there. It was new territory for me, and it was yet another desert that I wanted to see. After the gigs, the band returned to London, but I stayed on. I couldn't go home without seeing more of this mysterious, ancient land.

Alone in my Tel Aviv hotel I called several rental car agencies looking for a Jeep so I could drive north to the great Negev. No one would accommodate me, even though at the airport and in the center of Tel

don't let me be misunderstood

Aviv there were the regular Avis, Budget, and Dollar Rent-A-Car agencies. I'd come up against a brick wall. The country was still pretty much war-ravaged and very dangerous. The second day after the guys had left I got a telephone call from the local promoter. He said he would provide me with a bodyguard, Morty, who would also find transportation.

He had the classical Middle Eastern face, olive skin, hooked nose, jet-black curly hair, small, wiry, athletic. The obligatory gold chain dangled around his neck, and he carried a small traveling accessory which was really difficult to spot unless you knew what you were looking for—a Smith & Wesson .357 Magnum revolver.

"So how far do you want to go?" he asked smilingly as he shook my hand, his perfect set of teeth shining in the sun.

"To the end of the road," I said.

"OK. That's where we're going," he said. "Let's take a walk."

We left the hotel and made our way out into the crowded streets of Tel Aviv.

"The guys at the agency told me that you had been looking all over town for a Jeep."

"Yeah," I said. "I have this romantic idea of hitting the Negev Desert in an open Jeep. Is there a problem with that?"

"Well, yes there is," said Morty, "but nothing's impossible. Come with me. I want you to meet somebody."

We traveled across town in an old Mercedes, stopping at a white block of tenement houses. As we walked up the stairwell, he explained to me the guy we were going to meet was his onetime commander in Beirut, back in 1972. The door of the apartment swung open. A beautiful Israeli woman made us feel welcome. And I shook hands with Morty's ex-commander, a small, muscular, bald-headed, sun-tanned individual. "Morty was telling me that you guys served together in Beirut," I said as we sat cross-legged on the floor, Arab style, drinking mint tea.

"Yeah, we saw a lot of stuff together," he nodded slowly.

Morty nudged me and nodded toward the commander. "He was one of our best officers. Always took care of his guys. Never lost one. We all came back safe. And you know why that was?" he looked at me.

"No," I said, "pray tell."

"Because when we were on search duty on the borders, he always told us to look for the small packages and ignore the larger ones. That way nobody got a bomb, and we all got the best cocaine available." Everybody laughed.

The commander got up from the table, walked into his bedroom and returned. He sat down and looked me in the eye while he passed a set of keys to Morty.

"Here's the keys to my Jeep; you take care of this guy. And Eric, you make sure he doesn't bend my Jeep."

Then he shook hands with me, placing something in my palm, and sat drinking the strong mint tea.

I looked down into my hand; there was a small package containing a block of what appeared to be killer Afghani hash, moist and giving off a heady aroma.

Soon, Morty and I were traveling north, rolling across the Holy Badlands in an open CJ-7, painted blue and white to distinguish it from the regular military vehicles. I was looking forward to a smoke, but lacked the appropriate implement. I suggested to Morty that we stop at one of the many Arab shops that did brass work, including all kinds of wonderful plates, mugs, jugs, and, I hoped, water pipes.

We made a stop at such a shop. Morty parked the Jeep outside. He told me to stay in the vehicle and went inside to see if he could secure a pipe. The Jeep was instantly surrounded by a gang of young Arabic teenagers, totally in my face and staring me down, trying to make me feel as uncomfortable as possible. Six or seven of them stood motionless, staring at me and the vehicle. It was my first indication that things were very different here, and that I wasn't welcome.

Morty returned. "Excuse me," he said, pushing aside one of the kids, jumping into the driver's seat. "Well, they do have one pipe in there," he said, "but the guy won't sell it."

"Why not?" I said.

"He'll trade it but he won't sell it."

"What does he want in exchange?"

"The Jeep. Let's get the fuck out of here," he said, putting the Jeep into gear. We left the teenagers in a cloud of dust.

As we made our way out of the city, a veil was raised, revealing to me the real face of the Middle East. A military convoy passed, taking up the whole road. We pulled over to make room and watched the huge sand-colored tanks with their hatches open and young soldiers not even looking down at us. The army of God was on the move. Dust hung like fog in the wake of the convoy, and Morty handed me a pair of sand glasses to protect my eyes.

With evening, we made camp with several other travelers alongside a small, man-made lake. Morty went under the hood of the Jeep and disconnected the distributor cap, and slept with it underneath his pillow alongside his .357 Magnum. He told me we would arise before dawn and climb Masada.

As I lay in my sleeping bag looking at the star-filled sky, I felt somehow comfortably at home. I knew I was in good hands. It was great to have played music in such a diverse land. The Eric Burdon Band shows in Tel Aviv had been well received by an audience that was really international. There'd been young Jews from all over the world—lots of New Yorkers, and tourists from as far away as Australia.

The show at the University of Peace had been really special. After-ward, the principal showed me around the campus. He told me that on the morning prior to the show, the teachers and staff had risen at the crack of dawn and danced their traditional Yiddish dances while a stereo played Eric Burdon and War. I took this as a compliment of the highest order. After showing me around the campus, the principal, flanked by two assistants, gestured out beyond the edge of the university grounds. "Here is the University of Peace," said the principal. "Beyond, there is nothing but darkness, anarchy, and death, but here we are at peace."

I did well on the climb up Masada. It was the first time since I was in the nuns' care in Spain that I had walked any great distance, and it felt good. Morty set the pace, and he was making sure that I would complete the climb up the steep dusty road. When we reached the top we stopped and drank water, resting while he told me legends of this hill by the shores of the Dead Sea. I noticed a black scar on his arm and asked him about it. He said it was from an overheated machine gun, which he'd dropped on his arm as he was trying to take photographs while also shooting. The soldiers made extra money by selling combat pictures to the world's press.

"Incredible!" I said.

"Incredibly stupid," he replied, explaining it was better to buy photos from other soldiers and not endanger one's own life.

We'd made good time getting to the top, and it was still quite early. I wandered off on my own for a while and jumped down off a rock onto a concrete slab. Suddenly I heard Hebrew being spoken and saw a man in a uniform.

"Hey! I'm sorry!" I stammered.

"No, it's all right," the man answered in English. "Come on down."

I'd stumbled across a machine gun post manned by two soldiers and a huge .50 weapon. They were brewing coffee and offered me brandy. The alcohol surprised me, but it gets so cold there at night I guess they bent the rules.

Morty joined us as we drank and made small talk. I was amazed by their sense of brotherhood. Morty told me that years before, Arab soldiers used to camp there, and it was a rite of passage for young Jews to climb up, kill an Arab, and come back with the prize of his weapon.

Looking down at the Dead Sea from the top of Masada hearing these

stories, I knew this was the payoff. I had been right to stay and under-
take this journey.

Next we headed for Eilat, a small community on the Red Sea near
the Jordanian border. I was at the wheel of the Jeep, Morty giving me
driving tips. "Now stay in second gear most of the time, that's your
gas-saving gear and the best ratio for this terrain."

"Okay," I said, listening to every word he uttered. We came to a small
gully. In front of me was a hill with quite a steep climb.

"Hold it here," he said. He was checking his military maps, which
were wrapped in clear plastic. "Just continue up this hill and stay in
second gear if you can."

I reached the top of the dusty rise, and the Jeep was already rolling
down the other side when my heart stopped. At the bottom of the hill I
could see two oil drums and a wooden barrier. On the left side of the
barrier stood a soldier, naked to the waist, an AK-47 slung around his
brown frame.

"Jesus," I said, "It's the enemy."

The hill was so steep I couldn't have stopped even if I had wanted to
without skidding toward the barrier.

"Stay cool and stay in second gear," Morty yelled over the whine of
the engine, reaching down toward the gearshift to unzip the bag which
contained his .357. "Okay, let me handle this. I think he's Druse."

"You think he's what?"

"Druse," he said. "I'll do the talking, just stay behind the wheel."

"Right. Go ahead," I said.

There was a rapid exchange of Arabic between Morty and the soldier. To my left I could see a gasoline dock, some dirt bikes. And to my
right, a huge battle-scarred tank, its gun muzzle covered in canvas.
Somehow, in between the rapid-fire Arabic, Morty said to me in English, "He doesn't know where he is. He was dropped here by helicopter
in the middle of the night. And I was right, he is Druse."

"How can you tell?" I asked.

"By the color of his eyes. They're gray, see."

"Oh, yeah, gotcha," I said, confused as ever. I said to Morty, "Hey, I got a *Playboy* magazine I brought along for such an occasion. Should I get it?"

"Sure," he said, "but move slowly."

I turned around and from my zipped bag I took out a current issue of *Playboy* magazine, which, as luck would have it, contained a story on the leader of the Druse militia, to which this guy belonged. I flipped open the pages and showed the soldier the interview section. "Look," I said, "Walid Jamblat, your guy," pointing to him and then back to the magazine.

"Screw that," said Morty, "show him the centerfold."

I flipped out the centerfold. His gray eyes lit up. "For me?" he said.

"For you," I said.

"Thank you," he said, taking the magazine, rolling it up, and stuffing it inside his trousers.

He made a move toward the barrier. It swung up. "OK, pass," he said.

I gunned the Jeep, and we took off. "Wow," I said, "that was exciting. What's he doing out here?"

"You saw the tank?"

"Yeah."

"And the off-road bikes?"

"Yeah."

"Well, they're practising tracking out tanks with hand grenades. One person draws the fire from the tank and someone else speeds up on a bike and throws a grenade in the tracks. We tried it years ago," Morty said, "but we lost too many men. Let them find out for themselves."

I looked back at the lonely Druse soldier and waved.

"And, where the hell are we now?"

"Don't worry," said Morty. "Two clicks down this road we'll come to a two-lane tarmac. Hang a right and then you'll see."

Soon the tarmac loomed in front of us. I swung the Jeep off the dirt onto the main road and brought it to a stop. In the distance I could see the sun shining on the Red Sea.

"Look," said Morty, "Aqaba from the desert, just like Lawrence, I thought you'd like that."

"You bet," I said. I jumped up onto the seat. Leaning over the windscreen of the Jeep, I pointed and yelled at the top of my voice, "Lawrence, give no quarter!" I jumped into the passenger seat, Morty took the wheel, and we headed toward Aqaba, just like the great Lawrence had.

Morty had a wicked sense of humor. When we stopped at a set of three patched metal crosses, about 10 m apart, I asked Morty what they were. He replied that they pointed the way to the only Christian monastery enclave, across a ravine from where we were.

I was surprised that the Jewish state allowed such a thing. "Don't fool yourself," Morty said. "Our artillery uses them for gunnery practice. They're in a perfect place to test trajectory. The shells miss the monastery by a long shot, but it reminds them who we are."

A few minutes later, several shells streaked overhead and exploded in the sand beyond the monastery.

"Wow! I thought you were joking!" I said.

"No. It's no joking matter."

One morning while hiking, we rounded a bend on a high ridge and came across a patrol, two female officers and one male, that had stopped to make tea and eat breakfast. The man had a full beard and looked a little like Fidel Castro. The two women were beautiful—despite the Uzis hanging from around their necks. We approached and started talking. They asked about me, and where I was from. I talked a little of my family background in Northern England, and one of the girls asked if I had ever been in the British military.

"No," I said. But I regaled them with family war stories, especially of my Uncle Jack, who, it seemed, was at his best when he was a soldier traipsing through some jungle somewhere.

The man looked up at me with his deep brown eyes, a piece of pita bread in his beard.

"Yes, I knew of such a man as your uncle."

"Really?" I said.

"Yes. I had to kill him."

He handed me a fresh cup of mint tea.

As we began our journey back to Beersheba, I lay in the back of the Jeep on top of our rucksacks, sunning myself and watching the Negev desert roll by. Then the CJ-7's engine changed its tune. It was misfiring. We were ten clicks from the city. We crawled slowly the last few kilometers, counting our lucky stars that we weren't stranded out in the massive Holy Badlands. Morty went to work on the engine, and I took a stroll.

A motorcycle parked outside of a coffee shop caught my eye. I walked over to make a closer inspection. It was a lovable rat machine, a BMW R-6 with wonderful desert-weathered leather saddlebags, the paintwork scuffed and scratched up from many years of use. I wondered who this machine belonged to, and what kind of guy would take on this awesome desert on two wheels. One would have to be an ace mechanic to begin with, and a lot more to be able to ride a motorcycle across this gnarly terrain.

I walked into the coffee shop to take a look around. I ordered a mineral water and a double espresso. As the guy behind the counter was pulling the coffee, I noticed a Walther PPK sticking out of his back pocket, and on the other side of his belt a walkie-talkie. This is the answer, I thought. Give everybody a gun and a two-way radio, and thou shalt have peace.

Finishing my coffee, I walked outside again to look at the rat machine. Then I saw the CJ-7 come toward me, Morty behind the wheel.

don't let me be misunderstood

"We're okay, let's go!"

As we departed Beersheba I looked back at the R-6 standing there beneath the shade of a palm tree, wondering what kind of guy rode her.

Two days later, we pulled into Tel Aviv. In comparison with the last week and the open spaces of the Negev, the city seemed overcrowded, bursting with life. The sky was blue, there was a chill in the air, it was fresh and wonderful. Morty took me to his old neighborhood, introduced me to some of his childhood friends. We ate lunch in the place of honor, the booth in his favorite restaurant. The crest of the Israeli Special Forces was on the wall above us, along with a photograph of the boys in Beirut. I felt elated, I was with good company, and I had just completed the journey of a lifetime, another dream fulfilled, I looked out across the street, and lo and behold, I couldn't believe it—parked in front of the bar across the street was the rat BMW with the saddlebags, covered in dust.

"Excuse me, Morty," I said, "I want to go check out this bike."

I made my way across the street and stepped into the coolness of the bar. Sitting there was a huge, burly, bearded monster of a guy, a beer in his fist and a newspaper on the bar in front of him. He wore a British World War II tanker's leather waistcoat, army fatigues and combat boots. I sat next to him.

"Hey, how's it goin'?"

"It's goin' good," he said, wiping his beard. "And you?"

"Yeah, fine. That your machine outside?"

"Yes, it is," he said.

"Pardon me asking, but didn't I just see that machine in Beersheba two, three days ago?"

"That's me."

"Wow! You mean you actually travel this country alone on a motor-cycle? Bit fucking dangerous, isn't it?"

"That's what I do. Would you like a brew?" he said.

"Sure, would be nice."

229

He got another beer and we sat down outside in the shade, the bike in front of us.

"Yeah, you can say what you like about the Germans, but they sure know how to make a good machine. And you?"

"Yeah, I love motorcycles. In fact, seeing you, seeing this machine and knowing that you ride this desert, makes me realize that the first thing I'm going to do when I get back to America is buy myself a bike and ride my desert."

"Oh yeah, where would that be?"

"Southern California," I said. "It ain't the Negev, but it's beautiful."

"Yeah," he said. "A day wasted is a day wasted."

When we finally returned to the capital, Morty stopped and made a phone call only to receive some tragic news. His brother had been killed in a road accident. I didn't know what to say or do but I was amazed that Morty kept a stiff composure. We even stopped, further down the road, to help an old man whose aging Mercedes had overheated. Then Morty helped me pack for London and assisted me through Israeli customs.

As an officer inspected my passport and lifted a stamp to mark my exit, Morty yelled out for him to stop.

"You don't want them to stamp it," he told me. "Not if you ever want to enter an Arab country."

As I made my way toward my plane, he gestured to me in a secretive manner and pulled me aside.

"Don't let anyone see these until you get out of the country," he said, pressing two of his old army shoulder patches into my pocket as a farewell gift. "I could get into big trouble. See you, mate."

"Thanks, man," I said as we parted—me for London, and he for his brother's funeral.

CHAPTER 15

ghosts on the coast

After the disposal of the latest version of the Eric Burdon Band and the conclusion of my desert adventures, I couldn't face another long winter on the island of Menorca. I really loved it there, but my old enemy asthma grabbed me by the throat again. I got so freaked out I was afraid to face a trans-Atlantic flight, but my Spanish doctor loaded me up with syringes of cortizone just in case. My father's death also weighed heavily on me—a heart attack in his sleep. Would death jump up and grab me the same way? It sent me into a deep depression.

I sold the house in Spain in a lighting-quick deal that was financially a disaster. With what little money I had left, I headed back to California. My mother's fight with cancer was not over, but for my own health I had to get back to the desert.

The club scene in L.A. had changed. The bright shining star that was once the Whisky A Go Go had dimmed. The place was now a punk joint. There was a new place in town to hang out, the China Club, where the bouncers were radio-connected. The New York thing had come to L.A. The girls were outrageous, it was snowing coke, and everybody was wild. Big movie people slumming, video directors casting—it was a room full of victims—but the midweek jams at the China Club were definitely the place to be.

The list of familiar faces was endless, the particular mix depending on which band was in town that week. Some of the regulars were actor Bruce Willis blowing his blues harp, comedian Sam Kinison doing his wild thing, Jack Mack and the Heart Attack horn section, Terry Reid, sax player Jimmy Z. Zavala. Musicians, local and from out of town, stood in line to jam. I also ran into great players from my own bands, such as Tony Braunagel and Snuffy Walden. Regular raids by the fire department for overcrowding gave the place a '20s speakeasy feeling. But it sure was a different vibe from the 1970s. Sex, drugs, and rock 'n' roll were replaced with AIDS, Prozac, and Michael Bolton.

I was sleeping around town wherever I could: guesthouses, baby rooms, garages, friends' living room floors. I was broke, although I did have a Harley Davidson, which helped me save face somewhat: It was good, cheap, respectable transport.

On a jam night at the China Club I ran into Robby Krieger, the Doors guitar player, and we became running buddies. Robby had been given the job of musical director on Oliver Stone's movie *The Doors,* but, like all major movies, it was slow developing. In the months leading up to the production, Robby and I did gigs from coast to coast.

Robby had reason to be excited about the film. Stone was the director of the day, the guy who was taking on U.S. history and putting it into the medium that Americans relate to the best, the movies. He was planning to tell the inside story of musicians, as he had for the grunts with *Platoon.*

When Robby said there would be a juicy part for me in the film, my heart soared. I figured this was the break I needed to reenter the American scene. Robby said I'd play a poet friend of Jim Morrison's, a guy whom Jim had respected, an elder, Jim's missing father figure. It sounded like something right for me.

I hadn't seen a script yet, but found myself thinking often about Morrison, a singer whose good looks always helped hide what an asshole he could be.

After I'd met Jim up in San Francisco for the first time, he invited me down to the TTG Studios where the Doors were recording. I'd worked in the same studio with the New Animals and Frank Zappa.

Within the darkness of the main studio, the only faces I could see were those lit up by the lights of the sound board. The owner and engineer was Ami Ahid, an Israeli. He motioned for me to move to the rear of the control room and take a seat.

From inside the vocal booth, Jim looked up and said, "Ah, well, let's shut it down. We have visitors."

He always seemed so separate from the rest of the group. There was some milling around as Ahid brought up the studio lights. A girl from one of the fanzines stood near Jim, pencil and notebook in hand. She clearly wanted to talk with him, but he turned his head and leaned it against the acoustic tile of the wall. Then the zipper of his leather trousers came undone, and he pulled his dick out. The girl's face turned beet red. The band pretended there was nothing out of the ordinary going on.

What an asshole, I thought to myself.

Well, he was. But that didn't mean he wasn't interesting. I discussed these experiences with the actor Stone had hired to bring Morrison back to life, Val Kilmer.

The very first conversation I had with Jim was about his film studies. He loved movies, probably just as much as he loved creating mayhem. Jim's big thing seemed to be action street theater, a mix of movie making and live mayhem. Being a rock star just gave him a license to extend it—extend his whole life into one huge stunt.

As the shooting date approached, I still hadn't seen a script, though I still believed that I was to play this character of his old poet friend. Convinced of this, I trooped along to the wardrobe department early one morning to put on my '60s costume, ready to go to work in the movies. As a movie fan I was looking forward to the chance to watch a great director at work up close.

The production had taken over a few square blocks of West Hollywood to re-create the wild days of the Whisky. It did strange things to me, waiting for hours for the cameras to roll, looking at the dead faces pretending to be real, pretending to be emotionally involved in music that was canned, and seeing an actor playing someone whom I once knew.

The fake smoke that was pumped into the room by the special effects people made my asthma flare—but the Screen Actors Guild benefits that came with the good pay made up for it. So I hung in, behaved myself, did what I was told, and kept reminding myself this was a great thing to be a part of.

There was an extra on the set who captivated me. When she wasn't gazing in awe at Val performing, she was reading books on acting, so when the chance came to strike up a conversation with her, as I was sitting in the high chair having makeup applied to my mug, I opened the conversation: "Jesus, wasn't Val Kilmer's performance just perfect, I mean he really is Jim." She agreed. She was an angel. She had a map that led to my heart. Her name was Zola Cronos.

Her teeth were like white pearls against the darkness of her skin. She had that magic mix, that kiss of Indian along with Spanish blood. She was from East L.A., and she was proud of it. She wore her Chicana pride like the bracelets around her wrists.

"See you on the set," she smiled as she left the trailer and headed for the shoot.

That night we were recreating the scene in which The Doors, just about to make it, are playing their most notorious gig at the Whisky. It's the night that Jim goes into his "Mother, I want to fuck you" rap, and

Jim and the boys were ejected from the club by Elmer Valentine and his associate, Mario.

Mario must have read the script, because at about six o'clock that night he showed up on the set, I guess to give his guidance as to how the scene should play. This guy amazed me. Mario hadn't changed in thirty years, still the aggressive but warm-hearted doorman of the Whisky, a large cigar poking out of his sculptured Italian features. He looked as fit as a fiddle. And I was reminded of how much he and his boss had figured in our lives, in the lives of all the L.A. bands, during the '60s.

Mario saved my life one night. For some reason a drunken Scotsman was out to gut me with a knife. He seemed to be serious about it. As we stood facing each other down in the corridor leading to the dressing room, Mario came up behind him, disarmed him, then booted him down the stairs.

Seeing Mario and shaking his rigid hand brought back a flood of memories. Some good, some bad. I remembered one encounter with Jim when he was acting out his whole Lizard King persona and came staggering into the club dressed in the obligatory leather pants, black leather jacket, and torn T-shirt. He staggered up to the booth where I was sitting having a quiet drink with a sweet little stripper from Tulsa by the name of Kay. Morrison poured a can of beer over her head. I got up to punch his lights out, and he sprung backward, falling down. He then jumped up on the stage. The band that was playing recognized who he was and were only too pleased when Jim Morrison grabbed a microphone. The band, fresh in from Texas, slid into a twelve-bar blues which soon diminished, instrument by instrument, to a trickle as, player by player, they left the stage, disgusted by Morrison's angry rant.

"You're all niggers, you hear me? You'll never have a revolution. The country's had it's fuckin' revolution, and it'll never happen again. Why? Because you're all niggers. White niggers, yellow niggers, and black niggers," he went on.

The music had stopped, the lights had come up, and the place was beginning to clear. Jim kept on rapping. I sat there, glued to my seat, watching the great show. Jim went on, "When and if the great day should come when you niggers should wake up and really see what you really are, then I say unto you. . . ."

I saw movement up on the balcony, a flashlight. It was Otis, the club's old, black and, more importantly, armed, guard. He was leaning over the railing, his .38 Police Special aimed at Morrison, waiting for a point where Jim would take a pause. When he did, Otis cut loose: "Okay, Morrison! Get off my stage and out of my club before I plug your fuckin' ass."

At the sight of the uniform and the drawn weapon, Jim folded. He jumped from the stage, hit the dance floor, came up from all fours, and headed for the door. In the doorway stood two California Highway Patrol cops looking mean and pissed off. This is where Jim came into his own. He was actually in the hands of the two cops when somehow he slipped away. Wearing only his famous leather pants, he took off into the L.A. night, jumping from the roof of one car to the other, across four lanes of gridlocked traffic at the intersection of Sunset and Clark, and disappeared into the night. The cops stood there amazed, holding an empty leather jacket and torn T-shirt.

It was no wonder I thought of that night. I was in a time warp. Here I was in the Whisky again, all these years later, waiting to see Jim, in the form of Val Kilmer, take the stage. I don't recall Jim's ever really being as energetic and motivated as the movie portrayed him, but this energy was certainly important to the film.

A ripple of excitement ran through the whole crew. Cameras were ready to roll. Stone was outside on the sidewalk ensconced in his black tent watching the action on a monitor. A crowd of extras, the excited fans, stood around the small original Whisky stage as Val, in his leathers as Jim, climbed up and took the microphone. I was seated at a table full of heavies, not sure as yet who my character really was. I just went where I was directed by the assistant director.

Then I saw her on the far side of the stage. I couldn't take my eyes off of her, her black hair falling down around her shoulders, her upper lip raised in excitement as Kilmer began to dance around. The high volume, Kilmer's boots kicking up dust, beads of sweat beginning to appear on his forehead. . . he was really into it. He was the perfect Morrison. I was taken back to when the moment had really happened. The first take was over, and the crowd of extras broke into spontaneous applause. Everyone was amazed at Kilmer's performance.

"Take Two" came the call, and the cameras rolled again. "Break on through to the other side" came over the PA system, extremely loud, louder than The Doors ever played.

"We're gonna break on through to the other side,
break on through to the other side,
break on through, break on through, break on through."

The tempo and volume went through the roof. I looked at the beautiful brown-skinned girl. Her face lit up as she pushed back her hair, her lips pursed in sexual excitement. The dance came to an end, the cameras stopped, and everyone in the room broke out into wild applause again. Stone entered the room, headphones dangling from his neck, sweat on his brow, a beaming Cheshire cat smile on his face. Members of the crew helped Kilmer down from the stage, and he walked through the crowd pumping flesh, a smile on his face. He walked past the main camera and headed for his trailer outside, his leather trousers stained with sweat.

There was lots of activity outside on the corner of Clark and Sunset as the crew wrapped for the night. A full moon hung in the sky and it was quite cool. I stood there on the corner just lingering, absorbing the atmosphere, my mind going back to those days, which seemed like yesterday. I felt someone standing behind me. I turned, and her clear, beautiful brown eyes looked into mine.

"Eric," she said, swinging her body in an unconscious, nervous fashion.

"Yes," I said.

"You're Eric Burdon."

"That's right."

"I had no idea," she said.

"No idea of what?" I asked.

"You know, that you are the guy, that guy who sang "House of the Rising Sun." They always play that on the radio. You knew Jim, didn't you?"

"Yeah, I did," I said, rubbing my eyes.

"Are you tired?" she said, turning to press the walk button at the intersection.

"There's so much smoke in there, it's killing me."

"Let's walk," she said.

"I'm staying with a friend at her apartment on Doheney," I told her. "It's got the best rooftop view in the world if you want to check it out."

Zola told me as we approached the rooftop pool that she was working as an extra in movies but wanted to act seriously . She took her shoes off.

"Be careful," I warned her as she sat on the edge.

"Wow, this is great," she said. "Breathtaking."

"Yeah, I come up here with my field glasses sometimes," I said."It's great. The other evening there were cops all over the neighborhood. It was a bank robbery, I think. I watched the whole scene from here."

"Yeah, I can almost see where I was born," she said.

"Where's that?"

"Just off of Sunset, East L.A."

She struck a tough gangsta pose. "East Los, you know, Chicano land. And proud of it, man."

"I can see that," I said as she sat down again.

I took her naked foot in my hands. She didn't react. Just looked out at the city lights quivering in the warm Santa Ana wind.

"You've got warm hands," she said.

"Yeah, my mother always said I had toasty hands, even when it was deep winter."

We just listened to the silence, which was broken by a siren wailing against the night somewhere.

Due to high winds the air was clear enough for us to see the lights of the San Pedro docks.

"You still live there nowadays?" I asked.

"Oh, I can't tell you where I live," she said. "I'm married."

"That's a pity. Doesn't bother me if it doesn't bother you."

Changing the subject, she said, "God, I'm so lucky to be doing this movie. And you, you knew Jim, didn't you?"

I was on the verge of saying "Hey, if you just want me to tell you some Doors groupie Jim Morrison tales. . ." but I bit my tongue.

"Well, were you and he good buddies?"

"No, not exactly," I said.

"Well what, then?"

I stood up and faced her. My hands went around her waist, feeling the harsh fabric of her blue jeans, then the soft skin of her arms, brushing past her erect nipples under her white T-shirt, my left hand behind her long Rastafarian hair, her natural perfume. I kissed her neck and sank my teeth into one of her ears. She turned coolly and smiled.

"Yeah, my father was an activist for Cesar Chavez up in Northern California. He was arrested when I was just a baby."

"You ever been to Mexico?" I inquired.

"No, never," she said.

"Then we must go," I said.

She giggled to herself and turned again, looking out at the blaze of lights. Her arm went around my neck, and she said, "Do you think your friend has returned yet?"

This sounded like an invitation to go back downstairs. "Would you like a drink?" I asked as we entered the apartment.

"No thanks," she said. "I've got to be going."

"Then I'll walk you to your car."

"No, it's OK, just show me where you're going to sleep, and I'll tuck you in for the evening and then I must go."

We kissed and then walked together into the guest room. The two cats of the house, curious to see what was going on, joined us there in the half light.

"OK, get undressed," she said, pulling my shirt over my head.

As the week-long location shoot at the Whisky continued, we would meet during lunch breaks, and in the evening the rooftop was our rendezvous point. At the end of the week she invited me to Las Vegas to meet her parents. When I got off the plane, she was there waiting, looking like an Aztec goddess.

The taxi took the ring road around the town and arrived at an old section of downtown that hadn't yet been swallowed by the neon wave. This was her parents' northern home, she explained as we pulled up. They had another house in Chapultapec, Mexico.

"You said you'd never been to Mexico," I said, laughing.

"I was born there, señor," she laughed.

Her mother came to the door. She was slim and trim, dressed in a fake leopard-skin wrap and gold high-heel shoes, very much Frederick's of Hollywood. Her hair was so black it was almost blue, her skin in wonderful condition for an older woman. A moment after we shook hands and Zola made the introductions, she offered me a joint and whispered in my ear, "My husband is at work so I'm allowed to enjoy one of my few vices, but please, Eric, don't tell him."

"Yes," I said. "Mum's the word. Your secret is safe with me."

"She smokes and he drinks, and both do it in secret," interjected Zola. "They're both crazy."

Cuban music filled the air, and Jesus hung on the wall in his rightful place.

"Zola tells me you're an artist," she said.

"Singer," I said.

"Momma, he paints when he wants to. He wants me to model for him. . . don't you?"

"Sure, if your mother will give permission," I said.

"What would you like to drink?" asked Zola's mother.

There was a fully decked bar filled with her husband's private stock.

"Zola, get your man a drink," she said, pulling me aside and speaking quietly. "I, too, was once in love with an artist who was much older than I, so I can understand my child being attracted to such a man. But I warn you, Eric, my child. . . she is a psycho case. I allowed her to go to L.A. and stay at her grandmother's, but now I'm afraid of what goes on in that awful town, a dangerous town."

I toasted them both with the margarita that Zola had mixed.

"Salute!"

"So, I can trust you to look after my Zola in the big city, Eric?"

"Yeah, sure," I said.

"Good," she said as she walked by me, her perfume filling the room. "My husband, Juan, has a place picked out for us this evening."

The sun had gone down and all sorts of Vegas weirdness was coming out. We climbed inside a '57 Bel-Air, Zola in the rear seat.

"Would you like to drive my car?" her mother asked.

I noticed her fine, bird-like hands as she handed me the keys. Zola had told me her mother was a soap opera star in Mexico, and now I saw why. She was a Mexican Eartha Kitt look-alike. With perfect karmic timing, her mother turned up the radio and my voice came over the radio waves.

Mom was impressed.

Dinner, well, that was something I'll never forget. Her husband Juan worked at a local casino and took care of us personally as we dined in a chandeliered room, mirrors on the walls and an orchestra of about forty strings serenading us as we devoured lobster and white wine. It was just the three of us in that huge room.

"You must come and visit us in Mexico City," her mother said. "I would like to show you my town."

It was a great visit, and the next day—after Zola and I slept in separate rooms—I headed back to L.A.

There were many wonderful nights that summer and lots of pure weirdness on the *The Doors* shoot. It had a very strange effect on me, and spending time with Zola made it even more strange, especially her need to extract Jim Morrison tales out of me. It really shook me up. It was as if the bastard were still alive and pulling the strings from somewhere. Maybe he was getting revenge for the time I chased him out of my house with a gun.

It was like he owned this woman, like she was one of his angels sent to torment me. It was frustrating. We never spent a whole night together because she always had to get back to her grandmother's house in East L.A. before 1 A.M.

One night outside the Whisky, Oliver Stone was recreating the famous night of the Sunset Boulevard riots. Stone was tucked away beside us in his director's hut. I was just grooving on the overall scene, which included dozens of mint-condition, vintage cars filling several blocks of Sunset and the surrounding streets. It was a total recreation in the finest detail.

Harley engines began to rev, and Stone called "Action!" On the other side of the street, Val Kilmer and the other actors portraying the Doors crossed the crowded Sunset Strip.

Robby Krieger was spellbound as he watched a key moment in his own life recreated before his very eyes.

don't let me be misunderstood

I didn't bother to look at the shooting schedule, but when I got to the set the next day around three o'clock, I was sorely disappointed. The day's shoot would include only close-ups across the street from the Whisky. The extras had been sent home, and Zola had flown. My heart sank. The day dragged on. I spent most of it in my trailer reading. By nighttime, after dinner, I had a short conversation with Robby. He told me that after the movie was over, he'd be putting his own band together, and he wanted me to join him for some gigs.

"Sure," I said. It had been fun having Robby in my band before the movie got under way, and I looked forward to playing with him again.

"You seem down," said Robby.

"I am, kind of. This thing just didn't work out for me the way I expected it to."

"Hey, it'll be good for your career," he said. "And just think of the benefits."

He split, leaving me with my book. The end of the day rolled around, and everyone seemed to have something to do but me. Then Oliver poked his head through the door of the dressing room. "Hey, Eric, how's it going?"

"Oh, pretty good. Things working out for you the way you expected?" I asked.

"Oh, absolutely, I'm very happy. By the way, where did that accent of yours come from?"

"I'm a Geordie, from Northeastern England."

"Oh," he said. "Interesting." Then he was gone, closing the door behind him. The boredom dragged me down. When I finally was called to the set, it was for a little scene inside the Whisky. I had one line, ten seconds of screen time. Hardly what I'd been hanging around all this time waiting for.

I wish I could say it had been fun, I thought to myself as I packed up my gear in the small dressing room. I walked over to the makeup department for some cream and paper towels to remove the thick makeup. On my return to the trailer, I noticed a small envelope attached to the door handle. I excitedly tore it open. Inside was a note: "Dear Eric, Lots of love and good luck with your music. Zola."

The note included an address in Echo Park, in East L.A.—her grandmother's house.

I climbed into the car and headed for the I-10, endless lanes of L.A. traffic speeding by me. As I passed downtown, I looked out through the smoky horizon toward Echo Park. I pulled off and headed for the address on the note. I didn't imagine that Zola would be there, but maybe her grandmother could tell me where she was.

I pulled through the streets of East L.A., an obvious outsider, a target, and I felt it—the chilly stare from a crowd of gang members on a street corner, sidelong glances as I passed. When I found the right house, I went up and knocked on the door. After quite some time, an aged, matronly Mexican woman dressed in black answered the door. I fumbled with what little Spanish I know.

"Hola, buenos días. . . I am a friend of Zola's. Aquí?. . . Is she here?"

She smiled a yellowed, toothy grin and shook her head. "No here. In Hollywood. In movie. With husband."

"Husband?" I asked.

"Si," she said, still standing in the doorway and gesturing with her cane to a corner of the room behind her. With my puzzled look she stepped back and waved me into the room.

"You see," she said, gesturing.

I walked into the darkened, musky interior, and she shuffled ahead of me down a short hall. I followed her to a bedroom door, and she rested her cane against the wall as she tried the handle. The door finally swung inward, and the old lady reached around for the light switch. At first I couldn't make out anything as the overhead black light assaulted my eyes. The first thing I saw was a human skull on a pedestal. Above it was the famous Jim Morrison Lizard King portrait—Jim at his best. There were stacks of albums and magazines littering the room. Dead roses, and in the far corner an altar, at the center of which was a bust of Jim with a barbed-wire crown. A mirror behind the bust was a messy collage of photos and memorabilia.

"Husband," the old lady said again, pointing wildly with her cane.

I couldn't wait to get out of that house—and the neighborhood—and back on the highway to the sanity of the desert.

Shortly after *The Doors* wrapped, I got word from a Mexican promoter via my agent in the U.S. that I'd been invited to join a Woodstock-inspired festival with Jefferson Starship, Leon Russell, Edgar Winter, and Robby Krieger's new band. We would play Morales, Mazatlan, and wind up in the Plaza del Torres in Mexico City.

After Robby had left our band to do the movie, I'd brought in Larry Wilkins on guitar along with Brian Auger on keyboards, forming the Eric Burdon/Brian Auger Band. The festival tour sounded just right for us. Besides, I was due for a visit to Mexico.

Soon, I found myself on a hot afternoon in the marketplace of Mazatlan with Larry, just hanging out, grooving on the sights, sounds, and smells of the crowded market. There were plenty of local and federal police, as further south in the state of Chiapas revolution was taking place. Peasants were emerging from the jungles armed, wearing masks, and making impossible demands on the already overextended federal government.

The atmosphere freaked Larry out, but for me it was business as usual. In 1968, when I first played Mexico, I got my first taste of the ongoing strife. I had to perform in the wake of the slaughter of five-hundred students at the University of Mexico by government death squads. I'd nearly caused a riot when I went into a rap about how the Mexicans had given the world two precious things—marijuana and beautiful women. The crowd loved it, but I don't imagine the Mexican authorities did.

One stage with one of the finest guitarists I've ever known, Larry Wilkins, who lost his battle with cancer several years ago.

As Larry and I strolled around the market, I had kept my eye out for something that would always remind me of Mexico. I found a stall with children's toys, and in it was a display of wrestlers' masks, a popular cultural item throughout Mexico. The one I picked was a mask of a famous wrestler known as Octagon.

I knew I'd picked the right one when I tried it on, and little local kids swarmed around us, yelling "Octagon! Octagon!"

"It's a hit!" Larry said.

Right then and there I got the idea to use the mask in the show, to see if the audience would react—perhaps in the same way that the kids had reacted to my pot-and-beautiful-women rap thirty years before.

Before going on at the Plaza del Torres, I was backstage looking for something to smoke when two Mexican federales entered. One was in full quasi-gestapo uniform, and the other was in plain clothes. Brian Auger, in the process of getting into his stage clothes, looked on in horror, as did everyone else in the room, expecting this to be a bust. The guy in the uniform offered me a pull of tequila from a silver flask he had in his coat pocket.

I turned him down, saying, "Thanks, but no thanks."

Mr. Plainclothes, from the depths of his overcoat pocket, pulled out a ready-rolled spliff. There was silence throughout the tent. I gingerly accepted the offering, and then took a swig of the tequila so as not to offend.

"Salute!"

The cop who handed me the joint then took the bottle, also taking a swig with a thick-accented "Si! Salute! I remember you from '68. It was a fucking scandal! We love you, man!"

There was a palpable sigh of relief from everyone else backstage.

Thanks to the local officers, I was good and ready to take the stage before the thirty thousand fans who had gathered for their own version of Woodstock. Doors music remains hugely popular in Mexico, and the crowd was still singing "Come on baby light my fire" long after Robby's band had left the stage.

That would be tough to top, and it grew increasingly tougher as we were delayed taking the stage. Brian's specialized keyboard equipment wasn't working properly, and he wouldn't play until it was. I think almost a half hour passed as I cursed Jim Morrison, who seemed to haunt me from beyond the grave, as the audience continued to sing his words.

The restless crowd got even more restless, and I was sure we'd lost them. The momentum had slowed. Then I remembered the mask of

Octagon. I rushed back to the tent, stuffed the mask in my waistband and headed back to the stage. At last we were ready as Brian gave the thumbs up. Before walking out onstage I donned the mask, and as soon as they saw me, the crowd went wild. It had worked. They were ours.

When we left the stage triumphantly, I ran into my two new best friends in Mexican law enforcement.

"We remember, hombre! It was a scandal!" the now slightly drunken plainclothes officer said, shaking his finger at me.

The Mexican tour was a heartening experience after the letdown of *The Doors* movie, and I returned to Los Angeles in good spirits, looking forward to more touring and recording with Brian Auger.

I'd brought the Octagon mask back with me and once back in L.A. again my thoughts turned to Zola.

I got the idea to send the mask to her, if I could find her. After my haunting experience at her grandmother's place in East L.A., I figured it was better to send a package to her parents' place in Vegas.

I didn't hear anything from Zola, or her parents, for about a year. Then, out of the blue I got a letter postmarked Paris, France. I was disappointed to find there was no letter inside. Just a Polaroid of three people standing in front of Jim Morrison's graffiti-scarred grave in the famed Père Lachaise Cemetery. Two of them I didn't recognize. But in the middle was Zola, made obvious by her studded leather jacket and her beautiful bronze face obscured by the Octagon mask I'd mailed to Vegas.

Written on the back in a greasy eyebrow pencil were—what else—more words from the long-departed Jim Morrison.

"All the children. . . are insane."

CHAPTER 16

new orleans

 ay back in 1964, when I started out with MGM, I'd begun asking for some involvement in movies, since the company was at the time one of the biggest studios in Hollywood.

To keep me happy, they threw me a bone or two. One of these bones was a meeting with Burt Bacharach at his London apartment where we had dinner and talked over some of my musical movie ideas. Unfortunately, the one we ended up doing was *Beach Party A GoGo*. I guess the only memorable thing to come out of it was meeting his then-wife, Angie Dickenson. She looked radiant that night in a bright orange knit dress and shoes to match. I never forgot that dress.

Angie and I met again in the mid-'80s when I was doing "Larry King Live" in Washington, D.C. Among the guests appearing earlier on the show were Angie Dickenson and General Alexander Haig, which made for a fun evening of left and right ideologies. My interview went well, and there were lots of call-ins, and Larry seemed to be a sympathetic kind of guy. I was thrilled that Angie had stayed throughout the length of my interview. As I came off the set, I shook hands with her, and I reminded her of our first meeting, mentioning the orange dress; she was flattered that I'd remembered over such a long period of time, and from that point on we were talking like old friends.

I was getting ready to leave, putting on my jacket, when Angie came walking back toward me. "May I ask you a question?" she said.

"Of course."

"Have you seen the monuments here in D.C.?"

"No," I said. "I've never had that pleasure."

"Well," she said, "there's no time like the present."

I looked at my watch.

"Look, I have a limousine waiting outside," Angie said. "Come. Believe me I'm be the best guide that you could find."

Soon after, we were standing beneath the massive white marble image of Abe Lincoln. I was impressed with its size. It just didn't seem that big on film or in photographs. We stood at the top of the stairs in the warm night air and looked out over the lights of the city. Angie sat down on the marble stairs, took a deep breath, shook her hair back and looked into the sky. "Aahh, God, things were so different when Jack was around. He was just too good. It was all too good, too good to last."

"Yes," I said. "I can remember, as I guess everyone else who lived through it can remember, that very moment where I was when I head the news of Kennedy's death."

"Will we ever return?" she asked, her voice almost lost in the wind. The silence between us seemed to say more than anything.

Our next stop was the Vietnam memorial. As we approached the site, I was shocked. Angie linked arms with me as we walked slowly toward the shrine in silence. The sight of it humbled me. As we neared the spot, I saw three men wearing combat jackets with military patches on their shoulders. They had a small gas burner, blue flames hissing from it as they heated water for their coffee. A small battery-powered tape cassette was playing '60s music. We were invisible to them; they talked on in low tones, not even looking in our direction. I found it difficult to hold back the tears welling in my eyes.

Angie stepped forward: Her long, fine elegant fingers touched the dark black marble monument. We were fused in our silence. I'm English by birth, but have considered myself Californian for decades. Standing in front of that memorial made me think that, after Vietnam, the United States lost the dream and became just another piece of real estate.

Such things were on my mind, as it was at this time that I decided to become an American citizen. Back in L.A., I arranged to meet with an immigration inspector and my lawyer. I will always remember the inspector, Mrs. Lopez. She was a little Hispanic woman with huge teeth, efficient and officious in her task of rooting out devious, drunken communist spies like me, and she had before her a stuffed manila folder documenting all the evil I had done.

"Have you ever had a felony arrest?" she asked.

"No," I replied.

"Have you ever been arrested?" This was the loaded question. I looked at my lawyer, who nodded that I should answer.

"Sure," I said. "I've been in the hands of the police. I'm always in the hands of the police in the business I'm in!"

Mrs. Lopez didn't see humor in this or anything else I said, and she reached into her big envelope.

"OK. Do you remember this?" she began.

"You were stopped in the San Fernando Valley, wobbling from one lane to the next. You were drunk—under the influence of alcohol and probably chemicals. You failed the roadside test miserably. You were 43 years of age and you had a German national with you in the car who was only 19 years of age."

"This is America," I quipped, "I thought you got awards for stuff like that!"

Mrs. Lopez wasn't amused.

Actually, the incident itself wasn't all that funny, either. I'd been a real asshole with the police, but they had egged me on. They cuffed me and bounced my head off the roof of the cruiser, and they'd made the young girl walk the line too. She was just the passenger—but she had a killer body, a short, tight skirt, high-heel shoes, and the cops wanted to get a look at her incredible ass in action. I was out of control when they did this, but calmed down remarkably quickly when it looked like I was going to get a beating to tame my temper.

Lucky for me the breathalizer machine was on the blink. Somehow I managed to slither through the episode without getting charged, but it was a turning point for me. Ever since, I've been very careful to have a driver if I'm drinking.

As I was leaving the station, the cop in the lockup was handing me back my personal belongings—watch, credit cards, loose cash, and my wallet. As he handed the wallet to me, a tab of acid fell out and hit the table in front of him.

See what happens when you wind out your Porsche to 120 mph on California's Highway 101 ... busted again.

He looked at it and he looked at me and said, "You are a bad little motherfucker, aren't you?"

I shrugged. "Sorry."

"Trash it right now," he said.

For a split second I thought about wetting my finger and popping it into my mouth. That would be it—no evidence and I could walk out free and stoned.

"Don't even think about it!" he snapped, reading me like a book. "Trash it now."

I figured I'd gotten away with enough already and did as he asked.

Despite Mrs. Lopez's obvious disapproval as she reminded me about this embarrassing incident, it was insufficient grounds to refuse my petition for citizenship. Not long after, I found myself standing with dozens of other immigrants before a justice of the peace taking the oath of allegiance and becoming a U.S. citizen.

Angie Dickenson's tour of historic Washington gave me an added sense of "home." But there was another place in America that had been calling me, and the time was right to heed the call.

As soon as I arrived in the baggage claim area at the New Orleans airport I knew I'd done the right thing. There was the gang of Brit Boys: Keith Landells, Shelto, Craig, Mark Popkins, Tony Lyons from Boston, Lico from Guatemala; and the girls, Libby, Kate, and Lusanna, all there to welcome me. Lusanna had driven her Buick convertible for the occasion. Crazy Alex, at the wheel of his van, followed behind us as we rolled down the freeway toward the French Quarter. Lusanna looked wonderful in her black mini-skirt and low-cut tank top, beads of sweat rolling off her neck down to her soft, supple breasts. Her blonde hair waved in the wind as she sang along with the radio. I was back in the Big Easy and it felt good. L.A. and its ghosts didn't even cross my mind.

My friends had the evening's events all planned out. First we went to the projects and visited the Petroleum Lounge, where I ended up jamming with the Trem Band. I sang "St. Louis Blues," a song that I've held in my heart since I was a child. What a kick it was jamming with these guys, whose ages ranged from fifteen to seventy. A couple of huge tubas pumping away, two trombones, three trumpets and a marching snare drum. It was a wonderful feeling that took me back to my teenage years of club jams in Newcastle with Mighty Joe Young's Jazzmen.

Out of the Petroleum Lounge and back to the streets, we went cruising past the mansions and the trees hung with Spanish moss. The air smelled sweet; the night was dangerous and exciting.

It was the month of May, it was my birthday, and it was Jazz Fest time. My birthday gift was a large inflatable alligator, filled not with oxygen but with nitrous oxide. I took my new pal with me everywhere we went that night.

There I was at Tipatina's hanging off the balcony, one arm around Lusanna, my head in the sky, my soul bursting as the mighty Neville Brothers rocked the stage.

My belly ached from laughing.

When my British friend Keith Landells found me with the deflated alligator, he said, "Not to worry, lad, there's more." He introduced me to a wild Irishman, Paddy, who drove an MG with a large tank of nitrous, fitted with rubber air hoses that ran all the way up to the seats. We were losing it completely as we rolled along in the French Quarter.

Back on foot, we were staggering up Magazine Street, where we met kind-hearted Sister Mary. She was convinced I was possessed by the devil and made me get down on my hands and knees on the corner of Frenchman and Magazine and pray.

"Anybody who takes drugs in order to laugh has got to be in league with the devil!" she screamed at me. "Get down on your knees and pray for forgiveness."

The Brit boys all gathered around to witness this hilarious event. But she was right, it was time to clean up my act.

don't let me be misunderstood

I awoke the next morning in my elegant room in the Casa de Moraine, with Sister Mary lying next to me, fully clothed and snoring. On the floor was my wasted, twisted friend the alligator.

Then came the shocking phone call.

I've no idea how they found me because I didn't tell anyone I was going to New Orleans. But the phone rang and I got the news: My mother had died. It hit even harder to find out I couldn't get a flight for two days.

Rene had always been so joyous. It had been soul-destroying to see her in such pain and unable to laugh. I wandered slowly through the French Quarter; the smiling faces of people passing by made me envious.

It was peace at last for Rene, but for me it was time to step up to the plate and face the world for the first time really alone. I wished I could just disappear.

I trundled from place to place, heading in the general direction of Jimmy's club, where I knew Snooks Eglin was performing. I took a shot of alcohol in every bar on the way uptown. I knew if anyone could make me feel better, Snooks could. Blind, he'd started out as a street singer in the city of New Orleans at fourteen or fifteen. His influences were everything and anything that he heard coming from the doorways of that musical city—jukeboxes, radios, other musicians. The music came pouring back out through his fingers and throat. And though his voice aged to a weathered, soulful croak, his music remained forever youthful and strong. I knew he had the healing power, and the night my mother died I needed a shot of rhythm and blues. Within the smoky club, standing near the front row, the force of the crowd held me up. I fell under the influence of the blues chords and let the tears roll down my face onto my shirt. I went with the mighty river's flow.

"The greatest lesson to be learned in love is letting go." I kept telling myself this. My mother was now free of pain and, God willing, reunited with her beloved husband, my father Matt. I knew I was in the best possible place in the world to experience what I was going through. New Orleans is as much about death as it is about life. It's the spirit-world walking amongst us. No medications or meditations could serve to ease my mind at a time like this. So I let the Big Easy lift me up and carry me through. Snooks Eglin put me in the best possible place.

Eventually, I ended up back at Tipatina's to share the good medicine of the mighty Neville Brothers once more. They were rocking and the people were singing. Leaving the bar, I found myself shuffling my feet and doing a little dance. Later on, after the gig, I stood in the street barefoot, my hands in my pockets, looking up at the sky. A familiar face approached me. It was Art Neville.

"I heard about your trouble, Eric," he said. "You want to be able to go to that funeral and stand up like a man and do your thing. We've all been there," he said with a kindly smile. He was the first person I'd spoken to since I received the news some ten hours earlier. Art grabbed my hand and pumped it slowly in a fatherly handshake. He leaned over and whispered in my ear, "Look, I got a suggestion. Instead of trying to get up there and make a speech at the funeral, I want to give you a song, a song you can sing. You just tell that preacher up front, 'Hey, I won't be doing no talkin'. I'm a singer, you understand. I've got a song and want to sing it.' And then Art sang gently in my ear:

"Will the circle be unbroken,
By and by, Lord, by and by,
There's a better world a waitin',
In the sky, Lord, in the sky."

A gentle rain began to fall. Art leaned closer and said, "Do you understand? You got it?"

"Sure, I got it," I said. "I'm okay. You take care." And he was off into the night.

A friendly New Orleans cop stopped and said he was a fan. He gave me a ride home to Kate's, shining his powerful light onto the lock until I inserted the key and made my way inside.

The forty-eight hours passed slowly, but finally I was on a flight out of New Orleans to Miami, then on to Heathrow, then to Newcastle for my mother's funeral.

CHAPTER 17

lost within the halls
of fame

A fter my mother's death I got back on the road—the only place I felt even reasonably comfortable. For three years, the Eric Burdon/ Brian Auger Band played clubs, pubs, and theaters around the world.

While on the road, it's essential to my performance that I eat dinner at 5:30 each night, which gives me three or four hours to digest my food before singing.

On one occasion, we were working the Fire House in Seattle, staying at the Black Angus Motel, which was attached to a restaurant and lounge. I was headed toward my evening meal when I passed the lounge door and heard someone giving a great impersonation of Elvis Presley.

"Are you lonesome tonight? Do you miss me tonight?"

The guy was right on the button. He had a beautiful voice. I stood there in the doorway of the lounge looking in. The place was empty except for this one guy on the karaoke machine, and the barkeep who was getting ready for the evening.

I'd seen karaoke machines before on drunken nights in Japan, and

On stage with British keyboard veteran Brian Auger.

watched Japanese businessmen only too happy to make fools of themselves, but I'd never actually ever sung on one. When "Elvis" finished, I walked up to the machine to see what songs were listed. There was "House of the Rising Sun." Some perverse urge took over. The sounds came rolling at me, and I grabbed the mike, which had a lot of reverb on it. It felt good—and actually sounded better than some of the crappy sound systems I've been lumbered with over the years. I was halfway through the second verse when I thought, "Shit, no wonder people swing on these things!"

After I'd finished the tune the guy behind the bar called out, "Hey, that was pretty good! Here, have a free margarita. Why don't you come back later?"

A lark turns pathetic pretty quickly when a former No. 1 rock star is caught singing his own song on a karaoke machine. Talk about a Spinal Tap moment!

In the wake of my mother's death, I was drifting, sliding from gig to gig, not really feeling much interest in anything, including the band. Brian Auger ran everything, and I cut him a good deal when we produced a double live CD for a German record label. The lineup was Brian on keyboards, Dave Meros on bass, Larry Wilkins on guitar, and Brian's son Karma on drums. The band was a great jammin' outfit. A little too jazzy for my liking, but it served me well until I got my head and heart back together. Brian's family was good to me, and I was always welcome at their place in Venice, California. It is a crazy, wonderful household. His wife, Ella, is Italian and Brian couldn't be more British. They make a wonderful couple, have been married for years, and have three great children.

The band toured constantly, across the U.S. and Canada, Germany, Yugoslavia, Japan, and Hungary. In Budapest, we played an outdoor festival, which normally would have been a blast. But I had a summer flu and was suffering in the heat. After performing, I walked off stage and headed back to the dressing room area, where there was an open bar. I lay my head on the table, drained. Then I felt the touch of a cool hand, and looked up into the most beautiful, clear, blue eyes I'd ever seen, framed by gorgeous blonde hair.

"Hello, I am Judit," she said, adding something in German that I didn't understand.

"I think she said she wants to show you her wonderful city," said Brian, coming to my rescue.

"Welcome to Budapest," Judit said. "Would you like some French champagne?"

Backstage was packed with people, and I was sitting in my wet stage clothes. It seemed like everyone was looking at me and Judit.

Over in one corner, Larry Wilkins, the Indian in the band, was showing off his beads and his medicine pouch to three Hungarian beauties. I just sat there staring into the face of Judit. I gave her the name of my hotel and my room number.

She said "I call you, OK?"

"OK," I said.

As Judit disappeared, the band and a few locals piled onto the bus to continue the party. I lay in my bunk just thinking of her.

The next morning at 10:30, the phone rang. "I'm Judit, hello... in 45 minutes I will come. Please you will meet me?"

"Yes," I said.

When I went downstairs, there she was, looking radiant, with several old men waiting in line to kiss her on the cheek. She explained that she was a well-known fashion model in Hungary.

If her plan was to do me in, it worked. She took me to a High Mass at noon in the cathedral in the heart of the city. With the war heating up in Bosnia, the vibe was very heavy. A choir sang from a balcony, wondrous voices silenced for so long by communism, now vibrant once more. It brought tears to my eyes.

Later, sitting in a park that had once been reserved for the use of Communist Party officials, we sat and held each other and kissed.

"When do you must go?" she asked in her unusual, captivatingly sexy English.

"Tomorrow," I said.

"Then now do I make love to you."

Ever notice how grammar just doesn't matter sometimes? I took her by the hand and we went back across town to my hotel.

Love was being good to me, but business, as usual, was bad. When we set up the band's arrangements, Brian Auger had used an agent who subbed for a large conglomerate of agents, managers, and attorneys. These people would fuck a dead rat if they thought they could make a dime out of it. Our man, whom I call "Hoover," worked out of the San Fernando Valley. His office was an old, red English double-decker bus. As a booker he was unbelievably good and kept us working, if anything more than we wanted to. His girlfriend, soon to become his wife, confided in me that he was using massive amounts of cocaine, which worried me. But Brian didn't seem to mind, as long as we got our dough and the gigs kept coming.

I'd make unannounced visits to Hoover's place, and nothing seemed out of place, but his wife would take me aside and tell me horror stories about this guy doing crack and beating her up, covering the windows with cardboard because he was getting so paranoid. I couldn't figure out if it was real or all her imagination. But I did become concerned when a washed-up guitarist I'd fired years before started showing up at gigs and being overly friendly with Hoover.

Brian assumed that all was under control. When we were out touring, Brian's wife would keep an eye on things and make sure all was OK. The money was counted and checks were processed on time. Between Jeri in my office and Brian's office, things seemed to be all right.

Then something weird happened. Hoover and his wife were arrested in a bank by FBI agents, busted right there at the teller's window accused of being bank robbers. They weren't, of course. But Hoover kept a money satchel on his right calf, and he was unlucky enough to resemble a known felon. He and his wife were so wired on crack that their nervous behavior had everyone in the bank convinced they were about to stick up the joint.

Alarmed by this somewhat bizarre incident, we looked into the accounts and found that our agent and his wife had craftily managed to inhale about $20,000 of our money. That's why I call him Hoover. He divorced his wife and disappeared to Florida with my money dripping from his nose.

In stepped one of his business partners. Let's call him Lenny. He said that *his* boss wanted to sign me to a multi-media deal for recordings, videos, books, and more. I went to a meeting in their corporate office and was stunned by the amount of activity going on. There were several agents working away on computers. Phones were ringing and faxes flying. I decided I'd sign with them, but only if I had a solid "out" clause in my contract.

Naturally, they weren't so closely tied to "Hoover" that they were willing to cover my losses with him.

But I met the boss, and got the "nice to have you aboard" stroking, complete with "Springsteen has told us he'd like to produce your next album" and "How about an album of Randy Newman songs?"

I hired a lawyer to put the contract together, and once the deal was done I felt pretty optimistic once more. Springsteen, it turned out, really was interested in producing my next album, though nothing tangible ever arose. It didn't take long for me to realize that it was just the Eric Burdon/Brian Auger Band with a big agency behind it. Nothing had really changed. The gigs were about the same, we got the same amount of press, and made the same number of celebrity appearances.

After a year I was no closer to locking in a solid recording contract, so I decided I wanted out. But the lawyer I'd hired fucked up the deal. I didn't have the out-clause I'd asked for. The agency turned around and hit me with a bill for 20 percent of my past live shows and filed a lawsuit for breach of contract. Yet another lawyer managed to get the settlement down to $30,000.

With this depressing sequence of developments weighing on me, we were back out there on the road, somewhere in Germany in late 1993.

"Test, test."

I had my head in front of the monitors when Brian's smiling face appeared. "Hey, congratulations, mate. The Animals have just been voted into the Rock and Roll Hall of Fame."

"Nice," I said.

Brian handed me the telegram and shook my hand vigorously. "Cool, hey?"

"Yeah, thanks, man."

There I was in Germany, hard-pressed to deal with my latest finan-

Eric Burdon

Together again: Animals John Steel, me, Hilton Valentine and Dave Rowberry get
inducted into L.A.'s Rock Walk of Fame on my 60th birthday in May, 2001. We
played together for the first time in years later that night. Photo by Karen Monster.

cial disasters, and they wanted me to fly to Cleveland for the January
1994 induction ceremony. The plain truth was I couldn't afford to go. I
needed to make a living. I didn't expect anyone would believe or understand. Radio host Howard Stern complained, "That's Eric Burdon, he's
always doing that kind of stuff. He's just trying to piss people off, he
won't turn up."

What could I do about it? I was truly honored by the award, but I
couldn't attend without blowing a bunch of European dates. I found out
later that at the Rock and Roll Hall of Fame ceremony, Alan refused to
sit with Chas, Hilton, and John. A real team player to the end, eh?

A few years later, the Burdon/Auger Band had run its course. Larry
Wilkins and Dave Meros hung in there with me, and I hired a second
guitarist, Dean Restum, and Mark Craney to play drums. I called the
new group the I Band, inspired by California artist Von Dutch's "Flying
Eye" design. This band fit me like a glove and there was a feeling of
mutual respect. In the summer of 1995, we went out on the road doing

the full-tilt boogie. Once again, the Rock and Roll Hall of Fame came calling, asking if I would come to Cleveland for the concert celebrating the opening of the Rock and Roll Hall of Fame Museum, housed in a new building designed by I.M. Pei. "Hell, yes!" I said.

I wanted to do the show with my new band, but the museum wanted to make a big splash pairing me with Jon Bon Jovi and a selection of musicians that included Booker T. and Steve Cropper. It's kind of hard to turn that down.

As soon as I arrived in the city, I could feel a difference. My previous visit there had been dismal. We played in midwinter to half-filled houses, surprised that anyone came at all, it was so cold. Now it seemed somebody had turned the light back on. To walk on stage for the Rock and Roll Hall of Fame concert to a live audience of eighty thousand, with God knows how many watching on television, was indeed a thrill.

It was one of the best television productions that I have ever seen or been involved with. I was amazed the way they were able to turn over the stage. One act after another moved in and out, for hours, with no problems. The star-studded event included Jackson Browne, James Brown, Bruce Springsteen, Chuck Berry, Aretha Franklin, Little Richard, John Mellencamp, Chrissie Hynde, John Fogerty, Al Green . . . the list went on.

My two songs with Bon Jovi—"We Gotta Get Outta This Place" and "It's My Life"—were over in a flash. It would have been nice to do more, as Bon Jovi himself is a sweet man and an enormous vocal talent . . . one of the nice guys who finished first. The crowd seemed to like us, and after leaving the stage I kicked back to enjoy the rest of the evening. For awhile I hung out with Martha Reeves's grandmother and the rest of her family, sitting near a massive TV monitor watching the events unfold. When I heard that Al Green was coming up, I knew I had to get out there and immerse myself in the throng. Slipping away from my appointed bodyguard, who had been my shadow all day, I made my way past the side of the staging area, past a TV production truck, down a loading ramp, and into the massive stadium crowd. Just then the Kinks took the stage:

"Oh, yeah, you've really got me goin',
you've got me so I don't know what I'm doin', oh, yeah."

They really kicked it up, just like I remember them doing, circa '66, and the audience lit up. At one point, Ray Davies pulled off his silk British flag jacket, turned it inside out and put it back on as the flag of the United States. What a great, simple trick. They rocked the house. I was proud to be Brit.

The Steve Cropper/Booker T. band set down a smooth groove as I danced my way into the crowd and found my own space. When Al Green took the stage, I was swept away with emotion.

"Does anybody know what I'm talking about?
I go to my brother on my knees and I'm begging,
Please, it's all in his eyes, he's the preacher man."

It had such an effect on me that I promised myself the next book I'd pick up would be the Holy Bible—something I had never read. As Al's great Southern voice continued to caress, it seemed the whole world was moving in one vibe—"one love," as the great spirit dancer Bob Marley had put it.

The next day I visited the museum. As I stepped through the door I looked up and was greeted by a massive projection on the wall. It was the Animals in action, ancient BBC footage shot long before the crowd of kids that now surrounded me was born. How had I made the journey from that long-ago world to this one so quickly?

CHAPTER 18

not one thin dime from the fat man

I'm fortunate that I live in a place where I can begin the day at sunrise, take a cold mountain shower, feel the early morning sun on my back and ride my motorcycle into the high desert until the day gets too hot. In the evenings, I cruise past hundreds of perfectly tended palms, the smell of oranges in the air. Even one day like this a month and all the shit seems worth it.

On just such a night I was riding in downtown Palm Springs when, out of the corner of my eye, I spotted something in the window of a local record store. It was one of Elvis's gold suits—dusty and wrinkled, but unmistakable. And it was not unreasonable to see such a thing out in the desert, as Elvis had a long connection to Palm Springs. It was where he and Priscilla honeymooned, and where he liked to come when Graceland closed in on him and he needed some solid Harley time. I pulled up to the store and stopped. I'd met several people in the valley who claimed to have Elvis connections. A mate of mine said he had a Cadillac that was given to him by the King. There was a local guy who, for about $2,500, bought a secondhand Harley only to lift the saddle and find an engraved plate: "To Elvis, with love from Priscilla." Suddenly he had a Harley that was more valuable than his house.

The I Band was tight, and we were doing well on the club circuit, both in America and Europe. But it had been awhile since my face had appeared on television, and television exposure is how to get your music heard. I'd staggered out of the darkness of a local movie theater after seeing *To Die For.* The seductive red lips and pale white skin of Nicole Kidman spoke to me, saying, "You're nobody unless you're on a screen these days."

It was true. My only recent outing had been jamming with Paul Shaffer's band on Letterman's show. I'd done a couple of videos but they'd gone nowhere. The first one never even made it to the music networks. The second one (insert self-mocking laughter here) was for a song on the soundtrack of *Joe Versus the Volcano,* one of Tom Hanks's only box office bombs.

It's frustrating when your past is bigger than you are. The only thing that could change that for me, I believed, would be television.

It was then that I got a call from someone I'll call the Fat Man. He'd opened a new recording studio in downtown Palm Springs, called Sun Recorders. I wondered how he'd pulled that off without getting sued—there was only one Sun recording studio—Sam Phillips's legendary place in Memphis.

It was a hot summer morning as I parked my Harley outside and went through the swinging glass doors at the entrance to Sun Recorders. It was dark and cool inside, and there was that electric hum in the air. An attractive redhead sat behind a desk overseeing an array of phones. My eyes adjusting to the darkness, I took off my shades.

"Eric Burdon. I'm here to see [the Fat Man]."

She seemed protective of her boss.

"What's your name again?"

From down the darkened corridor I heard a roar of laughter. In a flash, the Fat Man embraced me as if we were old friends.

"Eric, how the hell ya been?"

He pumped my hand while a broad ringmaster's smile spread across his face. Suit pants with no jacket. The pants said he took care of business. Not having a jacket said, "Hey, I'll work with you."

In his inner sanctum, the Fat Man sat behind his glass-top desk and talked fast. He mentioned a publishing deal he'd made with several top country stars.

He explained, as if I didn't know, that if I used the Animals' name my earning power would double instantly. It was a painful subject with me. He dropped Sonny Bono's name here and there—at that time, Bono was mayor of Palm Springs—and made a phone call to Nashville to get me talking to some guitar player. He reminded me that he was close friends with Mike Curb, the head of MGM when I'd been there, but said with a huge smile that Curb held no grudges against me for having picketed MGM all those years ago.

I was suspicious of the Fat Man, and I had need to be. Of all the times there was a warning sign of trouble ahead, this was the one most blatant: The paper in Palm Springs, the *Desert Sun,* had sent a writer out to cover a show I was doing locally and he noticed the Fat Man at the gig.

"[The Fat Man] watched Burdon perform. . . with dollar bills in his eyes," the reporter wrote. Talk about foreshadowing! If I'd only read that column and paid heed I might have avoided stepping on another land mine.

But the Fat Man was one of those attractive hazards. He seemed to have all the tools to help me do what I wanted to at that point. It turned out he also owned the record store where I'd seen the Elvis suit, so I figured he was solidly settled in the community.

A few weeks after our first meeting, I stopped by the studios to talk some more. "Come on in," said the Fat Man, ear to the phone, putting his finger to his lips. "Sssshhh."

He covered the mouthpiece and whispered, "I'm talking to the Colonel in Vegas."

"Yeah, Yeah," he laughed into the receiver. "Yeah, boss, I see what you mean."

I sat there quietly going through a trade magazine as he talked away.

"That was the Colonel himself," said the Fat Man as he hung up. He was speaking of an even fatter man, the guy who had managed Elvis.

"I think I should introduce you to the Colonel." Before I could even think of what was going to happen next, the Fat Man was on the phone again, redialing Vegas. He quickly introduced me, and I heard an aging, wicked voice on the other end of the line. He said something about coming down to Palm Springs.

"You're a singer, are ya?"

"Yes," I said.

"Well, keep singing those songs. And remember, get a good lawyer."

After I'd hung up, the Fat Man and I went out for lunch. Inside the cool interior of a Japanese restaurant, he laid it all out for me. He was going to own the new local NBC TV affiliate, he said. We'd record a new CD of all the old Animals' hits, hawk it on the Home Shopping Network and license the new recordings to Hollywood. Why would anyone want the old mono recordings, he asked, when they could have a new digital stereo version?

After lunch he showed me around his facility, and I was impressed. He stroked me good. I was all ears.

A week or so later we had a meeting with two guys from L.A. who were pioneers in the CD-ROM revolution, and I got a comprehensive demonstration on the possibilities of interactive media. I was impressed.

So I sold my soul to the Fat Man.

Soon after, the Colonel came calling. The old guy was in town for the unveiling of a star on Palm Springs's new Walk of Fame. The star was for Ricky Nelson, and there was a major media event, attended by thousands of fans. Everyone was there to see the Colonel up close. In his days, he'd been a big, cigar-chomping dude, the ringmaster of his own circus. But age had reduced him to a little old man in a wheelchair, peering out from under the straw hat that protected him from the afternoon desert sun.

He was flanked by Elvis clones. In their multicolored, sparkling, caped-crusader uniforms, they stood with arms folded and heads bowed. And there, standing behind the Colonel with a huge smile on his face was the Fat Man. A microphone howled. "Testing, one, two, three." The Colonel was going to say a few words about Elvis.

His nasal voice drifted over the crowd as he read "My Memories of Elvis," a poem he wrote soon after Elvis's death. He was half done before I noticed how bizarre the words were.

"It was Elvis here and Elvis there.
And teddy bears were everywhere.
It was Don't Be Cruel and Such A Night.
And he sang Mamma, That's All Right.
He was All Shook Up and G.I. Blues.
And Girls, Girls, Girls and potluck too.
Kissin' Cousins and roustabout.
And then we knew what he was all about."

It was a hilarious, if a little pathetic. But there were a lot of moist eyes among the faithful on the street that day.

I had a good feeling about the Fat Man, as it seemed his business was firmly established in Palm Springs. As soon as the ink was dry on the contract I moved my guys from L.A. to begin recording. It was the first time I'd heard this band in the studio. Live onstage is one thing. In the studio, it's different. I was having fun again. We were recording. We cut "Fever," a Little Willie John classic, a song dedicated to Robert Johnson, and a track written by John Bunderick known as "Rabbit, I

271

Don't Mind." The tracks were cool. They were clean. Now I could begin to write and record in earnest and return to the arena where I belonged, Maybe the bad spell was over. It was with this optimistic hope that I did something my heart told me not to do: I rerecorded a handful of Animals' tunes.

The band and I then hit the road for a European tour, and I soon found out, to my horror, that the Fat Man had done me in.

As soon as I'd left Palm Springs, he'd bootlegged the tapes to a small Italian label called Disky. It only made it worse that the final mixing and mastering was so bad that the programmed drum click tracks spilled over the ends of the songs. It was an embarrassment. When I returned to Palm Springs, the Fat Man, his whole family and his whole business had disappeared. The only bright spot in the whole mess was that Martin Scorcese somehow got a hold of my rerecording of "House of the Rising Sun" and used it in a prominent place in the movie *Casino*. I was honored that the great director had graced the drama with my voice—but I didn't receive one thin dime. Fucked again—fucked twice over the same song!

The check went to the Fat Man, who, I assume, is still out there somewhere, selling my voice out of the trunk of his car.

It's taken me such a long time to learn that every time I sit in front of a microphone, whatever comes out of my mouth is likely to be ripped off by someone who will find a way to sell it without my control.

In this new world of MP3 downloads and the culture of fan tape trading that the Grateful Dead so generously encouraged, I may be swimming against the tide—but I've been taken advantage of by bootleggers to such an extent that I can never abide the practice. In fact it was when I realized how badly I'd been ripped off that I really reached my low point, back in the mid-1980s.

For awhile, I didn't care if I lived or died. Only the existence of my daughter and all the kind fans who continued to attend my shows kept me going.

On stage at my 60th birthday gig at L.A.'s El Rey Theater, me and by beautiful daughter Alex. Photo by Karen Monster.

Over the years, I recorded countless times, during writing sessions, at rehearsals, and during auditions for new musicians. Many of these tapes have been ripped off, copied or, in some cases, released as legitimate albums by record companies. In one case, a washed-up guitarist I fired years ago flooded the market with illegitimate material. Besides the pain, disgust, and anguish it causes, this leakage and deception also undermine record companies' interest in new, legitimate recordings. But the tide is turning.

One night in Germany, I was halfway through a set when I noticed a set of white-knuckled hands holding a tape recorder aloft. I brought the show to a screeching halt.

"You! You there! I want that cassette or the show's over. No more songs 'til I get that fucking tape!"

The kid tried to run and I yelled at the crowd to stop him. They did—his machine crashed to the floor and was then passed, like the body of a mosher, to the foot of the stage. I picked it up and threw it down on the

273

stage. The crowd loved it. I went over and grabbed our monitor man Ullie's Zippo and a can of lighter fluid. With the crowd cheering, I doused the tape machine. After a moment I dropped the Zippo and the recorder erupted in a putrid tower of rancid plastic- smoke.

I can't deal personally with every bootlegger that way, but I wish I could.

In Europe, in early 2000, I won a big case involving some stolen and illegally licensed material, and I currently have my sights on one particular thieving bastard in the U.S.

Let me say this directly to my fans: If it ain't in this book's discography or on a major label, it's probably an illegal release. And there are dozens of them out there. Whether they're called *Baltimore Live* or *Live in Pasadena, Japan or Australia,* they're stolen, and if you buy them you're putting cash in my enemies' pockets.

Still, I'm a realist. I know the stuff's out there—even my never-officially released *Mirage* project—and it isn't going away. So I'm working to gather all this bootlegged material and will offer it to my fans to download for free on my official Web site (ericburdon.com) so collectors can enjoy it. And so certain thieving fuckers no longer make a dime off my voice.

CHAPTER 19

house of the rising
sun

A rainy day in New Orleans can be really special, and it had been raining all day. My girlfriend Lusanna looked out the window into the yard. It was deep, deep green out there—tropical. It could have been Thailand, or perhaps Guam. But this was the Big Easy.

"See, that's what I'm talking about," she said, applying lipstick. "That's why the people of New Orleans have the blues. It's always raining."

I hadn't seen Lusanna for about two years. She was looking good, getting her act together. She was working the bar at the old Absinthe House and had nearly finished her studies to become a nurse.

I was in New Orleans to play at the Shrimp Festival. I'd flown in early to enjoy a lazy, rainy day kicking back and indulging in the wonders of Lusanna.

Marvin Gaye was on the box.

"Umm, nice," she said as she tripped through the room.

"Yeah, St. Marvin of the brokenhearted," I said.

"Yeah," she agreed. "Great music for a rainy day." She stopped to put on a little more lipstick. "I really gotta go. I gotta work tonight until at least one-thirty. Unless you want to stop by around two, I won't see you until tomorrow."

"I have a dinner appointment tonight, and that's going to go until ten, ten-thirty. If I'm still up I'll come by and get you, okay?"

"Okay, baby," she said, and she was out the door.

The rain was coming down heavily, bouncing off the sidewalk. Lusanna rushed toward the open door of her cab, a newspaper over her head. I smiled as I realized I'd watched her grow from a girl of seventeen into a woman.

My longtime guitarist Dean Restum, his girlfriend Tracy, and I had been invited to dinner by Darlene Jacobs Levy. I'd met Darlene through my friend Jan Densmore, a girl who had all the contacts in New Orleans and whom I'd known for years. She was a writer for Hollywood, working in the French Quarter. Whatever there was to be seen and done in the city of New Orleans, Jan knew exactly where it was located.

So I had reason to believe her when she said the original House of the Rising Sun had been found. For years I'd hoped to find the actual building that inspired the song that had meant so much to me. My quest had taken me to some strange places.

The phone rang. I grabbed for a towel, and it was Jan on the line.

"Hi, baby, what's happening?"

"Oh, nothing, just toweling off, staying cool. I'm ready for tonight, looking forward to it."

"Yes," said Jan. "Listen, hey, you and Dean make sure you wear a jacket, you know, a little on the smart side, because Darleen tells me she's having some respected guests around for dinner, and she knows what you rock 'n' roll boys are like, OK?"

"Fine," I said. "No problem. So you'll pick me up?"

"Yeah, in about an hour."

As the rain eased, I looked out the window and could see a patch of blue. Still, I grabbed my small umbrella, stuck it under my arm and headed toward the door. Jan's little white car pulled up.

"You won't need that," Jan called out when she saw my umbrella. "It's all over."

"Y'all guarantee that?" I asked in a phony southern accent.

"I guarantee it," she said. "Let's go."

Soon we were on our way, speeding down Magazine Street to the French Quarter. The sky was magnificent. I'd never seen such light. Well, maybe in Holland.

"It's the water in the air," said Jan.

"By God, it's beautiful," I said, sticking my head out the window. "It's not the same kind of blue as we get in the desert on the West Coast. It's a different kind of light."

Suddenly a rainbow burst out, stretching from horizon to horizon. "Wow," I said, grabbing Dean's camera.

"Don't waste film," he said. "We'll need it for the party."

"OK, OK," I said, "hold your horses." After a couple of shots from the speeding vehicle I realized I wasting his film. One could not photograph such things. You could only open your eyes, let your mouth drop in amazement and drool. "It's pure Salvador Dali," I said.

It was the prelude to a magical night.

As we circled the block looking for a place to park I caught a glimpse of the House of the Rising Sun. It was all I'd dreamt it would be. A palace in the New Orleans heat. It was a wondrous feeling learning that the place I'd fantasized about for thirty years wasn't some run-down shack but was in fact a place of beauty.

As we reached the main entrance, Darleen was there to greet us and took us warmly into the house. After some chat, she took my hand, pulled me aside, and said, "Come, I want to show you something downstairs."

Jan and Dean following, we moved through the crowded room, out through the double doors, onto a landing and down a flight of stairs to the courtyard.

"Here," Darleen said, "this is what I wanted to show you, this mural here." She pointed to the wall behind two parked cars. "This was originally done in vegetable oils, and it's meant to depict the voodoo gods," she said. Her hands swept the length of the wall as she stepped around the cars to get closer. The paint was in an advanced state of decay. She pointed to the lower part of the mural. "You see the black roots down here beginning underneath the ground? If you look closely enough, you can see the fruits on the trees, the blue sky beyond."

Darlene returned to her hosting duties, leaving us to stare at the mural. Dean studied the wall closely for awhile, then turned and smiled. "You could scan this with a computer and really bring it alive."

"Yeah, you bet," I said. As I put my hand out to touch the wall, Darleen reappeared at the entrance of the corridor. "Come over here, there's something else I want to show you."

We walked the length of the yard. The sun had slipped beneath the horizon and it was getting dark. Darleen waved her hand toward some huge, wet banana trees and beyond, to where there was a Christian cross embossed on the wall.

"This here is a voodoo altar on which you can see a cross," Darleen explained. "The slaves knew that if they didn't accept Christianity their religion would probably disappear. So they adopted the cross and Christian saints, and mixed them in with their own religion, voodoo."

Jan, Tracy, Dean, and I stood in the darkness of the bushes looking at the embossed brick cross as Darleen continued.

"The thing they would do is one would make an offering at the altar. Sometimes small animals were sacrificed and offered to the gods in appeasement. And of course," she said with a smile, "I'm quite sure that the animals were cooked and devoured by the members of the family and visitors to the house."

don't let me be misunderstood

Darleen lit a candle in the growing darkness of the garden and placed it near the altar. I looked back toward the main room of the house one floor up. Distinguished party guests stood inside under a crystal chandelier with drinks in their hands, talking, moving through the room. Suddenly, I was beginning to see the house in a whole new light. The place was coming alive for me. I imagined the human traffic that came through this place two centuries before, the difference between the lifestyle of the people who lived down in the yard and that of the prostitutes and clients upstairs in the main house. I thought of the ties that bound the two together—the Christian gentlemen who worshiped the same flesh as those who practised voodoo down in the darkness of the yard.

As if reading my thoughts, Darleen turned and said, "Don't let anybody fool ya, honey, we all got black blood down here, we're all tarred with the same brush." She laughed as she moved toward the upper house.

We followed her back up the stairs. Once more we were back in the thick of the party as nuns and high society folk milled about with city dignitaries, smiling faces everywhere. Darleen took me by the hand. "One more thing I'm gonna show you before you can sit down and eat. During the restoration of the house we uncovered this."

She pointed up to the ceiling. There, painted high above our heads, was a golden sun, on the rise, surrounded by three cherubs.

"It was that little mural up there that first made us believe we really had found the House of the Rising Sun," she said.

Against the wall nearby stood a large, Oriental medicine cabinet about six feet high with many tiny drawers and brass handles. Darleen explained that in the old days the ladies who worked here would also administer medicines and give treatments to ailing guests. I began to realize that the more deeply you could see into it, the more interesting the story of this house became.

I got through the excellent dinner as quickly as I could, then picked up a glass of wine. I wanted to wander around the house by myself to pick up the vibes.

The house was talking to me. The walls were breathing. I smiled to myself as I walked. Almost every night since I was 20 years old, I had sung a song about this very house, and now that I'd found it I was happy to discover that it was a place of beauty.

Thirty years ago, I'd walked right by this place after the Animals' first concert in New Orleans. What a great adventure that first tour had been. What a great time to be alive—and to have come this far!

My mind drifted back to Newcastle when I was a kid and my father worked for the Northeastern Electricity Board. During the holiday when the miners would take their summer breaks, he would go down into the dark, deserted pit to check the electrical equipment and service the running gear of the lifts. The name of the pit was "Rising Sun," and the first time I'd heard those words I was about seven. He took me down to the pit face one day, just to give me a dose of what it's like to be underground. As I stood there in the darkness I felt true fear for the first time, and I wondered how anyone could name such a dark, dank, gloomy place the Rising Sun Colliery. I also knew, at that moment, that I would never work in a factory or mining pit in Newcastle or anywhere else.

It wasn't that long before I was singing "We gotta get outta this place" with conviction, as the Animals hit the road in search of our dreams.

All those years later, in New Orleans, I'd finally arrived at the heart of the matter. As I walked around I realized the House of the Rising Sun was having an effect on me. The mural downstairs in the alley had come alive before my eyes. I turned around, and suddenly there was Darleen, her wonderful soft blue eyes dancing as she slid her diamond-fingered hand around my arm.

"Darling," she said, "I have a favor to ask you. I was wondering if you would grace us by singing that song of yours. Maybe we could get our violinist to accompany you."

"Well, of course," I said. At the same time I was thinking, Jesus! What am I letting myself in for, singing a capella in a whorehouse with only one violin to back me, in a room full of nuns and city officials?

But it was too late, the audience was already gathering.

A short talk with the violin player, a dead ringer for Zero Mostel, left me convinced I was pretty much on my own. But he said he'd do his best.

As we walked down the corridor into the main parlor and took our place at the center of the room, Darleen made an introduction. "Ladies and gentlemen, we have a guest here from California—originally from England. He's going to sing a song which some of you may know. It's about this very house. Ladies and gentlemen, Mr. Eric Burdon."

I took a deep breath, my hands thrust into my pockets, my head toward the mural of the rising sun and three cherubs. I sang for all I was worth. As I finished, the applause in the room was tremendous. "Thank you very much, ladies and gentlemen," I took a bow. Off the hook, I was now free to resume my explorations.

Jan swooped by, her eyes sparkling behind cat's-eye glasses. "Isn't this great? Isn't this so New Orleans? There's a fresh batch of crawfish coming up. I'm off to get some, how about you?"

"No," I said, "I'm going to take a walk around."

I wandered into an empty room. There was a red-and-gold, ornate divan against the wall, and above it an old portrait of a smooth-skinned, brown beauty. I know this woman, I immediately thought. I took a closer look. "I know this woman."

A thin white wrap of silk looked like it had just slid down, revealing her breasts. Her hair was piled high upon her head, her eyes wide and intelligent, her nose long and thin, and, yet, the lips African. I know this woman, I thought. Yes. She was a celebrated beauty known from L.A.

A long, strange trip indeed: Me in the foyer of the real House of the Rising Sun in New Orleans' French Quarter.

to London, a onetime model for Salvador Dali who'd danced on the stage in Paris to the music of my band War. I was staring at an eerie, century-old doppelganger of my old girlfriend, Alvenia Bridges, the very same woman who was with me the morning we got the call that Jimi Hendrix was dying.

My head flooded with these twenty-year-old memories and recalled the note that Jimi had written before he died.

"I've seen angels from heaven, flying saucers in the sun,
And must make my Easter Sunday in the name
of the rising sun."

I found myself in the darkness of the yard, facing the voodoo altar. I pulled a joint from my pocket, lit it up and smoked it quietly, alone, watching the activity in the upstairs parlor.

I put out the joint, rubbed some of the ash onto my fingers and applied the soot to the wall of the altar, which, Darleen had said, was what one did when making an offering.

Soon, the party drew to a close and the guests were departing. I hung back, breathing in the Louisiana night. There were genuine smiles and embraces upstairs as I joined everyone in bidding farewell. It had been a great evening.

For me, New Orleans is the deep root of the real American story. The walls of this house had spoken, and a key had been handed to me. As I stood there dreaming on the balcony, Darleen smiled at me, walked over and shook my hand.

"I was so glad that you could come and join us here today," she said in her fine New Orleans accent. "I want y'all to come back to see us again some time. It was wonderful, and I thank you for the entertainment."

"My pleasure," I said.

She walked me downstairs with my friends. As we emerged onto the sidewalk. She called from the open doorway, "Be careful out there, it's dangerous."

We thanked her once more and headed off toward Jan's car. I'd found deep peace within the walls of that house. We had been to another world for a few hours, and now we were heading back to the fury and fire of life, ready to face a new millennium and whatever its new night would bring. And we were better for having made the journey.

CHAPTER 20
saying goodbye

Postcard from the Caribbean: Black children on a white beach. Crashing surf, mist blowing toward the dark palms of Barbados. The postcard came to my place in California in early 1997. Scrawled on the back was a short note: "Lots of love to you. Of course you can use my photos for your next book. We all say hello and hope to see you one of these days. Love, Linda."

I had no idea how sick Linda McCartney had become. The last time I'd seen her was when she and her beloved Paul visited backstage after one of my shows at London's Hammersmith Theater. Those two were perfect together, woven tight like a many-colored Shetland sweater.

Paul is the only man I've ever known who can hold three conversations at once, on three different subjects, with three different people, and never miss a beat. That night, backstage, they smelled of the farm. They brought their kitchen smells with them. . . parsley, garlic and the country freshness. Shy smiles and a wave from Paul, who was nailed to the wall by press and fans. Linda came straight to me, elbowing her way through the crowd. I was in the corner, drinking an ice-cold vodka after my set.

"Hello, my dear. Long time, no see. Still enjoying a drink from time to time?"

"Yeah," I answered. "I try to keep it down, but. . . ." I gave her a bear hug and said, "Good to see you."

"Ah, memories, sweet memories," she said, smiling. "Well, I guess you're doing very well for yourself."

"Yes, this is the way life should be." We made small talk over the din as she held on to my hand with a light touch, Paul still stranded on the other side of the room, up to his eyes in people.

New York in the mid-'60s is where I remember Linda best, years before she ever met her Beatle. Dearing Howe's apartment in Manhattan was the place to hang. It was at this time that I remember Linda getting very serious about photography.

Because of my noted love for Black American culture, *Ebony* magazine wanted to do an in-depth article on me. They had us take the A train up to Harlem accompanied by a staff photographer. Along for the ride came Linda, drummer Barry Jenkins, and a girlfriend who'd come out to join me from the coast. Linda seemed a little shy in front of the lens, but she was quick to learn the power of still images.

Linda showed me how to move through the city of cities. New York. The Big Apple. It was there that we got our first tabs of LSD, passed to me by Brian Jones on the floor of Ondine's nightclub. Never a participant, Linda was always there to make sure we got home safely after tripping the light psychedelic in our favorite place: Central Park. One morning as Barry Jenkins and I marveled at the skyscraper walls that loomed over the city's green sanctuary, Linda snapped away, capturing some of my favorite images of that time.

They were days of wonder in a world without fear; we were out to change the world. We looked on in saddened amazement at young men standing in line, willing if not eager to go off to the horror movie known as Vietnam. I had tried to capture some of these images in the studio when I cut the album *Every One of Us:*

"And when I got to America
I said it blew my mind.
And when I got to America
I said it blew my mind.
The Apollo Theater on 125th Street
The place was closed it was pouring rain
I had a feeling I'd go there again
and the taxi driver thought I was insane.
Brown girl from the Bronx
showed me her home
We went there by subway train
She took me there time and time again
Love was our sweet summer's game
And when I got to America
I say it blew my mind
And when I got to America
I say it blew my mind"

We were open-minded, young, and free. We were up all night, and as we'd make our way to the Carnegie Cafe for breakfast, we'd link arms, Jenkins, Linda, Dearing Howe, guitar player Hilton Valentine, and myself, laughing at the gray-faced workers on their way to their dreary offices. We loved every minute of it, everything and everybody. It's as if we were living in a cosmic movie, with Beatles music as a soundtrack.

There were a lot of strong women around at the time, and Linda introduced me to the strongest. The baddest. Nina Simone. We attended her show at Hunter College in New York, and Linda had

On stage at Hunter College in the early days. Photo by Linda McCartney.

arranged for us to go backstage and meet the great lady. We were in a crowded room loaded with fans, well-wishers, students and press. I was all for getting out of there, envisioning a heavy atmosphere, but Linda insisted, "No, hang about. Here's a drink. Chill out. It will be worth it."

Eventually, people drained out until the only strangers left in the room were me, Linda, and Hilton. Sitting at a table in the corner of the room was the star of the night, the great Nina Simone. She was a tigress. Her eyes flashed as she looked me up and down and spat out a curse: "So you're the honky motherfucker that stole my song and got a hit out of it."

don't let me be misunderstood

Apparently she'd heard my version of "Don't Let Me Be Misunderstood!" I was thunderstruck. Lost for words—and beginning to think that I should indeed have fled this scene long before. But after a silence, I came back at her. "Hey, listen, if you will admit that the work song in your set this evening probably belongs to the bones of some poor unfortunate buried in an unmarked grave in Angola State Penitentiary—then I'll admit that your rendition inspired us to record the song. Besides, the Animals' having a hit with it has paved the way for you in Europe. They're waiting for you. You'll find out when you get there." She turned in her seat and slowly stood up. Linda nudged me from behind as Nina put her hand out toward mine and said, "My name's Nina Simone."

"Eric Burdon," I said.

"Well, pleased to meet you. Sit down."

Suddenly everyone in the room could breathe again.

After this meeting, Nina and I became friends and some time later, when she arrived in London to do a television special, I was asked by the producers to be her minder, as everyone else was too unnerved to deal with her.

I shared many other magical moments with Linda Eastman. One was a trip in more ways than one. A couple of years later, Dearing Howe had invited me, members of the new Animals, and Linda for a journey on his powerboat, and most of us were well-dosed on LSD before we left. Dearing was a rich kid, heir to the John Deere tractor fortune. He loved music, and his apartment in Manhattan was always filled with familiar music and faces. . . Jimi Hendrix, Noel Redding, Mitch Mitchell, and the rest of our extended gang.

As we shoved off from the Manhattan docks and headed up river, Dearing put on a reel-to-reel tape of *Sgt. Pepper's Lonely Hearts Club Band,* which blasted out through giant stage speakers he'd placed on the stern. I was on the bow, holding onto the brass rail. As the George

Washington Bridge came into view, we were enveloped in "A Day in the Life." It came at me from behind, into my ears, moved through my body, and emerged through the top of my head. Singing along with the track, I could actually see my voice leave the boat, bounce off the water, head up toward the footings of the bridge, up into the sky—circling the Earth and returning to me.

"I'd love to turn you on. . . ."

It was the last time I saw Linda in America. The Animals went off on a tour to Japan and beyond, and she headed for London, where she would meet and fall in love with Paul McCartney. The next time I saw her at all was—to my shock and surprise—on TV, onstage with Wings in 1976. She'd gone beyond the expected and became a musician, touring the world at her husband's side and, later, with their whole closely knit family.

"The family that plays together stays together" is an old hippie slogan. It came to mind when I saw Linda up there on the TV screen, playing in concert with Wings. I was sure it would have been with Paul's insistence, assistance and coaching.

Exposed to as much bullshit as the Beatles were, I'm not surprised Paul hung on for dear life once he found his true love. (John Lennon quite publicly did the same thing. And no matter what crap has circulated over the years, I know that John loved Yoko.) For Paul, this would be enjoying the two things he loved best—his family and his music. He's been criticized by some, but so what! If you want a good marriage and life on the road, you usually have to make a lot of sacrifices. Paul figured out how to have it all, and was able to give it his all with his wife at his side, touring into the '80s.

If you can't admire their life and music together, then you're one cynical, miserable prick. I am sure their gypsy family had wonderful times on the road. And, in retrospect, I think Linda played a part in paving the way for more female performers to join the boys' club called rock 'n' roll. Her legacy of now-historic photographs—among the first and best of early rock music—firmly established her as an artistic talent, and she found acclaim even before finding her soulmate in a Beatle.

Over the years, there would be kind and thoughtful postcards from their assorted homes around the globe, the most recent giving me her blessing to use those photos from our heady early days in New York. Then, on the morning of April 21, 1998, came the phone call. It was from my friend Dana in Santa Barbara.

"Have you heard?"

"Yes," I said "I saw it on the news last night."

Dana had been Paul's personal secretary for several years before becoming an enormously successful businesswoman. "Look," she said. "I want to have a memorial service for Linda up here. She used to ride horses with Paul, and they had a lot of good times in this part of the world. Would you be able to get here by tonight, say a few words, and sing a song? I'll provide the piano player." I thought about it for a second and said, "Of course." My Hungarian girlfriend Judit was staying in Palm Springs with me. I leaned over and whispered to the just-waking beauty, "Fancy a trip to Santa Barbara?"

As Judit was showering and getting dressed, I went to my CD collection and, thinking of what Paul might choose to perform, I made a cassette recording of "The Long and Winding Road," copying it several times in a row on a cassette so I could listen to it non-stop and memorize the words during the journey north.

We arrived in Santa Barbara as the sun was beginning to set. We weren't sure exactly where we were going, but as we turned a corner in the heart of the city, we were amazed to see more than a dozen satellite news trucks representing media from all over the world. Luckily I found a parking space right behind one of the trucks. We walked into the Sunken Gardens of the city hall grounds, stepping over the power cables that snaked their way from the trucks to the stage area. As Judit and I entered the Sunken Gardens, there was Dana, surrounded by TV reporters, looking very smart in a jet-black suit and black sunglasses. I walked straight up to her, embraced her and asked, "Jesus, how did you manage all this?"

"Amazing, I know," she said, "The *L.A. Times* picked it up and now. . . look."

As I turned around, I saw that Judit, who seems to attract cameras wherever she goes, was being confronted by a small woman with a New York accent, dressed in a white outfit with a plastic press pass on her lapel. A recent visitor to the U.S., Judit was still learning American culture. The woman with the New York accent said, "I'm from *Hard Copy.*"

Judit, taking the show title literally, jumped in immediately with her new English and asked, "What is a porno movie maker doing here?" I cracked up and turned away as the reporter, with a very serious look, tried to explain that, since Princess Diana's death, her program was now aimed at more wholesome coverage. From that point on, we were besieged by crews from around the world.

Martin Lewis was there as the evening's MC. Elegantly dressed, making himself very busy, he was in his element. And it was due to his presence that the affair ran smoothly. It was hard to believe how Dana had pulled this farewell to a friend together. The crowd arrived, including many younger girls, and everyone was handed a candle. The sun set, and as darkness fell over the somber scene, the children's faces reflected the candle light.

Backstage, Jimmy Massina was tuning his guitar. I met the piano player who was to accompany me on "Long and Winding Road." I also had written a remembrance that I would read before sliding into the song.

don't let me be misunderstood

Wildflower
I walked the road up to my neck in bright yellow blooms. I saw the
very same road from a jet plane at 12,000 feet the day before yesterday,
returning from a gig in Mississippi. And now, I walk, breathing out
the toxins I collected in the smoky joint. . . the sound of slot machines
still ringing in my ears.
I notice a rise in the temperature.
This could signal the beginning of the end for the desert flora in this
year of El Niño.
The colors were spectacular.
And here I was without a camera.
I met this girl one time in New York in 1966. She told me quite seri-
ously that to become a photographer, one should carry one's camera at
all times. Just like a soldier carries his weapon. Because the action is all
around you. Everywhere. Every day. I have photographic images
ingrained in my head of our gang and our trips to Harlem, taking the
A train uptown to visit the High Church of black music, the Apollo
Theatre on 125th street. One Saturday night, we saw James Brown.
She threw flowers, red roses, at the stage.
Wildflowers. Wild times.
It was the same girl who introduced me to Nina Simone, backstage at
Hunter College. I was terrified. Face the tiger. Face your fears. I think
that's what she was telling me. She was one of the girls who became
one of the boys by becoming a woman upon the road.
Go Linda, go.

Saying goodbye to friends does not get easier with experience. I've had
to do it a lot these days, and when I'm asked to attend and sing at serv-
ices, I always think: Am I up to this? Can I make it through this without
faltering? Because now, people are relying on me to make sense of the
nonsense of a premature, unexpected death of a friend.

Backstage before going on at Linda's memorial, I felt lightness in the occasion. It was the beauty of the surroundings, the faces of the young people, the flowers they held, the way their faces were illuminated by candles. Linda McCartney's own spirit had made the affair an enjoyable experience. Not even the press, trying to catch a whiff of scandal as it became unclear where Linda actually passed away, could spoil it.

The family had announced that she'd died in Santa Barbara, but in fact she died at the McCartney farm in Arizona. They wanted to keep that location secret for privacy's sake. But everyone attending the service had only one thing in mind—saying goodbye to a friend. We knew she had enjoyed a great life and this was the best possible place for us to say farewell to her.

Nothing else mattered.

After the ceremony, the core of close friends followed me and Martin Lewis to a restaurant bar in Montecito, where, after dinner, Martin and I told Beatles stories until the place closed.

Linda's death was the second in recent years that truly hit me hard. The first was that of the great guitarist Larry Wilkins. I'd met Larry through Brian Auger, and he had become the lead guitarist in my band for years. We travelled the world and had many spectacular times, both off the stage and on. But he was a pretty private guy, and never let on when he, like Linda, had cancer. He kept up a facade until the end. None of us knew he was dying until he was in the hospital in Santa Monica, the melanoma leaching his life away. I drove in from Palm Springs to see him but, in one of those cruel twists, he died less than an hour before I got there.

When I returned home I went up onto the roof of my house, which has a small cactus garden and a shady place to meditate under some huge palm leaves. Much to my surprise, I found that a rare cactus had exploded in a burst of purple flowers. It blooms only once every two years.

Larry had given it to me.

CHAPTER 21

eastern bloc party

At a gig in Detroit I ran into a guy named Redencko, a Bosnian refugee who'd been rescued by a Catholic charity of some sort and relocated to Canada with his wife and three young boys.

He was one of the most enthusiastic fans I'd ever met. The reason, he explained, was that during the nightmarish nights of the Bosnian conflict, the one thing that kept him and his friends going had been my music.

"Bosnia was time and place where the cheapest thing was human life," he told me. "And the most expensive thing was an Eric Burdon record."

Some weeks later he sent me a letter. In his broken English he wrote: "Eric Burdon & Animals & War in the war was the best thing for escape from dying & crying. In my hometown there is no house, no restaurant, or coffee place without Burdon's music for almost 20 years."

I was flattered when he asked me when I was going to play Bosnia, but I wasn't sure what to say.

"One of these days, maybe, if they ask us. You never know."

A few months later, Ringo Starr & his All-Starr Band were playing at the Universal Amphitheater. I arranged backstage passes so a friend of mine and his eleven-year-old son could meet Ringo. The boy had just gotten a drum kit and was a big Beatles fan. Backstage before the show, it was a circus. Ringo's manager, David Fishoff, came and introduced himself, and asked me if I'd do a walk-on with the band to sing "With a Little Help from My Friends." Sure, I said.

Just before I went onstage, Fishoff dangled a bit of carrot—he asked if I would participate in a special event he was promoting in Sarajevo with the Sarajevo Philharmonic. I was excited at the prospect, and told him I'd love to join in, if it fit my schedule and he could work out all the logistics.

Soon after, I was in the back of a limo on my way from a recording session in L.A. when my secretary Jeri called from Palm Springs.

"You're being asked to call an Ambassador Mohammed Sacirbey in New York."

I immediately dialed and, quite quickly, Bosnia's ambassador to the Balkans came on the line. He and Fishoff had been working together to arrange the concert in Sarajevo. It would be known as The Bridge. He explained that in the city a beautiful bridge, one of the country's finest works of architecture, had been destroyed in the shelling. The ambassador and his people hoped that holding a music festival there would lift peoples' spirits for the work ahead, rebuilding the culture that had been destroyed in the war.

His people would take care of the tickets. We would board a special flight to Frankfurt in about two weeks.

I needed the help of one of the musicians in my band, and felt like I was in a war movie when I pulled the curtain aside in the dressing room at one of our gigs and told the guys "I need a volunteer to go to Sarajevo. Any takers?"

With only a few moments of hesitation, Neal Morse, a great Nashville musician who was with me for a short time, spoke up from the darkest corner of the room. "Yeah man, sounds like fun. I'm up for it."

"Good," I said, "Here's a tape. Have a listen. These are the songs you're going to have to know."

Two weeks later Neal and I were in Frankfurt. We drank tea and looked out bleary-eyed at the empty runway, which was covered in a veil of early morning fog. We were waiting for the daily plane from Sarajevo so we could board for the return trip. It was the only non-military flight going in and out of the country at this time.

As we left German airspace heading east, the gray weather suddenly changed, and, as we dipped in for our final approach, the sun broke through. We could see the green hills of Bosnia below us. Sharp ridges and high hills draped in almost jungle-like green, a carpet of lushness. A country to fight for, I thought. A country to die for. And we had brought the sun with us. After all, that was our job.

As soon as the jet touched down on the runway, my pulse began to rise. "Welcome to Sarajevo," said the stewardess in several languages, adding the equivalent of "Have a nice day."

Looking out the window, I noticed that there was no control tower. Just military vehicles. Beyond the runway were farm houses with red and white squares painted on the roofs. Once we came off the plane, I stood there on the tarmac, my face to the sun, feeling the heat.

Another massive white-and-blue flying machine was parked alongside our jet. Property of the U.S. Air Force, it was waiting for then-Secretary of State Madeleine Albright.

The arrival-shed was abuzz with all kinds of faces and uniforms. There was no customs and no passport check, and we were soon outside on the street. A gray-haired, gray-faced old man in a pinstripe suit helped us load our luggage into the back of his red Fiat. Then an announcement was made: all traffic for five miles must stop as Albright was on her way to the airport. For fifteen minutes, all was frozen in time as an incredible motorcade of armored personnel carriers, one limo, and several helicopter gunships in the sky made sure that Albright made it to the big blue jet.

As Neal and I hung out in the sun waiting for this event to wrap up, we surveyed the destruction in the surrounding hills. We were mesmerized, waiting, as Albright arrived safely and boarded her plane. The convoy broke up, someone yelled, and, as if we were at a Formula One race, engines all around us kicked to life, dust flew into the air, and the town kicked into action once more.

Soon we were driving through concrete dust and exhaust fumes toward Sarajevo, passing buildings that had been reduced to rubble. Washing lines were strung from crate to crate and children played in bomb craters and dirty pools of water left by recent rains. we were getting a closeup view of what a civil war can do to a country and a people. As we reached the crossroads on the edge of the city, Neal turned to me. "Shit, I left my camera in the trunk."

Then I saw an Italian armored car, which was bristling with radio whips and antennas. A couple of crew members turned our way. They looked to be real cowboys—automatics tied down with string to the legs of their personally tailored combat suits. They were tight-assed and cocky, their helmets sprouting majestic black feathers, gleaming in the sun. Across the street was a tank from the new, united Germany, the black cross painted across its hull. It was a shock to me.

"I wonder what that is," I said, looking at a bombed-out building.

"I wonder what it used to be," said Neal. The driver heard us talking and looked back. "Television."

It had been the national television station, once a new concrete and glass structure, it was now a pockmarked pile of rubble. Bits of plastic blinds dangled in the open window frames. Then we saw something that made us both laugh. The highest building left standing—freshly replastered to hide bullet holes, and painted pink—stood there in proud glory, shining in the sun. It was the Holiday Inn.

Yeah! Business as usual. First in and last out, no matter where you are, it's always the Holiday Inn.

Several lanes of traffic began to merge into one as we got closer to the old downtown section. Traffic finally came to a standstill. Neal and I made small talk and tried to behave, but both of us knew we were playing the game called "normal." There was nothing normal about this situation. As we sat at the traffic light watching a crowd of people leaving their offices, we noticed that many people had limbs missing. At another major intersection, there was an armored personnel carrier on each corner. The multinational troops held their weapons locked and loaded, pointed at the pedestrians as they crossed the street on their way home.

In bizarre contrast, the downtown was also filled with people attending the film festival.

Our driver looked relieved and turned to smile, assuring us that it wouldn't be long before we arrived at the hotel. We began to climb a hill, leaving behind the madness of downtown Sarajevo.

The taxi made a hard left, its tires screeching on the cobblestones and we came to a stop. We unloaded the luggage and made our way to the front desk. There were a couple of overly cheerful, sharp-featured Serbian girls working behind the desk.

"Mr. Burdon," she said. "I have a message for you." She handed me a slip of paper and the keys to my room.

"I'll see you later, Neal."

"Yeah, I'm going to put my head down for awhile."

"I put in a wake-up call for 7:30."

"See you then."

The room was a pleasant surprise. The interior was bright. There was a medium-sized bed and a piece of lattice work that acted as a room divider. Beyond that, a U-shaped window seat, potted plants on a shelf, and a large bay window. I opened it and looked out into the night. In the valley below was a deserted Olympic-sized swimming

pool. Beyond that, a massive dark hill loomed above us. On its very top perched an Islamic temple. Stars were beginning to twinkle in the clear sky.

I'd already unpacked when I remembered the note I'd been handed at the front desk: "I am here. I am Judit. My mother and sister come with me. We are shopping. Will be back soon." I couldn't believe it.

I'd been seeing Judit on and off for about five years. We'd meet and travel from border to border, town to town, country to country. Our wild romance unfolded in Berlin, Los Angeles, Mexico City, Hawaii, and Budapest. I'd last seen her when she spent some time with me at my place in California, but after she returned to Hungary I hadn't heard from her in about six months. Recently we'd reconnected, and she'd told me she wanted to come see the Sarajevo event, but there were no flights. She vowed she'd attend one way or another.

I was supposed to be mad at her. I'd promised myself that the next time we met we'd have it out face to face. I'd promised myself that I was through with all the craziness from this woman, who hadn't called me for nearly half a year. But the reality of the situation dawned on me. She must have driven here. There were no flights, no trains. I made sure my door was unlocked, then crashed into the bed, pulling the blanket around me and falling into a deep slumber. I woke to the feeling of her long blonde hair moving across my cheek, down my shoulders, and down my arm to my hands. I looked down, and she was kissing the back of my hand. She looked up at me and smiled, and those deep blue eyes lit up.

"Please don't be angry with me," she smiled. "Please."

Then she slid back up toward me and buried her face in my neck, her hair covering me. I slipped back into the darkness of my love for her.

"How the hell did you get here?" I asked her, whispering in her ear.

"We drove here—my sister, my mother, and I. We came in my Mercedes."

"Jesus, how far?"

"About 300 kilometers from Budapest."

"What were the roads like?"

"It was terrible. Don't ask. I'm here, you're here. That's all that matters. My momma is looking forward to seeing you."

As I held her in my arms, I realized that it was true: She was probably doing this more for her mother than for me. That's the way she was. She provided everything for her mother and sister, and her sister's child. She had been the breadwinner for the family for years, ever since becoming a model.

We lay there, just holding each other until the telephone snapped me back to reality. It was the front desk with my wake-up call.

"Oh, God," I said, "Judit, I have to go. I have a meeting in town with the conductor of the orchestra and the ambassador and the promoter. We have to talk about the show tomorrow night. Do you want to come with me?"

"No, I'll stay here with my momma. We'll have dinner but then we'll see you later, yes?"

"Yeah, for sure," I said.

We kissed and she was gone. As I slowly got dressed, I couldn't believe that she was in Sarajevo. In the distance I heard the Muslim calls from the hill and the sound of a NATO jet fighter screeching across the sky. Down in the lobby of the hotel I met Neal, sitting in the corner smoking a cigarette and chewing gum, as usual.

Transportation arrived to take us downtown for our meeting. It was smoky, noisy, and crowded in the small production office. I was glad that a couple of months earlier I had rerecorded "House of the Rising Sun" with a string quartet, so at least we had a basic strings chart to work from. I'd never sung with a symphonic orchestra in my life. But I understood one thing: Once the conductor gives the count, the massive machinery begins to churn. An orchestra performing live is like a railroad train—there's no stopping it.

For a soloist this can be disastrous, so I paid close attention to what was being said. From the moment I first heard the Led Zeppelin song "Kashmir," I'd desperately wanted to sing it. It was surely the best string arrangement that Fishoff had among his orchestrations. There was a crack of excitement in the air, and a great feeling of comradeship as we began to discuss the music for the event.

Fishoff, a giant of a man with a round, smiling face, was proud of his involvement in this affair. An Orthodox Jew, he cared passionately about people, about Europe, and about this region of the world especially, which had seemingly slipped into a holocaustic-like nightmare.

After the meeting we were shown the place we were going to play. The stage was still under construction, with people climbing all over the place hammering nails. They were erecting a massive wooden platform that would accommodate the full Sarajevo Philharmonic, along with several other performers. The stage was being constructed on what appeared to be the remains of a bombed-out building. Surrounded on all four corners by ancient-looking high-rise apartments, this was to be our theatre. As we strolled around the venue, I told Fishoff that Judit and her family had arrived from Budapest by road.

"My God, you're joking," he said.

"No, I'm not. They drove here through 300 miles of war-torn territory."

"How did they make it?"

"I don't know, the girl's amazing."

"We must call her and get her to come down and meet us for coffee."

He called the hotel and Judit and her mother and sister headed down to meet our group in a small smoke-filled restaurant. As we crowded around the table, the ambassador, with his movie-star looks, introduced everyone and helped order food off a strange menu.

When Judit and her family arrived, the air was filled with laughter, hugs, and kisses.

I leaned over to Judit and told her I thought she looked beautiful. "I've never seen you look so healthy," I said.

"Four weeks on a health farm in northern Italy, darling. It costs money to be beautiful."

"I guess it does," I said, kissing her on the cheek. She turned away in embarrassment. I looked across the table.

"Eric," said her mother, over and over again. "Eric."

Then her sister, smiling, leaned over and said to me, "Tell me, Eric, do you really love Judit?"

"Of course I do," I said. "Doesn't everyone?"

"Will we ever see you in Budapest again?"

"I certainly hope so," I said.

The meal was surprisingly good. It was a wonderful evening among people who could still believe in peace.

A taxi arrived to take us back to the hotel. Outside in the street, the city lights seemed to shine extra brightly. The film festival screening ended, and people stumbled out into the night air.

I was extremely jet-lagged and looking forward to my bed, but on the other hand I wanted to absorb as much as I could during my forty-eight hours in the war zone.

Once Judit and I were alone in the room, things chilled. I couldn't forget all that had gone on before, and I found it difficult to forgive the six months of silence. We ended up sitting in the open window, leaning against the ledge, looking out into the night.

I started to speak, then held my voice. Then started again.

"I'm sorry, I don't want to be mad at you. It's just that I'd like an answer to my question: Why haven't you called me for the last six months?"

"There's this other man, this Italian. He's there for me. He's good for my son. He behaves like a father to my son."

Well, ask a stupid question, I thought.

Like myself, she'd been through a rotten divorce and had lost contact with her kid. And like myself, she was trying desperately to correct this problem, and needed someone to help her out along this road. But it wasn't me.

It wasn't me.

I had no business thinking of marriage. The memories of the bad days with my second wife were still so strong that I'd never marry again. And that's what she wanted, a husband, and a father for her son.

We embraced and lay there for an hour or so, and she quietly got up, put her finger to her lips and said, "Shhh. Go to bed."

She walked across the room and put out the candle. Then she said, "We see you tomorrow. Sleep good, darling. Good night."

And she was gone.

I awoke with the sun in my face, looking around for the clock. It was 9:30. There was just enough time for a quick breakfast and a quick rendezvous with Neal. Soon a minivan picked us up and took us down into the heart of Sarajevo. Backstage, there was a warm feeling of optimism among the Serbs, Croats, Muslims, and infidels like myself. All grooved nicely with white wine and blue cigarette smoke. I tried my best not to think of what was going on in the countryside surrounding this small patch of dirt where we were about to take the stage.

Backstage, one can always tell when musicians feel it's getting close to showtime—there is a collective search for a place to take a piss. The closest toilets were near the entrance to the yard, and it would have taken at least fifteen minutes to get through the crowd and back. I slipped into the shadows at the rear of the tent that had been erected to house the players backstage. Relieving myself, I heard the sounds of shuffling feet, and I saw that many members of the orchestra had followed me. What a way to bond! Forty penguins pissing against a wall.

Then there was a crack in the air. Showtime. As the violins began the Stones song, "Ruby Tuesday," the mood changed instantly. The rigid, shell-shocked crowd slowly but surely began to loosen up and go with the music. By the time they got to the chorus the crowd began to sing along.

We made it through "House of the Rising Sun" and then an impromptu "Tobacco Road." But the song that seemed to sum up the feeling, the mood, and the atmosphere of the moment, and touched the souls of the people gathered in this yard of destruction was the Plant-Page rearrangement of "Kashmir."

The opening chords were pure magic. The memory of that night and of that particular song will remain with me forever. And although I knew that in the morning we would all separate and most probably never see each other again, for that moment I was never more in love in my life, with everything.

Afterward, I looked at Judit and asked her if she wanted to return to the hotel.

"Sure, darling, I'd love to spend some time with you."

"OK," I said, "I know it's going to be difficult to get a taxi, but why don't you and your momma and your sister go out front and see if you can. I'll go backstage, get my clothes and meet you outside."

"If there are no taxis," she said, "we'll be in the coffee house next to the cinema."

Backstage I ran into Neal, who was already packed and ready to go back up the hill to the hotel, eager to get to bed. We'd have to rise early to catch the plane out.

As he left, Neal turned to me, "Hey, don't go for any walks up that hill—it's mined. The girls at the front desk told me."

"Jesus," I said. "What a mess."

He smiled and waved goodnight.

As I loaded up my bag backstage and grabbed some bottles of water, I shook hands and said goodbye to several guys from the orchestra. I wondered what life would be like for them when things went back to normal.

As I made my way out past the side of the stage, I was hit by a shock-wave of terror. Hot white stage lights pointed straight up into the sky like World War II searchlights, hitting the faces of the punk band that was now on the stage. Dressed in black combat gear with shaved heads, earrings, nose rings, and tattoos they raised their fists to the sky above.

The noise coming from the amplifiers was deafening, as were their voices. But what shook me was the crowd that suddenly emerged at the front of the stage—skinheads, all of them, their hands raised in a Nazi salute, yelling at the top of their voices.

"Serbia! Serbia! Serbia!"

I was thunderstruck, horrified, never thinking for a moment that the extreme right would be here. This was the second half of the show. The dusty square was not as full now as it has been previously, but the skinheads were packed in against the front of the stage like wolves.

"Serbia! Serbia! Serbia!"

People in the surrounding apartments began closing their windows. I stood there rigid for a few moments, absorbing the scene. When I couldn't take it anymore I headed through the crowd to the back of the place and made my way down the alley into the street. I could see the three women holding a taxi. The alley was packed with people coming and going, and we were lucky to have scored a taxi. I broke into a trot, my bag slung over my back. Then I bumped into a young guy dressed in a black leather jacket. His face was ashen white, a look of panic on it. A blonde with shoulder length hair stood behind him. In his arms he held some sheets of paper.

"Mr. Eric," he said, "please give me a moment. I must talk with you."

I reached for a pen to sign my name, then realized he wasn't an autograph hunter.

"Mr. Eric, please you must come to Kosovo. We need you in Kosovo."

"Kosovo?" I said. "Where's that?"

"Is my home, I have just come from there. Please, take these papers with you and read them. Please, we need your help."

"Okay, but I have to go, my friends are waiting," I said, as I took the wad of paper and left him with tears streaming down his face.

We piled into the taxi, the women in back, me up front, and headed up the hill toward the hotel. I turned back to Judit and said, "Listen, tomorrow, when you drive home, if anything happens, let your mother do the talking. Don't do anything. Promise?"

"I promise," she said, and then translated to her mother.

Judit looked at me and said, "Don't worry, it won't be a problem."

I folded the papers that the kid had given me and stuffed them into my bag. Soon we were back at the hotel. The three women headed up to their rooms to pack, for they were leaving early on their journey back to Budapest.

When I got back to my room I removed my shirt and remembered that someone onstage had passed me a leather necklace with a circular medallion. It was a mysterious piece of jewelry. I held it in my hands and looked at it. In the center was a blue dot. Turquoise. And around it was Islamic writing. It was a beautiful piece. I began to do my packing and remembered the papers the boy had handed me. After I'd finished packing my clothes, I laid them on top, the last thing I packed. I was too tired to look at them.

I opened the windows wide and looked down at the Olympic-sized pool, green with algae. I felt I was in the darkest corner of Europe.

Then there was a knock at the door. Judit stood there.

"Hi, darling, remember these?"

She held up a black slip I'd bought for her in Hollywood.

"I'll take a shower and be right with you," I said as she lit a candle. I came out, and the night was still. I swore that this was the last long-distance love affair that I'd ever be involved in. We'd met more than five years earlier, yet I really didn't know this woman. I remembered what a friend in Berlin had told me. "She's a communist. She came up dirt poor, no shoes, no food on the table. She had to provide for the whole family."

I found myself moving toward her slowly. I pulled her toward me, and told her I was happy she'd found somebody. We slid down onto the bed and slowly made love. When I woke up, the bed was empty. She was gone. I ran toward the window and looked down into the parking lot. The old Mercedes was gone, along with another chapter in my life.

don't let me be misunderstood

I looked up in the daylight at the hill that had loomed so darkly the
night before and saw for the first time that it was dotted with little
white crosses. I prayed that Judit and her family would return safely to
Budapest. Then the telephone rang from downstairs. It was Neal. The
taxi was waiting.

Downstairs, he, too, was staring at the white crosses on the black
mountain. "God," he said. "I miss my kids. Let's go."

We piled our luggage into the taxi and headed for the airport.

Both of us slept all the way to Frankfurt.

On arrival at LAX, I found that my luggage was missing. I was
pissed off but not surprised. Neal's was missing, too. I was sure some kid
in Sarajevo was wearing my silk jacket. Another kid, throwing rocks at
a UN tank, was probably wearing my stage shoes.

I called Budapest to make sure Judit and her family had made it to
Hungary safely. She told me that their old Mercedes had broken
down late at night on the Bosnian side of the border. When she
looked for her money so she could call for help, she discovered that
all of it—the cash in her pockets as well as a secret stash she'd hidden
in a suitcase—had been stolen, probably by the hotel staff. They had
sat there until morning, Judit told me, until a farmer came along in a
truck. He was soon followed by a local policeman. At first, the cop
tried to fix the car. When he couldn't, he helped the farmer hook the
old Mercedes up to a tow rope on his truck. The women were towed
in their dead car all the way to the Hungarian border—but not over
it. The Hungarians on the other side warned them not to approach,
and Judit feared they'd be stuck in no-man's land. But she was so
pissed off and fed up with the whole experience that she, her mother,
and sister just pushed their car across the border, while the Hungarian guards watched in disbelief.

I was happy she and her family were safe, but felt bittersweet about
our failed affair.

Nearly two months after my return, my secretary knocked on my door. "Guess what?" she said. "Your suitcase has turned up."

I pulled the errant container into the house and dumped it out in front of the TV set, which was blazing away with CNN reports on the growing carnage in Kosovo. As I unzipped the bag the first thing that fell out was the bunch of papers the kid in Sarajevo had given me. I began flipping through the pages. They were from some Eastern European news agency, and contained a list of the dead, the dying, and the raped, casualties from the monstrous civil war that was taking place in Kosovo. As I flipped through the papers, mesmerized by the list of names, CNN reported that NATO was to begin a bombing campaign. All hell was about to break loose.

The last, weird chapter to my love affair with Judit came when I got a postcard, postmarked Budapest, depicting a beautiful Italian beach. On the back it read: "There is no street, no car, you have to have a small boat to get to the place, no winter. This will be my new home. You have to learn to swim if you want to visit me."

That's all it said. It was unsigned, but dated nearly six months before—on Valentine's Day.

CHAPTER 22

epilogue

id I choose the life I've lived or did It choose me? Just about anyone might ask himself that question and be unable to come up with a definitive answer. In my case, I can. My life chose me—and I came by it all very honestly; I am just another chapter in an old family saga.

I hadn't thought about it for years, but at some point my sister reminded me of the stories our father used to tell us about one of our ancestors, one George "Geordie" Ridley. Our great uncle through my father's side, Ridley was born in February 1835. He "always had a taste for entertainment," the story went. As a boy, he'd won an amateur singing contest at the Wheat Sheaf Music Hall and went on to become what was in those days a singing star: His song "The Blaydon Races" is still one of the favorite local tunes. More than one hundred years after his death, it's sung wherever locals meet en masse. I have fond memories of tens of thousands of people singing the tune at the St. James soccer ground in Newcastle before a game.

On stage at the House of Blues on L.A.'s Sunset Strip.

> *"Ooohhh me lads*
> *Ya shoulda seen us gainin'*
> *gaining along the Scotsland Road*
> *Just to see them standin'*
> *all the lads 'n' lasses there*
> *with all their smiling faces*
> *gaining along the Scotsland Road*
> *to see the Blaydon Races. . ."*

My mother's father, Grandfather Jack, was a gambler. A fanatical gambler. If he didn't get a horse "up" in a week, the whole household was made to suffer. But when he had some winnings, he would come home with bottles of Brown, smoke his cigarettes, and spin tales about Geordie.

There had been two Ridley brothers, actually. Geordie's brother held the record for the mile run in England. Geordie worked in the mines as a young man, from the age of eight to eighteen. But he was crushed by a runaway ore wagon and seriously injured, and was forced to quit. That's when the singing became the career.

Grandfather Jack used to talk about Geordie's pals, a colorful group of local legends such as Coffee Johnny, who was black, and Johnny on the Bridge. They were street entertainers, the latter of whom, true to his name, performed on the Tyne Bridge, hopping the imaginary line dividing the counties of Northumberland and Durham in the belief that the authorities from neither county would be able to arrest him.

The group's most memorable caper involved conspiring with a local promoter to fix the Blaydon races by lead-weighting the saddle of the favored horse.

After suspicions were raised, the weighted saddle was discovered, and a riot ensued at the race park. Ridley and his mates were never pinned with the deed and got away with their winnings.

Around this time Robert Peel was instrumental in creating the first police force in Britain, the peelers, later known as the bobbys. Geordie commented on this development in a song called "The Bobby Cure," questioning the sanity of having a force of men sanctioned by the state to wield clubs against the citizenry. The population of northeast England responded wildly and Geordie had a "hit" in every dance hall he played.

When I was last in Tyneside visiting my sister, I strolled into the Newcastle Public Library to do a little research on Geordie. What I found floored me. Except for his early stint in the mine, our lives have run surprisingly parallel for men born more than a hundred years apart.

Most of what's documented on Ridley now comes down to us courtesy of one Thomas Allan, who collected local songs and published them in a book called *Tyneside Songs,* which appeared in various editions from 1863 to 1891.

According to this source, Geordie also had "hits" with songs about well-known local characters of the day, Johnny Luik-Up and Joey Jones. On July 30th, 1861, Geordie got one of his first newspaper mentions when the *Daily Chronicle* said he was "an especial favourite with the juvenile portion of the audience."

Sounds familiar.

A review of a performance at Tyne Concert Hall in the same period said, "Mr. Ridley's songs are given with an ease and freedom from restraint that proves beyond all doubt that he is to the manner born."

By the next year he'd written a number of popular songs, including what would go on to be his most enduring, "The Blaydon Races."

There in the library I also discovered a document that is so eerie it gives me a chill.

It's a contract with a manager. In exchange for being managed, Geordie signed away the ownership of his songs. The manager then took him to the nineteenth-century cleaners.

The manager? One Thomas Allen.

The contract is dated November 10, 1862. One hundred years later, I would pick up a pen and sign away my life to Mike Jeffery in the bad original Animals' deal.

Geordie Ridley died at the age of 30 in 1864. He never made a penny from "The Blaydon Races." I got screwed on "House of the Rising Sun"—but at least so far I've already lived twice as long as Geordie!

When Allen began publishing Ridley's songs, he's said to have made a fortune, all at the expense of his dead, broke client.

It all sounds familiar. Too fucking familiar.

I've had the fame. I've had and lost several fortunes. And I'm bittersweet, I suppose. I'm still alive, which can't be said for many of my friends and colleagues. The rock 'n' roll road is dotted with a lot of little white crosses. There's Buddy Holly, Elvis, Jim Morrison, Brian Jones, Janis Joplin, Keith Moon, John Bonham, Kurt Cobain, Mal Evans,

An old friend still missed—me with Rolling Stone Brian Jones in 1967.

Peter Grant, Jimi Hendrix, the great Otis Redding. . . and so many more, including the sweet, sweet Linda McCartney, whose cancer took her far too soon.

I'm fiercely proud of some of what I've done—embarrassed by and regretful of other events. I wish I'd been able to be a good husband and good father. I wish Jimi had made it through that morning all those years ago. These things just weren't in the cards.

Another version of the New Animals: Aynsley Dunbar, Dean Restum, me, Martin Gerschwitz and Dave Meros in 2001. Near the end of 2001, Dunbar was replaced by Bernie Pershey on drums.

But, ultimately, I'm grateful. Through it all, this wild life on and off the road, through Jordanian deserts, Spanish islands, German prisons, Caribbean tax scams, halls of fame, wine, women, and all the drugs under the sun—one constant companion has never abandoned me.

My first true love: singing.

It's been the *savior* of many a poor boy, and God I know I'm one.

Animals and Eric Burdon discography and band history

DISCLAIMER: This is not an exhaustive, authoritative discography of Animals/Eric Burdon material. This list includes the initial, original releases but does not include best-of collections or box sets, foreign releases, or rereleases. Several original Animals LPs had the same names in the U.S. and the U.K., but contained different tracks, so they're included here. To catalogue the rest would take hundreds of pages—and has, in fact: Dionisio Castello's *Good Times: The Ultimate Eric Burdon Audio-Videography* is the book for the serious collector. It contains the myriad releases, compilations, and imports from 1963 to 1991 (when it was published).

discography

The Animals / 1964
Eric Burdon, vocals
Hilton Valentine, guitar
Alan Price, keyboards
  (replaced by Dave Rowberry, 1965)
Bryan "Chas" Chandler, bass
John Steel, drums
  (replaced by Barry Jenkins, 1966)

ALBUMS:
The Animals
Animal Tracks
The Animals on Tour
Animalisms
Animalization
Animalism
In the Beginning
Night Time Is the Right Time
Before We Were So Rudely Interrupted
Ark
Rip It to Shreds

Eric Burdon & The Animals / 1966
Eric Burdon, vocals
  (with studio musicians)

ALBUM:
Eric Is Here

Eric Burdon

Eric Burdon & The Animals / 1966
Eric Burdon, vocals
John Weider, guitar and violin
Vic Briggs, guitar
Danny McCulloch, bass
Barry Jenkins, drums

ALBUMS:
Winds of Change

**Eric Burdon
& The New Animals / 1968**
Eric Burdon, vocals
John Weider, guitar and violin
Vic Briggs, guitar
Andy Summers, guitar
Danny McCulloch, bass
Barry Jenkins, drums
Zoot Money, Hammond organ

ALBUMS:
The Twain Shall Meet
Everyone of Us
Love Is
Roadrunners

Eric Burdon and War / 1970
Eric Burdon, vocals
Howard Scott, guitar and violin
Lee Oskar, harmonica
B. B. Dickerson, bass
Harold Brown, drums
Papa Dee Allen, percussion
Charles Miller, tenor sax and flute
Lonnie Jordan, organ and piano

ALBUMS:
Eric Burdon Declares War
The Black Man's Burdon
Love Is All Around

**Eric Burdon/Jimmy
Witherspoon / 1971**
Eric Burdon, vocals
Jimmy Witherspoon, vocals
(with studio musicians and various
members of War)

ALBUM:
Guilty! (re-released on CD as *Black
& White Blues*)

**Eric Burdon Mirage Project /
1972-1974**
Eric Burdon, vocals and illustrations
(with studio musicians)

MULTI-MEDIA AUDIO-VISUAL PROJECT,
NEVER RELEASED

don't let me be misunderstood

The Eric Burdon Band / 1974

Eric Burdon, vocals
Aalon Butler, guitars
Alvin Taylor, drums, percussion
George Suranovich, drums
Moses Wheelock, percussion
Kim Kesterson, bass
Terry Ryan, keyboards

ALBUMS:
Sun Secrets
Stop
(These were released by Capitol
Records without my permission and
now appear together on one CD, *Sun
Secrets/Stop.*)

Solo Releases

I worked with many talented musicians throughout the '70s and '80s, some in the studio, and others on the road. Among the most influential are Snuffy Walden, Tony Braunagel, Randy Rice, Bill McCubbin, Ronnie Barron, and Bobby Martin.

ALBUMS:
Survivor, 1977
Darkness, Darkness, 1980
The Last Drive, 1980
The Comeback Soundtrack, 1982
Crawling King Snake, 1982
Power Company, 1984
That's Live, 1985
Wicked Man, 1988
I Used to Be an Animal, 1988

**Eric Burdon/Brian Auger
  Band / 1991**

Eric Burdon, vocals
Dave Meros, bass
Don Kirkpatrick, guitar
  (replaced by Larry Wilkins, 1992)
Brian Auger, keyboard
Paul Crowder, drums
  (replaced by Kharma Auger, 1992)
Richard Regueira, percussion
  (1993-1994)

ALBUM:
Access All Areas

Eric Burdon's Flying I Band / 1994

Eric Burdon, vocals
Dave Meros, bass
Dean Restum, guitar
Larry Wilkins, guitar (died 1997)
Neal Morse, guitar, keyboard
  (replaced by Martin Gerschwitz, 1999)
Mark Craney, drums
  (replaced by Aynsley Dunbar, 1996)

ALBUMS:
Official Live Bootleg-Vol. I
Official Live Bootleg-Vol. II

Solo releases

ALBUM:
Lost Within the Halls of Fame, 1995

**Eric Burdon & The New
  Animals / 2000**

Eric Burdon, vocals
Dave Meros, bass
Dean Restum, guitar
Martin Gerschwitz, keyboard, violin
Aynsley Dunbar, drums
  (replaced by Bernie Pershey, 2001)

ALBUMS:
Official Live Bootleg, 2000
untitled CD, October 2001
(with selection of guest stars and
  studio musicians)

chart history

The Animals:

Baby Let Me Take You Home	1964, #15 Pop
House of the Rising Sun	1964, #1 Pop
I'm Crying	1964, #19 Pop
Don't Let Me Be Misunderstood	1965, #15 Pop
Bring It on Home to Me	1965, #32 Pop
We Gotta Get out of this Place	1965, #13 Pop
It's My Life	1965, #23 Pop
Inside-Looking Out	1966, #34 Pop
Don't Bring Me Down	1966, # 12 Pop

Eric Burdon & the New Animals:

See See Rider	1966, #10 Pop
Help Me Girl	1966, #29 Pop
When I Was Young	1967, #15 Pop
San Franciscan Nights	1967, #9 Pop
Monterey	1967, #15 Pop
Sky Pilot (Part One)	1968, #14 Pop

War:

Spill the Wine	1970, #3 Pop

index

don't let me be misunderstood